Concepts in Physical Education

ext. 360

LAB 22

Concepts in Physical Education

th Laboratories and Experiments

ourth Edition

Charles B. Corbin
Kansas State University

Linus J. Dowell
Texas A & M University

Ruth Lindsey
California State University
Long Beach

Homer Tolson
Texas A & M University

wcb

Wm. C. Brown Company Publishers
Dubuque, Iowa

wcb group

Wm. C. Brown
Chairman of the Board
Mark C. Falb
Corporate Vice President/Operations

Book Team

Judith A. Clayton
Assistant Developmental Editor

Anthony L. Saizon
Designer
Bob McGuill
Production Editor
Mary M. Heller
Visual Research Manager
Mavis M. Oeth
Permissions Editor

wcb

Wm. C. Brown Company
Publishers College Division

Lawrence E. Cremer
President
Raymond C. Deveaux
Vice President/Product Development
David Wm. Smith
Assistant Vice President/National Sales Manager
David A. Corona
Director of Production Development and Design
Matthew T. Coghlan
National Marketing Manager
Janis Machala
Director of Marketing Research
Marilyn A. Phelps
Manager of Design
William A. Moss
Production Editorial Manager

Second Printing, 1981

Contents

Preface

This text is designed primarily for an introductory course in physical education at the college level. In this, the fourth edition, new material has been added. Up-to-date references are provided to document the facts presented in the book, and one new concept and one new lab were added. As with the first three editions, an attempt has been made to provide the reader with the best scientific evidence in the area of physical education. Though it covers many areas in the broad field of physical education, this book primarily deals with the specific areas of physical activity, exercise, health, physical fitness, skill learning, and body mechanics.

An outline format is used to give the reader a concise and factual presentation with regard to the HOW, WHAT, and WHY of physical activity and exercise. Discussion has been kept to a minimum; bibliographies, suggested readings, and extensive documentation are provided for the reader who wishes to further pursue a specific topic.

There are twenty concepts and forty accompanying laboratory exercises that are appropriate for both men and women. In an attempt to make the text materials as easy to use as possible, all self-evaluation materials, exercise programs, and laboratory information is incorporated into one lab section of the text. In the lab section, some material is meant to be torn out to be handed in as lab reports. However, where possible exercises, rating charts, and other similar information are provided on separate sheets from lab reports so that this information can be kept in the book for future reference. The reader is encouraged to keep the book for future use in selecting exercise programs and for doing self-evaluations. An understanding and appreciation of the information presented in these pages should provide the foundation for an intelligent selection of activities and health practices to aid the individual in leading a useful and productive life.

A comprehensive Instructor's Manual is available to teachers who use the text in their classes. It includes suggestions for organizing the classes, grading, lecture outlines, and laboratory instructions, as well as suggested supplementary activities. A master set of illustrations suitable for transparencies is available to accompany the lectures.

The authors wish to extend a special thanks to Robert Clayton, Melvin Ezell Jr., Connie Fye, John W. Jones, Marjorie Avery Willard, Robert L. Pugh, Tony Jadin, Betty McVaigh, James Harvey, John Hayes, David Laurie, Ron Lawman, Al Leister, Mary Rice, Roberta Stokes, and Dennis Wilson all of whom provided important advice and suggestions for improving this book.

A Note to the Reader

This book is not exactly like other textbooks you may have used in the past. To make the book as easy to use as possible, we have organized the book in a unique way.

First, the book is written in a outline format. For this reason, the book does not read like most texts. However, the information will be useful and precise. Secondly, references are listed to support the facts presented in the text. While we do not expect you to look up each reference, we do want you to know where to look for more information about the facts that are presented if you want additional knowledge.

Another important feature of the book is the "tear out" lab sheets. These sheets have been perforated so that you can hand them in to your instructor, if requested. We have made sure that important testing or exercise information will not be torn out with these sheets, because we feel that you will want to keep this information for future use. Finally, special "program" appendixes are included at the end of the book. Many different exercise programs are presented in this section, and, in each case, the advantages and disadvantages of the various exercises are discussed.

This book is intended to help you make important decisions about your own personal exercise program and your personal physical fitness for now and for the rest of your life. We trust that you will find the book interesting and useful.

The Authors

Concepts in Physical Education

Introduction

Concept 1

Being physically educated is an important part of one's total education.

Introduction

Automation and technology have freed many people from the exhausting physical labor required of earlier generations. The fatiguing physical labor of the farmer and manual laborer is not part of the normal daily activity pattern for the majority of individuals. However, the need for sound physical and mental health and physical fitness, which result from regular exercise, is still quite necessary for every individual. In addition, the "free time" that has been made available to the average individual has created a need for the development of recreational skills that can be used for a lifetime. The physically educated man or woman must be able to make intelligent decisions concerning health, physical fitness, and recreational pursuits and must be able to recognize the role of exercise and physical activity in daily life. It is encouraging that a recent survey indicated that 59 percent of American adults now participate in some form of regular exercise as compared with 24 percent twenty years ago (Harris and assoc. 1979). Americans appear to be committed to the importance of regular exercise and regular physical education. Research results indicate that more than 90 percent of all American adults feel that ". . . people should have physical education . . ." as part of their regular school experience (Pres. Council 1973).

The Facts

Too many American adults are not as active as they should be.

Though as many as 59 percent of adults surveyed indicate that they participate in some form of regular physical activity, only 15 percent get as much as 300 minutes of exercise each week. Only 16 percent get 200 minutes a week and 69 percent do no exercise at all or get less than 150 minutes a week (Harris and assoc. 1979).

Too many Americans suffer from "hypokinetic diseases."

A "hypokinetic disease" is a disease that relates to or is caused by the lack of regular physical activity (Kraus 1961). These diseases of sedentary man include coronary heart disease, high blood pressure, low back pain, and obesity, to name just a few. While recent advances in modern medicine have been quite effective in eliminating infectious diseases, the degenerative diseases, characterized by sedentary or "take-it-easy" living, have increased. Heart disease is the leading cause of death in the United States, accounting for 55 percent of all deaths (Cooper 1977). One man out of every three will have heart disease before the age of 60. The percentage of women to be stricken with heart disease is only slightly lower than it is for men (Turner and Ball 1976). As many as 46 percent of Americans are considered to be obese (Pollock et al. 1978), and low back pain is a leading medical complaint (Feffer 1971 and Kraus 1965). Apparently, the onset of these diseases can begin in youth. The fact that too many American children score poorly on tests of physical fitness suggests that the future will not see a reduced rate of "hypokinetic disease" in our culture.

Regular physical activity and exercise can reduce the risk of "hypokinetic disease."

Scientific evidence, including a long-range study of an entire community, shows that people who exercise regularly are less likely to have degenerative diseases (Kannel 1971). In fact, the death rate among active people is approximately one-half that of those who exhibit an inactive life-style (Fox 1971). At least one of every five adult Americans has been advised by a physician to get involved in regular exercise (Pres. Council 1973).

Many Americans are ignorant of important facts concerning exercise and physical fitness.

While a recent study (Pres. Council 1973) shows that as many as 90 percent of all Americans believe that regular exercise is important to good health and fitness, more than half have miconceptions about exercise (Harris and assoc. 1979). Fifty-seven percent of adults who are inactive feel that sports such as baseball and bowling provide enough exercise to develop good health and physical fitness. Though the facts indicate otherwise, those who do not exercise regularly believe that they get all the exercise they need. Interestingly, those who report that they participate in regular exercise are more likely to feel that they do not get enough exercise for their own good health (Pres. Council 1973; Harris and assoc. 1979).

Physical activity, including games and sports, is an enjoyable way to spend one's leisure hours.

Labor Department statistics indicate that in the past century the average workweek has been reduced by about thirteen hours, netting the average person 675 more hours of free time annually. With vacations and holidays added, the typical worker has 800 more free hours per year (Hodgson 1972). Increased sales of boats, campers, and other lifetime sports equipment indicate that many Americans are enjoying their leisure through participation in these activities.

Efficient movement is essential to effective living.

Although movement is unique to each individual, there are general guidelines for the efficient performance of movement skills used in the course of daily living. Whether it be walking, working on an assembly line, or performing household chores, learning to move efficiently is important to avoid strain and to conserve energy.

The physical skills that an individual learns should be applicable for a lifetime of recreational use.

Most American adults who do exercise regularly indicate that they walk, do calisthenics, ride a bike, jog, or swim. Among sports, bowling, golf, basketball, and tennis are the most popular (Harris and assoc. 1979). Every individual should possess skills in "lifetime" sports and should have a knowledge of general exercises that could be used to promote health and physical fitness.

An individual should know *why* physical activity and exercise are important as well as *how* to perform various exercises and physical activities.

A study by Brunner (1969) showed that 63 percent of the adults he interviewed felt the exercises and activities they learned as children and young adults were not applicable for use as adults. A more recent study indicates that very few people participate in competitive sports as adults (Pres. Council 1973). Many of those interviewed in these studies have indicated that it would be desirable to learn *why* exercise is important to every adult so that the decision as to *what* to do and *how* to do it would be more meaningful.

The choice of exercises and physical activities should be unique to each individual.

No two people are alike; therefore, physical activity patterns should be based on individual needs and interests. The decision concerning choice of exercise and physical activities should be made only after carrying out the following five steps:

1. Assess current health and physical fitness status to determine individual needs.
2. Examine current interests. (Physical activity should be enjoyable.)
3. Acquire a knowledge and understanding of the values of physical activity and exercise.
4. Determine which activities will best meet individual needs and interests.
5. Acquire skill and knowledge in the activities selected.

Physical Fitness

Concept 2

"Physical fitness is not only one of the most important keys to a healthy body; it is also the basis of dynamic and creative activity" (Kennedy 1960).

Introduction

Physical fitness has been defined by many people in many different ways. It is difficult to adequately define such a complex human characteristic. One point of consensus is that physical fitness is a desirable quality to possess. The following information is presented not only to aid the individual in developing a personal definition of physical fitness, but also to aid in developing a better understanding of the nature of physical fitness.

Health-Related Fitness Terms

Body Composition—The relative makeup of the body in muscle, fat, bone, and other vital parts.

Cardiovascular Fitness—The ability of the circulatory and respiratory systems to supply fuel (most importantly, oxygen) during sustained physical activity.

Flexibility—The range of motion available in a joint.

Muscular Endurance—The ability of muscle groups to exert external force for many repetitions or successive exertions.

Strength—The amount of external force that a muscle can exert.

Skill-Related Fitness Terms

Agility—The ability to rapidly change position of the entire body in space with speed and accuracy.

Balance—The maintenance of equilibrium while stationary or moving.

Coordination—The ability to use the senses, such as sight or hearing, together with the body parts in performing motor tasks smoothly and accurately.

Power—The ability to transfer energy into force at a fast rate of speed.

Reaction Time—The time elapsed between stimulation and the beginning of the reaction to it.

Speed—The ability to perform a movement in a short period of time.

The Facts

Physical fitness is a part of total fitness.

Aspects of total fitness include emotional, social, spiritual, and mental as well as physical.

Physical fitness consists of many components each of which is specific in nature.

Physical fitness is a combination of several aspects rather than a single characteristic. It is possible to possess any one of the following physical fitness aspects in varying degrees: cardiovascular fitness, muscular endurance, strength, body composition, power, speed, agility, balance, coordination, reaction time, and flexibility.

Cardiovascular fitness, musuclar endurance, strength, body composition, and flexibility may be considered the health-related aspects of physical fitness.

The health-related fitness aspects as listed above can contribute to a state of positive health by reducing chances of degenerative diseases, increasing work efficiency, and eliminating muscle soreness. Because of the importance of the health-related fitness components, the physical fitness test most commonly given to children in our schools has been recently revised to focus on these five parts of fitness. For good health it is important to develop and maintain the health-related aspects of fitness beginning early in life.

Power, speed, agility, coordination, balance, and reaction time contribute to one's ability to perform skills and to participate in enjoyable leisure-time activities.

These aspects of physical fitness are considered to be motor or skill-related.

Physical fitness is important to optimal health.

Optimal health is more than freedom from disease. According to the World Health Organization (Pollock, Purdy, and Carroll 1979) health is "a state of complete physical, mental, and social well being and not merely the absence of disease and infirmity." Healthy people are full of vitality and have a zest for living.

Physical fitness contributes to positive physical health.

Many of the contributions of physical fitness to good health will be described elsewhere in this book. However, the physical health benefits of regular exercise are summarized in Table 2.1.

Table 2.1 The Physical Health Benefits of Activity

Major Benefit	Related Benefits
Improved cardiovascular fitness	• Stronger heart muscle Lower heart rate Possible reduction in blood pressure Reduced blood fat Possible resistance to atherosclerosis Possible improved peripheral circulation Improved coronary circulation Resistance to "emotional storm" Less chance of heart attack Greater chance of surviving a heart attack
Greater lean body mass and lesser body fat	• Greater work efficiency Less susceptibility to disease Improved appearance Less incidence of self-concept problems related to obesity
Improved strength and muscular endurance	• Greater work efficiency Less chance of muscle injury Decreased chance of low back problems Improved performance in sports Improved ability to meet emergencies
Improved flexibility	• Greater work efficiency Less chance of muscle injury Less chance of joint injury Decreased chance of low back problems Improved sports performance
Other health benefits of exercise and physical activity	• Increased ability to use oxygen Quicker recovery after hard work Delay in the aging process Greater respiratory efficiency Possible increase in efficiency of the vital organs other than the heart and muscles. Decreased muscle tension

Physical fitness contributes to positive mental health.

Mental illness is now recognized as a health problem and not a personal weakness or reason for social disgrace. The serious nature of mental health problems is illustrated by the following facts: approximately twenty-five thousand suicides occur in this country each year (Frederick 1977); doctors estimate that as many as 70 percent of all illnesses are psychosomatic or emotionally related (Pollock, Purdy, and Carroll 1979); statistics show dramatic increases in cost for care of those with mental illnesses (Carroll and Miller 1979). Some of the benefits to mental health that are derived from regular physical activity and good physical fitness are summarized in Table 2.2.

Table 2.2 The Mental Health Benefits of Activity

Major Benefit	Related Benefits
Reduction in mental tension	Relief of depression Fewer stress symptoms Ability to enjoy leisure Possible work improvement
Opportunity for social interactions	Improved quality of life
Resistance to fatigue	Ability to enjoy leisure Improved quality of life Improved ability to meet some stressors
Opportunity for successful experience	Improved self-concept Opportunity to recognize and accept personal limitations
Improved physical fitness	Improved sense of well-being Improved self-concept Improved appearance

Physical fitness is the basis for dynamic and creative activity.

"The relationship between the soundness of the body and the activity of the mind is subtle and complex. Much is not yet understood, but we know what the Greeks knew: that intelligence and skill can only function at the peak of their capacity when the body is healthy and strong and that hardy spirits and tough minds usually inhabit sound bodies. In this sense, physical fitness is the basis of all activities in our society; if our bodies grow soft and inactive, if we fail to encourage physical development and prowess, we will undermine our capacity for thought, for work, and for the use of those skills vital to an expanding and complex America" (Kennedy 1960).

Physical fitness needs depend upon the individual.

Several generations ago Americans performed vigorous physical activity as a way of life. More recently the need for physical exertion as part of one's job has decreased. For this reason, many individuals feel little need for physical fitness for efficient daily work. While it is true that an individual's occupation will affect his or her need for physical fitness, it is not true that there is little need for physical fitness for those employed in sedentary occupations. *Every individual* has a need for fitness for living. The following factors should be considered.

1. Every individual should possess enough physical fitness to meet the needs of his or her occupation and regular daily activities.
2. In addition to normal daily physical fitness requirements, every individual should possess enough physical fitness to be capable of meeting emergency situations.
3. Finally, the individual should possess enough physical fitness to enjoy leisure-time activities at the end of a normal workday.

Suggested Readings

Cooper, K. H. *The Aerobics Way.* New York: M. Evans and Co., 1977.
Pollock, M. L.; Wilmore, J. H.; and Fox, S. M. *Health and Fitness Through Physical Activity.* New York: John Wiley and Sons, 1978.

Threshold of Training and Fitness Target Zones

3

Concept 3

There is an optimal amount of physical activity that is necessary for developing each of the different parts of physical fitness.

Introduction

Just as there is a correct dosage of medicine for treating an illness, there is a correct dosage of exercise for developing physical fitness. The minimum effective "dose" of exercise is called the *threshold of training* and the *fitness target zone* is the optimal amount of physical activity for developing physical fitness.

Terms

Fitness Target Zones—A range of exercise from the minimum necessary to cause improvements in fitness to the maximum amount of exercise, beyond which exercise may be counterproductive. If you exercise above the minimum and below the maximum you are exercising in the fitness target zone.

The Overload Principle—A basic principle of physical fitness that specifies that for an aspect of fitness to improve, one must "overload" or do more than normal exercise relating to that aspect of fitness.

Threshold of Training—The minimum amount of exercise that will produce improvements in physical fitness.

The Facts

The overload principle is the basis for improving physical fitness.

In order for a muscle (including the heart muscle) to get stronger, it must work against a greater than normal load. To increase flexibility, a muscle must be stretched beyond its normal length. To increase muscular endurance, muscles must be exposed to sustained work. If a muscle is used less than normal, it will atrophy, resulting in loss of strength, endurance, and flexibility.

There is no substitute for overload in developing physical fitness.

During childhood and adolescence, physical fitness aspects may be developed through the vigorous play activities of youth. The more sedentary adult must make a special effort to find activities that overload the muscles and cardiovascular system.

To get fit you must overload above the threshold of training (Pollock, Wilmore, and Fox 1978).

Threshold of training refers to the minimum amount of exercise necessary to produce gains in fitness. What you normally do or just a little more than your normal exercise is not enough to cause improvements in fitness. The illustration that follows shows the threshold of training and target zones for physical fitness improvement.

Laurie, D. R., and Corbin, C. B. *How Much Exercise Is Enough?;* Manhattan, Ks.: An audiovisual slide tape program, Master Teacher, 1980.

To get optimal benefits of regular exercise, you should exercise in the fitness target zone (Corbin and Laurie 1980).

The fitness target zone begins at the threshold of training and stops at the point where the benefits of exercise become counterproductive, as shown in the illustration.

Concept 3

There is a threshold of training and a fitness target zone for each of the different aspects of fitness (Pollock 1978).

The amount of exercise necessary to develop one aspect of fitness is not the same as the amount necessary to develop another aspect of fitness. Each part of fitness has a different threshold of training and target zone. Further details of the specifics for different aspects of fitness are presented in the following chapters.

There are three important variables to consider in determining threshold of training and fitness target zones (Pollock 1978).

1. *Intensity*—Exercise must be hard enough to require more exertion than normal.
2. *Duration*—Exercise must be done for a significant length of time to be effective. As duration increases, intensity may be decreased.
3. *Frequency*—Exercise must be performed regularly to be effective. Even exercise of enough intensity and duration may not be effective in improving health-related fitness if not performed regularly.

Overload should be progressive.

Exercises should be specifically selected to meet specific purposes. Too little exercise may not be any more valuable than no exercise at all. Too much exercise may be less valuable than no exercise at all and can be dangerous. It is better to start too slowly than to do too much when you first begin exercising. You should start below the threshold and work up to the threshold and into the target zone.

Threshold levels and target zones change as your fitness level changes.

As you become more fit by doing correct exercises, your threshold of training and fitness target zones may change. Likewise, if you stop exercising for a period of time they will also change. Your threshold of training and fitness target zones are based on your current physical fitness levels and your current exercise patterns.

Suggested Readings

de Vries, H. A. *Physiology of Exercise*. 3d ed. Dubuque, Ia.: Wm. C. Brown Company Publishers, 1980.
Pollock, M. L. "How Much Exercise Is Enough?" *The Physician and Sports Medicine* 6 (June 1978): 50.

Health-Related Fitness

4

Concept 4

Cardiovascular fitness, muscular endurance, strength, body composition, and flexibility are health-related aspects of physical fitness.

Introduction

As previously indicated, physical fitness consists of at least eleven specific aspects. An individual might perform well in one area without performing well in others. All aspects of physical fitness are important; however, the aspects of cardiovascular fitness, muscular endurance, strength, body composition, and flexibility are most important to good health. An individual must possess more than minimal amounts of these fitness aspects if "hypokinetic diseases" are to be prevented.

The Facts

People with a body composition consisting of high amounts of lean muscle have less disease and other health problems than those who are overfat (Clarke 1975).

There is evidence that those people who are too fat have a higher death rate than lean people. Among the diseases more common to obese people are coronary heart disease, hypertension, and diabetes.

A skin caliper

Body Composition—the relative percentage of muscle, fat, bone, and other tissue of which the body is composed. A fit person has a relatively low percentage of body fat.

People who possess cardiovascular fitness have less risk of coronary heart disease and other hypokinetic diseases than people who do not possess good cardiovascular fitness (Boyer July 1972; Oct. 1972; Clarke 1976; 1979).

Cardiovascular Fitness—the ability of the heart, blood vessels, blood, and respiratory system to supply fuel, especially oxygen, to the muscles during sustained exercise. A fit person can persist in exercise for relatively long periods of time without undue distress.

People who possess good flexibility are less likely to injure muscles and joints and have less risk of contracting hypokinetic diseases, such as back, leg, and neck pain, than people who do not possess good flexibility (Corbin and Noble 1980).

Flexibility—the range of motion available in a joint. It is affected by muscle length, joint structure, and other factors. A fit person can move the body joints through a full range of movement in work or play.

People who possess good muscular endurance have a greater working capacity, less chance of injury, and less risk of getting hypokinetic diseases, such as low back pain, than do people who do not possess good muscular endurance (Clarke July 1973; Jan. 1974).

Muscular Endurance—the ability of the muscles to repeat muscle exertion. A fit person can repeat strength performances without undue fatigue.

People who possess good muscle strength have greater working capacity, less chance of injury, and less risk of contracting hypokinetic diseases, such as low back pain, than do people who do not possess good muscle strength (Clarke Jan. 1973; Jan. 1974; Oct. 1974).

Strength—the ability to exert external force or to lift a heavy weight. A fit person can do work or play that involves exerting force, such as lifting or controlling one's own body weight.

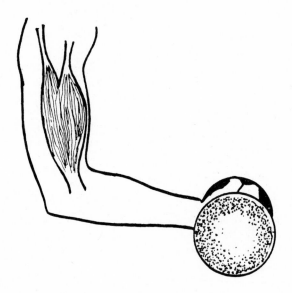

People who possess one aspect of health-related fitness do not necessarily possess all aspects of health-related fitness.

Each aspect of health-related fitness is separate and different from the other aspects. There is some relationship between the different aspects of fitness but for example, people who possess strength do not necessarily possess cardio-vascular fitness and people who possess muscular endurance do not necessarily possess flexibility.

To develop all aspects of health-related fitness you must exercise above threshold levels and in the target fitness zone for each part of fitness.

Since there is a separate threshold and target zone for each aspect of fitness, you must do specific exercises designed to develop each of the different fitness aspects. Specific threshold levels, target zones, and exercises for developing each aspect of fitness are presented in Concepts 5,6,7,8, and 9, as well as in the appendixes.

All individuals can gain health-related fitness as a result of regular vigorous exercise.

Regardless of age, sex, or even current fitness status, progressive overload can benefit almost all individuals. It does not take skill in sports and games to become fit. There are cardiovascular fitness, strength, muscular endurance, and flexibility exercises, as well as exercises for reducing body fatness, which are appropriate for *all* individuals. Even those who have previously experienced heart attacks can benefit from regular progressive exercise (Clarke Jan. 1974; Oct. 1974; 1975; 1979; Corbin and Noble 1980).

Regular exercise is very beneficial, but it is not a panacea.

While research does support many values of exercise, it is not a cure-all. For example, there is no evidence that exercise can reduce viral or bacterial infection. Accordingly, each person should carefully evaluate all claims before making exercise decisions.

Suggested Readings

Clarke, H. H., ed. "Update: Exercise and Some Coronary Risk Factors." *Physical Fitness Research Digest* 9 (July 1979): 1.

Corbin, C. B., and Noble, L. "Flexibility." *Journal of Physical Education and Recreation,* Vol. 51, page 23 (June 1980).

de Vries, H. A. *Physiology of Exercise.* 3d ed. chaps. 17 and 18. Dubuque: Wm. C. Brown Company Publishers, 1980.

Katch, F. I., and McArdle, W. D. *Nutrition, Weight Control, and Exercise.* Boston: Houghton Mifflin Co., 1977.

Cardiovascular Fitness

5

Concept 5

Cardiovascular fitness, the ability of the blood, heart, lungs, and other systems of the body to effectively persist in effort, is probably the most important aspect of physical fitness and can be developed and assessed in many different ways.

Introduction

Cardiovascular fitness is frequently considered the most important aspect of physical fitness because those who possess it are likely to have a lessened risk of coronary heart disease. Cardiovascular fitness is also referred to as cardiovascular endurance, cardiorespiratory capacity, and circulatory fitness. Regardless of the word used to describe it physical fitness is complex because good cardiovascular fitness requires fitness of many different body systems.

Terms

Aerobic Exercise—Exercise for which the body is able to supply adequate oxygen to sustain performance for long periods of time.

Anaerobic Exercise—Exercise that requires the use of the body's high energy fuel. This type of exercise is of short duration and does not depend on the body's ability to supply oxygen.

Continuous Exercise (aerobic exercise)—Exercise that is maintained at a fairly constant intensity for the entire exercise period.

Hemoglobin—Oxygen-carrying pigment of the red blood cells.

Intermittent Exercise (anaerobic exercise)—Relatively taxing exercise that is alternated regularly with periods of rest or mild exercise.

Liter—A metric measure of volume slightly larger than one quart.

Maximal Oxygen Uptake—A laboratory measure of fitness commonly held to be the best measure of cardiovascular fitness.

The Facts

Because of its importance to a healthy life, cardiovascular fitness is one of the most important aspects of physical fitness.

Considerable evidence exists to indicate that people who exercise regularly have a lower incidence of heart disease (Boyer 1972; Dawber 1973; Morris et al. 1973; Paffenbarger et al. 1979) and that exercise is one type of effective prescription for those who have already suffered heart attacks (Cantwell, Watt, and Piper 1979; Shepard 1975).

Good cardiovascular fitness requires a fit heart muscle.

The heart is a muscle; to become stronger it must be exercised like any other muscle in the body. If the heart is exercised regularly, its strength increases; if not, it becomes weaker. Contrary to the belief that strenuous work harms the heart, research has found no evidence that regular progressive exercise is bad for the normal heart (Corbin 1980). In fact, the heart muscle will increase in size and power when called upon to extend itself. The increase in size and power allows the heart to pump a greater volume of blood with fewer strokes per minute. For example, the average individual has a resting heart rate of between seventy and eighty beats per minute, while it is not uncommon for a trained athlete's pulse to be in the low fifties or even in the forties.

The healthy heart is efficient in the work that it does.

The fit heart can convert about half of its fuel into energy. An autombile engine in good running condition converts about one-fourth of its fuel into energy. By comparison, the heart is an efficient machine.

The heart of a normal individual beats reflexively about 40 million times a year. During this time, over 4,000 gallons or 10 tons of blood are circulated each day, and every night the heart accomplishes a work load equivalent to carrying a thirty-pound pack to the top of the 102-story Empire State Building.

Good cardiovascular fitness requires a fit vascular system.

Blood flows in a sequence of arteries to capillaries, to veins, and back to the heart. Arteries always carry blood away from the heart. Healthy arteries are elastic, free of obstruction, and expand to permit the flow of blood. Muscle layers line the arteries and on impulse from nerve fibers control the size of the arterial opening. Unfit arteries may have a reduced internal diameter (atherosclerosis) because of deposits on the interior of their walls or they may have hardened, nonelastic walls (arteriosclerosis).

Fit coronary arteries are especially important to good health. The blood in the four chambers of the heart does not directly nourish the heart. Rather, numerous small arteries within the heart muscle provide for coronary circulation. Poor coronary circulation precipitated by unhealthy arteries can be the cause of a heart attack. (See illustrations of a healthy and an unhealthy artery.)

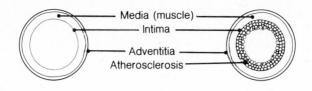

A healthy elastic artery   An unhealthy artery

Veins have thinner, less elastic walls than arteries and contain small valves to prevent the backward flow of blood as shown in the illustration of a healthy nonelastic vein. Skeletal muscles assist the return of blood to the heart. The veins are intertwined in the muscle, and when contraction of the muscle occurs, the vein is squeezed pushing the blood on its way back to the heart. A malfunction of the valves results in a failure of used blood to be removed at the proper rate. As a result, venous blood pools in the legs causing a condition known as varicose veins.

A healthy nonelastic vein

Capillaries are the transfer stations where oxygen and fuel are released to the tissues and waste products are removed from the tissues. The veins receive the blood from the capillaries for the return trip to the heart.

Good cardiovascular fitness requires a fit respiratory system, fit blood, and fit muscles capable of using oxygen (deVries 1980).

In order for a healthy heart to transmit oxygen through a healthy artery, the blood must also be healthy. It must contain adequate hemoglobin in the red blood cells (erythrocytes). Lack of oxygen-carrying capacity of the blood is called anemia.

As fit blood travels through the lungs, adequate oxygen must be transmitted from the lungs to the blood. A limited respiratory system will limit cardiovascular fitness.

If cardiovascular fitness is to be developed, one must exercise regularly above the cardiovascular threshold of training and in the cardiovascular fitness target zone.

Research shows that three factors must be considered in designing exercise programs for developing cardiovascular fitness: frequency, intensity, and duration (American College of Sports Medicine 1978; Gench 1975; Pollock 1978).

There is a threshold of training and a fitness target zone for each of two different types of cardiovascular training (deVries 1980).

Specific amounts of exercise necessary to achieve increases in cardiovascular fitness are outlined in Tables 5.1 and 5.2.

Table 5.1   Cardiovascular Fitness Threshold of Training and Target Zones for Continuous or Aerobic Exercise*

	Threshold of Training	Target Zone
Intensity	Exercise until the heart rate is elevated to the appropriate level. Your resting and maximal heart rate are used to determine this level. These heart rates are determined for you and are located in the chart of page 159. Use the threshold heart rate from the chart and keep your heart rate above that level for the proper duration.	The heart rate should be elevated to the minimum threshold level but not beyond the highest level shown in the chart on page 159. For young adults the target zone is generally between *135 to 160 beats per minute.*
Duration	Exercise above the proper intensity for a minimum of *15 to 30 minutes.* As the intensity of exercise periods increase, the length of exercise periods may decrease. Another way to determine duration is by the amount of calories you expend. Exercise of the proper intensity and frequency that causes you to expend 1,500 to 2,000 extra calories a week is enough to improve cardiovascular fitness.	Exercise above the minimum threshold of 15 to 30 minutes. The recommended amount of time is from *30 to 60 minutes.* Exercise of the proper intensity and frequency that causes you to expend 1,500 to 3,000 calories represents the target for most people.
Frequency	Three days a week	Exercise at least to the threshold three times a week and up to six days a week. Seven days a week may be counterproductive.

*The threshold of training and target zone values depicted in this table are for typical young adults and may need to be modified for individuals of exceptionally low or high levels of cardiovascular fitness.

Table 5.2 Cardiovascular Fitness Threshold of Training and Target Zones for Intermittent or Anaerobic Exercise*

	Threshold of Training	Target Zone
Intensity	Short interval exercise: 90% to maximum speed running, swimming, or other exercise for a short distance; then rest by walking or mild exercise until the heart rate returns to 120 beats per minute. Repeat as desired.	Short interval exercise: Exercise above the minimum threshold of 90% and up to maximal speed running, swimming, or other exercise for short distances. Rest with walking or mild exercise until the heart rate returns to 120 beats per minute. Repeat as desired.
	Long interval exercise: Exercise at 80% of maximum speed running, swimming, or other exercise for three to five minutes. Walk or perform mild exercise for the same length of time.	Long interval exercise: Exercise above the minimum threshold of 80% and up to 90% of maximum running, swimming, or other exercise speed for three to five minutes. Walk or perform mild exercise for the same length of time.
Duration	Exercise above the proper intensity for a minimum of *15 to 30 minutes.*	Exercise above the minimum threshold of 15 to 30 minutes. The recommended time is from *30 to 60 minutes.*
Frequency	Three days a week.	Exercise at least to the threshold of *three times a week and up to six days a week.* Seven days a week may be counterproductive.

*The threshold of training and target zone values depicted in this table are for typical young adults and may need to be modified for individuals of exceptionally low or high levels of cardiovascular fitness.

Cardiovascular fitness can be achieved by doing either aerobic or anaerobic exercise.

Both aerobic (continuous) and anaerobic (intermittent) exercise are effective in promoting cardiovascular fitness. Cooper (1977) and others advocate the *continuous* type program, while Astrand (1977) and others recommend the *intermittent* type program. Table 5.3 summarizes the strengths and weaknesses of each.

Though cardiovascular fitness can be measured in many ways, maximal oxygen uptake is the best method for its evaluation (deVries 1980).

A person's maximal oxygen uptake is determined in a laboratory by measuring how much oxygen one can use in one minute of maximal work. Great endurance athletes can extract five or six liters of oxygen per minute from the

Table 5.3 Advantages of Continuous and Intermittent Fitness Programs

Continuous	Intermittent
Less intense—may be better for beginners, especially those who are older and are beginning exercise after a long layoff.	May be best approach for preparing for competition, especially in such sports as track and swimming.
Not so intense as intermittent exercise and may be easier for some people to perform regularly.	Saves time—allows a person to do more work in a given period of time.
Produces aerobic fitness or the ability to do sustained exercise.	Produces anaerobic fitness or the ability to do exercise involving short bursts.
Less risk to middle-aged people with less than very good levels of fitness.	Some feel intermittent exercise is more interesting because it provides a "change" resulting from alternate work and rest.

environment during an all-out treadmill run or bicycle ride, as opposed to the average person who can extract only two or three liters. In order to extract a large amount of oxygen during maximal work a person must have a fit heart muscle, capable of pumping large amounts of blood; fit blood, capable of carrying adequate amounts of O_2; fit arteries, free from congestion and capable of carrying large amounts of blood; and fit muscles, capable of using the oxygen supplied to the muscle. Less sophisticated tests such as the twelve-minute run, the step test, or the Astrand-Ryhming Bicycle Test may also be used to measure cardiovascular endurance (see Labs 5, 6, and 7).

There is evidence that the heart should be "warmed up" before moderate to vigorous exercise.

Recent research suggests (especially for middle-aged adults) the need for an adequate warm up before vigorous activity to stimulate the flow of blood to the heart muscle. This exercise should be last among warm-up exercises and should be done immediately before your planned activity begins.

Before exercising, especially with exercises involving sudden stopping and starting like in handball and basketball, you should jog easily for at least *two to three minutes*.

Suggested Readings

American College of Sports Medicine. "Position Statement on the Recommended Quantity and Quality of Exercise For Developing and Maintaining Fitness in Healthy Adults." *Medicine and Science in Sports* 10 (Fall 1978): vii.

deVries, H. A. *Physiology of Exercise.* 3d ed., chaps. 13 and 14. Dubuque, Ia.: Wm. C. Brown Company Publishers, 1980.

Pollock, M. L. "How Much Exercise Is Enough?" *The Physician and Sports Medicine* 6 (June 1978): 50.

Exercise and Heart Disease 6

Concept 6

Regular exercise is *one* important factor in reducing the risk of coronary heart disease as well as other hypokinetic diseases.

Introduction

There is little doubt that regular exercise is one of several important factors in reducing the risk of coronary heart disease. Statistical evidence shows "better odds" for the active individual. Presented in this unit is statistical as well as theoretical evidence relating heart disease to inactive living. Further, this unit will discuss the relationship between inactivity and other heart disease risk factors.

Terms

Angina Pectoris—Chest pain associated with lack of oxygen supply to the heart muscle.

Arteriosclerosis—A term used to describe conditions that cause the arterial walls to become thick, hard, and nonelastic; hardening of the arteries.

Atherosclerosis—A term used to describe the deposition of materials along the arterial walls; a type of arteriosclerosis.

Collateral Circulation—Development of auxiliary blood vessels that may take over normal coronary blood circulation during diminished blood flow through obstructed vessels.

Congestive Heart Failure—The inability of the heart muscle to pump the blood at a rate adequate to sustain life.

Coronary Occlusion—The blocking of the coronary blood vessels.

Coronary Thrombosis—The formation of a clot that occludes a coronary artery.

Emotional Storm—A traumatic emotional experience that is likely to affect the human organism physiologically.

Fibrin—The substance that forms a blood clot in combination with blood cells.

Hypertension—High blood pressure.

Lipid—A term used for all fats and fatty substances.

Lipoprotein—Fat-carrying proteins in the blood.

Parasympathetic Nervous System—A branch of the autonomic nervous system that slows the heart.

Risk Factor—Any of the conditions that predispose to heart disease.

Sympathetic Nervous System—A branch of the autonomic nervous system that prepares the body for activity by speeding up the heart.

The Facts

There are many different types of heart disease.

Hypertension (high blood pressure), atherosclerosis, arteriosclerosis, coronary occlusion, angina pectoris, and congestive heart failure are among the more prevalent forms of heart disease. Evidence indicates that inactivity may relate in some way to each of these types of heart disease (Boyer 1972).

There is a wealth of statistical evidence indicating that active people are less likely to have coronary heart disease than inactive people (Cooper 1977; Dawber 1973; Dedmon 1979; Fox 1971; Paffenbarger 1979).

Much of the research relating inactivity to heart disease has come from occupational studies that show a high incidence of heart disease for people in occupations involving only sedentary work. Even with the limitations inherent in these types of studies, the findings of more and more occupational studies present convincing evidence that the inactive individual has an increased risk of coronary heart disease.

Studies also indicate that people who are physically active in their leisure time have a reduced risk of coronary heart disease if the exercise they choose is done above the cardiovascular threshold of training and in the cardiovascular fitness target zones.

Regular exercise is one effective means of rehabilitation for a person who has coronary heart disease or who had a heart attack (Cunningham 1979; Rechnitzer 1975).

Not only does regular exercise seem to reduce the risk of getting coronary heart disease, there is also evidence that those who already have it may reduce the symptoms of the disease through regular exercise. For those who have had heart attacks, regular and progressive exercise can be one effective prescription when carried out under the supervision of a physician.

Recent decreases in the incidence of heart disease in the United States may be, in part, due to recent increases in activity levels of American adults (Cooper 1977).

In 1961, only 24 percent of Americans participated in regular physical activity. In 1979, 59 percent of American adults reported involvement in regular physical activity (Harris and assoc. 1979). During this same period of time the incidence of heart disease decreased by 14 percent. While heart disease is still present in epidemic proportions, many experts feel that the increase in regular exercise by previously sedentary Americans is one reason for the modest decreases in heart disease in the last two decades.

Contrary to popular belief, exercise does not cause "athlete's heart" nor does it injure the hearts of children (Corbin 1980).

The term *athlete's heart* is a misnomer. While some investigators have found increases in heart size as a result of training, this is not the pathological increase in size associated with heart disease. There is no evidence that heavy exercise injures a normal heart.

Many parents suggest that strenuous exercise is harmful to their children. To be sure, overstrenuous activity for long periods of time may have deleterious effects, but regular activity holds no harmful effects for children's hearts. Perhaps it is the psychological and social pressures that accompany juvenile athletics that may cause unwanted results.

There are many theories that attempt to explain the causes of coronary heart disease and the reasons why regular exercise reduces the risk of this disease.

Six of the most plausible theories of heart disease are the "Oxygen Pump Theory," the "Lipid Deposit Theory," the "Protective Protein Theory," the "Fibrin Deposit Theory," the "Coronary Collateral Circulation Theory," and the "Loafer's Heart Theory." There is evidence that regular exercise relates in some way to each of these theories.

The Oxygen Pump Theory

There is evidence that regular exercise will increase the ability of the heart muscle to pump blood as well as oxygen.

The "Oxygen Pump Theory" suggests that a fit heart muscle is one that is able to handle any *extra* demands placed on it. Through regular exercise the heart muscle gets stronger and therefore pumps more blood with each beat, resulting in a lessened heart rate and a greater heart efficiency. Of importance is the fact that the heart is just like any other muscle—it must be exercised regularly if it is to stay fit. The fit heart pumps more blood, thus supplying more oxygen during physical exertion and times of emotional stress (deVries 1980).

The Lipid Deposit Theory

There is evidence that exercise can reduce lipid deposit atherosclerosis, thus helping to reduce the risk of heart disease (Clarke 1979; Costill et al. 1979; Dressendorfer 1979; Shepard 1977; Simonelli, 1978).

The heart has its own arteries that supply blood to the heart muscle. If these vessels become clogged, there is danger of a heart attack. The "Lipid Deposit Theory" of heart disease suggests that one of the causes of heart disease may be the narrowing of the artery within the heart resulting from fat or lipid deposits on the walls of these arteries (atherosclerosis). If the deposits on the inner walls of the arteries become excessive, there is a diminished blood flow to the heart. Also, there is increased danger of a heart attack as a result of a clot lodging in the already narrowed coronary artery (coronary thrombosis). (Refer to the accompanying illustrations.)

There are many different kinds of blood fats including lipoproteins, phospholipids, triglycerides, and cholesterol. While cholesterol is the most well known, it may be no more the culprit than the other fats. Whatever fat is involved, the following conclusions are warranted based on recent research:

1. Exercise can reduce blood fat levels, particularly for individuals who have above normal blood fat levels.
2. There is evidence that there is an increased risk of coronary heart disease with increased blood fat levels.

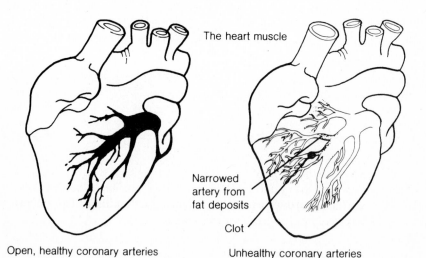

The heart muscle

Narrowed artery from fat deposits

Clot

Open, healthy coronary arteries   Unhealthy coronary arteries

The Protective Protein Theory

There is evidence that exercise can increase levels of protective proteins in the blood and thus help reduce the risk of heart disease.

The "Lipid Deposit Theory" suggests that excess fats in the blood may result in atherosclerosis and may contribute to coronary heart disease. The "Protective Protein Theory" suggests that the levels of fat-carrying proteins (called lipoproteins) in the blood may be related to the incidence of coronary heart disease. Lipoproteins are of several sizes including large or very low density (VLDL), medium or low density (LDL), and small or high density (HDL). It appears that the medium-sized lipoproteins (LDL) are undesirable because they may be deposited on the wall of the artery just as other fats described in the "Lipid Deposit Theory." It also appears that the small lipoproteins (HDL) are protective proteins. People who have high levels of the small lipoproteins (HDL) in the blood have a lessened risk of coronary heart disease (Costill 1979; Lehtonen 1979).

At this time, the best evidence suggests that high density lipoproteins (HDL) or protective blood proteins pick up excess fats in the bloodstream and carry them to the liver where they are eliminated from the body (Clarke 1979). There is good evidence that those who exercise regularly have increased levels of protective proteins in the blood (Hartung and Squires 1980; Hartung et al. 1980).

The Fibrin Deposit Theory

There is evidence that regular exercise can reduce fibrin deposit atherosclerosis and thus help reduce the risk of heart disease (Boyer 1972; Burt, Blyth, and Rierson 1964; Williams et al. 1980).

Fibrin is a sticky threadlike particle that is present in the bloodstream. It is an important substance in the blood-clotting process. The "Fibrin Deposit Theory" of heart disease suggests that the narrowing of the wall of the artery (atherosclerosis) may result from fibrin deposits. A heart attack may result from the diminished flow of blood to the heart resulting from the fibrin deposits or as a result of a clot lodged in the *now* narrowed artery.

The fibrin and lipid deposit theories are compatible, since it may be the deposits of both the sticky fibrin and fat that are responsible for atherosclerosis. If this is correct, exercise may help prevent a heart attack. The following research findings form the basis for this statement:

1. Exercise causes the breakdown of fibrin in the blood, thus reducing fibrin levels in the blood.

2. Reduced blood fibrin may diminish the chances of development of fibrin atherosclerosis.
3. Reduced blood fibrin as a result of exercise may reduce the chance of a clot forming in the blood vessel.

Coronary Collateral Circulation Theory

There is evidence that regular exercise can improve coronary collateral circulation and thus reduce the risk of heart disease (Clarke 1979; Conner et al. 1976; Eckstein 1957).

Within the heart, there are many tiny branches of the coronary arteries that supply blood to the heart muscle, as can be seen in the accompanying illustrations. These interconnecting arteries can supply blood to any region of the heart as it is needed. "If a person is relatively inactive these interconnecting arteries are functionally closed." During regular exercise these extra blood vessels are opened up to provide the heart muscle with the necessary blood and oxygen. For a person with atherosclerosis (and evidence suggests most of us have some atherosclerosis beginning early in life) or a person who has suffered a heart attack, coronary collateral circulation may be very important. There is also evidence that the size of the coronary arteries increase as a result of exercise.

Improved coronary circulation may provide protection against a heart attack because a larger artery would require more atherosclerosis to occlude it.

The heart muscle

Dormant coronary arteries   Open coronary collateral arteries

In addition, the development of collateral blood vessels supplying the heart may diminish the effects of an attack if one does occur. These "extra" (or collateral) blood vessels may take over the function of regular blood vessels during a heart attack.

The Loafer's Heart Theory

The heart of the inactive person is less able to resist stress and is more susceptible to "an emotional storm" that may precipitate a heart attack (Boyer 1972; Kraus and Raab 1961; Raab 1958).

The heart is rendered inefficient by the following circumstances: high heart rate, high blood pressure, and excessive stimulation. Any of the above conditions requires the heart to use more oxygen than is normally necessary and decreases the heart's ability to adapt to stressful situations.

The "Loafer's Heart" is one that beats rapidly because it is dominated by the sympathetic nervous system, which speeds up the heart rate. Thus, the heart continually beats rapidly, even in resting situations, and never has a true rest period. Further, high blood pressure makes the heart work harder and contributes to its inefficiency.

Research indicates the following concerning exercise and the "Loafer's Heart."

1. Regular exercise leads to parasympathetic dominance rather than sympathetic dominance; thus heart rate is reduced and the heart works efficiently.
2. Regular exercise helps the heart rate return to normal faster after emotional stress.
3. Regular exercise strengthens the "Loafer's Heart," making the heart better able to weather "emotional storms."
4. Regular exercise may be one effective method of reducing high blood pressure.
5. Regular exercise decreases sympathetic dominance and its associated hormonal effects on the heart, thus lessening the chances of altered heart contractibility and the likelihood of the circulatory problems that accompany this state.

The theories of heart disease are compatible and it is likely that most cases of coronary heart disease may be related in some way to more than one theory.

It is likely that any or all of the listed theories are correct and that exercise may help reduce the incidence of coronary heart disease in several ways. Since recent evidence indicates a decreased age for the onset of coronary heart disease, it seems especially important that we consider any factor that might reduce heart attacks (Boyer 1972).

There is no single cause or prevention of coronary heart disease. However, exercise is one of several factors that significantly relates to the incidence of coronary heart disease.

Exercise may alter certain coronary risk factors and thus reduce the chances of heart disease.

Certain factors or characteristics have been identified or associated with susceptibility to coronary heart disease.

While the relationship between these risk factors and coronary heart disease is of a statistically associative nature, sufficient data have been collected from a number of independent sources that suggest that physical activity may have a definite influence on several of these risk factors, if not directly on coronary heart disease. See Table 6.1.

Table 6.1 Exercise and Coronary Heart Disease Risk Factors

Risk Factors	Effect of Exercise
Obesity and overfatness	Loss of fat, or maintenance of weight
Excess stress and tension	Release of and increased tolerance for stress
High blood fat level	Reduction of lipid levels
Lack of exercise (activity)	Negates this factor
Age	Retards aging process
Hypertension	May reduce blood pressure for some

In addition to reducing the risk of coronary heart disease by reducing the risk factors suggested in Table 6.1, there are other benefits to the circulatory system that may result from regular exercise.

1. Regular exercise may be *one* effective method of reducing high blood pressure (hypertension) (Clarke 1979).
2. Regular exercise is necessary for the efficient return of venous blood to the heart after it is pumped to the body parts. People in standing occupations, such as barbers, dentists, etc., can improve venous return by regular exercise, especially exercise of the leg muscles. Excessive pooling of the blood in the legs resulting from inactivity may result in varicose veins.

3. There is some evidence that regular exercise may improve peripheral circulation (circulation to the arms, legs, and body parts other than the heart) (Clarke 1979).
4. There is evidence that regular exercise may result in greater blood volume and a greater number of red blood cells, thus making the delivery of oxygen to the body more efficient (Clarke 1979).

Exercise is only one of many factors that relates to reducing the risk of coronary heart disease.

Other major risk factors include family history of heart disease, smoking, sex, age, diet, stress, and blood pressure.

Suggested Readings

Clarke, H. H., ed. "Update: Exercise and Some Coronary Risk Factors," *Physical Fitness Research Digest* 9 (July 1979): 1.
Cooper, K. H. *The Aerobics Way,* chap. 3. New York: M. Evans and Co., 1977.

Strength and Muscular Endurance

7

Concept 7

Strength and muscular endurance are two important components of physical fitness and are needed in varying degrees in all types of work and play.

Introduction

The development and maintenance of strength and muscular endurance are essential for a healthy life, since both strength and muscular endurance are needed to perform normal daily functions. The purpose of this concept is to clarify strength and muscular endurance terminology, present information concerning muscular contractions, and present methods of developing strength and muscular endurance.

Terms

Anabolic Steroid—A synthetic hormone similar to the male sex hormone testosterone.

Antagonist Muscle—The muscle or muscle group that must relax in order that movement can take place.

Concentric—An isotonic contraction in which the length of a muscle decreases.

Eccentric—An isotonic contraction in which the muscle length increases.

Fast Twitch Muscle Fiber—A type of muscle fiber with fast contractile properties and a high capacity for anaerobic metabolism.

Isokinetic—A contraction against a controlled maximum resistance throughout the full range of motion.

Isometric—A type of muscular contraction in which the muscle's length does not change and no movement occurs.

Isotonic—A type of muscular contraction in which the muscle length changes and movement occurs.

Muscle Fiber—A single muscle cell.

Muscular Endurance—The capacity of a muscle to continue contracting over a period of time.

Repetitions—The number of consecutive times a particular movement or exercise is performed.

Set—The number of groups of repetitions of a particular movement or exercise.

Slow Twitch Muscle Fibers—A type of muscle fiber with slow contractile properties and a high capacity for aerobic metabolism.

Strength—A measure of the amount of external force that a muscle or group of muscles can exert.

The Facts

There are three types of muscle tissue.

The three types of muscle tissue—smooth, cardiac, and skeletal—have different structures and functions. Smooth muscle tissue consists of long spindle-shaped fibers; each fiber usually contains only one nucleus. The fibers function as the movers of internal organs since they are located in the walls of these body parts. Cardiac muscle tissue, as the name implies, is found only in the heart and its fibers are interwoven. Smooth muscles and cardiac muscles operate involuntarily. Skeletal muscle tissues consist of long, cylindrical, multinucleated fibers. They provide the force for the movement of the skeletal system and may be controlled voluntarily (deVries 1980).

There are several different types of skeletal muscle fibers (Armstrong et al. 1977; deVries 1980; Gollnick 1980).

The skeletal muscles are the muscles that do the work when a person runs, does calisthenics, dances, or participates in a sport. Skeletal muscles are made up of two different types of fibers, slow twitch and fast twitch. There are at least two different kinds of fast twich fibers. While slow twich fibers are used for prolonged or aerobic work, fast twitch fibers are used in strength and power activities.

Studies indicate that distance runners have a high number of slow twitch fibers in their muscles, and sprinters have a high number of fast twitch fibers. As a muscle is overloaded, the muscle fibers grow larger and circulation to the fibers increases. Apparently, strength training using high resistance exercises tends to selectively build fast twitch fibers. Muscular endurance training seems to promote increased functioning of the slow twitch fibers. While some people have tried to use muscle biopsies (a method of counting fast twitch and slow twitch fibers) to determine their potential for success in various sports, there is good evidence that counting the numbers of different kinds of muscle fibers is *not* an effective way to predict athletic success (Cambell et al. 1979; Costill et al. 1976; Gollnick 1980).

There are several different effective methods of exercising to develop muscle strength (Clarke, H. H. 1973; Jan. 1974; Oct. 1974; Hinson and Rosenswieg 1972; Hinson et al. 1979; Pipes and Wilmore 1975).

Most strength and muscular endurance exercises can be classified as either isotonic, isometric, or isokinetic. All three methods of exercise as well as combinations of isometric and isotonic exercises are effective in developing strength and muscular endurance. Since the most popular forms of exercises requiring the least equipment are isotonic and isometric, these types of exercises will be emphasized in this unit.

Isotonic Exercise

Isotonics are contractions of muscles against a movable resistance. Exercising with barbells or weight machines, or using your own body weight as resistance, such as in push-ups or chin-ups are examples of isotonics.

Isotonic exercise

Isometric Exercise

Isometrics are static muscle contractions performed against an immovable object, such as a wall or doorjamb, or against one's own antagonistic muscles.

Isometric exercise

Strength and Muscular Endurance

Isokinetic Exercise

Isokinetic exercises are isotonic exercises done slowly throughout the full range of joint movement and against a constant resistance. Special machines have been developed to regulate the resistance and keep it constant.

Isokinetic exercise

There is a minimum amount of exercise (threshold of training) and an optimal amount of exercise (target zone) necessary for developing muscular strength (deVries 1980).

As in other aspects of fitness, developing strength requires that the basic principles of exercise be followed. A muscle must be overloaded (overload principle) if it is to get stronger, and to be most effective, the overload must be progressive (principle of progression). The best way to progressively overload a muscle is to exercise it above the threshold of training and in the fitness target zone. Threshold levels and target zones for strength are presented in Table 7.1. Since thresholds and target zones are different for isometric and isotonic exercises, each is discussed separately.

Each form of strength exercise has its advantages and disadvantages.

The advantages and disadvantages of isotonic and isometric exercises are presented in Table 7.2. While both are effective in developing strength, for most people isotonics is the preferred type of exercise.

Table 7.1 Strength Threshold of Training and Fitness Target Zones

| | Threshold of Training | | Target Zone | |
	Isometrics	Isotonics	Isometrics	Isotonics
Intensity	Use maximal contractions.	During the first set,* lift one half of maximum; during the second set, lift three-fourths maximum; and during the third set, lift maximum weight.	Use maximal contractions.	Same as for threshold.
Duration	Hold for 5 to 8 seconds. Repeat once a day.	Perform two sets of each exercise. Do 4 repetitions of each exercise.	Hold for 5 to 8 seconds. Repeat three times a day.	Perform three sets of each exercise. Do 4–10 repetitions.
Frequency	Three days a week.	Three days a week.	Every other day.	Every other day.

Adapted from deVries, H. A. *Physiology of Exercise.* (3d ed.) Dubuque, Ia.: Wm. C. Brown Company Publishers, 1980, p. 406.

*A set refers to a group of repetitions of an exercise. If you do five push-ups, this could be one set. If you did another group of five after a rest, you would have done a second set. A set can include any number of repetitions of an exercise.

Table 7.2 Advantages and Disadvantages of Isometric and Isotonic Exercise

Isometrics	Isotonics
1. The major advantage is the fact that isometrics can be done in small areas without equipment.	1. While both methods build strength, comparisons show that isotonics promote more gain.
2. One problem with this type exercise is the inability of some to be motivated to maximal performance.	2. Most work involves movement. Since isotonic exercises are movement exercises, they are most likely to improve one's ability to do work.
3. Isometric contractions may impair endurance and circulatory blood flow.	3. Isotonic exercises provide some aid to endurance performances.
4. Isometrics do not build strength at all joint angles unless practiced at all angles.	4. When used through a full range of motion, isotonic exercises build strength at all joint angles.

Isometric and isotonic exercises can be combined to serve as an effective method of developing strength.

In order to incorporate the advantages of both isotonic and isometric exercises many isometric-isotonic exercises have been developed along with various machines employing the characteristics of both. Studies show that isotonic training is superior to isometric training in developing muscular strength and muscular endurance. In addition, motivation has been found to be greater in isotonic training than in isometric training.

Concentric isotonic exercises are most effective in building strength.

It has been found that the numbers of fibers involved in muscular contractions applied to a given load differ with types of contractions used. Concentric contractions are shortening contractions of the muscle. For example, when you do a chin-up you concentrically contract the muscle. When the muscle shortens, the chin is lifted to the bar. Eccentric contractions are lengthening contractions. For example, when you lower yourself slowly after you have done a chin-up you are doing an eccentric contraction. The muscles are working to keep your body from dropping quickly, but the muscles are lengthening rather than shortening. Both concentric and eccentric contractions are isotonic exercises. Isometric exercises do not involve either shortening or lengthening of the muscles. Concentric contractions involve the greatest number of muscle fibers with isometric contractions involving the next greatest number. Eccentric contractions involve the least number of the three types of contractions. Since tension exerted by a muscle is the important factor in building strength (Goldberg 1975), one can conclude that isotonic concentric contractions are most effective in developing strength, followed by isometric contractions and eccentric contractions (Rasch 1974).

There is a minimal amount of exercise (threshold of training) and an optimal amount of exercise (target zone) necessary for developing muscular endurance (Clarke, D. H., 1973; Clarke, H. H., Jan. 1974; Corbin and Lindsey 1979).

Though muscular endurance can be developed isometrically or isotonically, most exercises for the development of muscular endurance are isotonic in nature. The threshold of training and target zone for developing muscular endurance through isotonic exercise are presented in Table 7.3.

There is a proper way to perform strength and muscular endurance exercises (Jesse 1976; Mamaliga 1976).

In utilizing different types of muscle contraction to develop strength, there are certain guidelines to which one should adhere in order to obtain maximum benefit. General guidelines for performing any type of strength or muscular endurance exercises are summarized in Table 7.4.

Table 7.3 Muscular Endurance Threshold of Training and Fitness Target Zone

	Threshold of Training	Target Zone
Intensity	The intensity of exercise for developing muscular endurance varies widely. It may require merely lifting your arms or legs, doing an exercise such as the side-straddle hop (jumping jack), jogging, or lifting your total body weight such as in doing a chin-up or push-up. You can develop muscular endurance by repeating any of these tasks. Unlike strength, the amount of weight you lift is not as important as the duration of the effort.	
Duration	Tasks of low intensity, such as jumping jacks, trunk bends, etc., should be done for at least 30 seconds duration.	Low intensity tasks: 30 seconds to several minutes.
	Tasks of higher intensity, such as sit-ups, push-ups, etc., should be repeated at least 8 times.	Higher intensity tasks: These tasks should be repeated from 8 to 25 times. For most people there is no advantage in repeating such exercises more than 25 times.*
Frequency	Three days a week.	Three to five days a week.

*For those who are exceptionally fit and who need exceptional levels of muscular endurance, more than one set of many repetitions may be used.

Table 7.4 General Guidelines for Muscular Endurance or Strength Development

1. Obtain and record body measurements in order that areas needing improvement can be identified and progress charted.
2. Warm up slowly and completely. Supplement with flexibility exercises.
3. Perform exercises at a moderate pace.
4. Select exercises for all body parts and muscle groups.
5. Perform a complete set of an exercise before proceeding to the next exercise.
6. Do not stop a workout abruptly; cool down by continuing mild exercise of the large muscles.
7. Do not expect changes overnight.
8. Do all isotonic and isokinetic exercises through a full range of joint movement.

The development of strength and muscular endurance in women can be accomplished without loss of femininity.

While women need to strengthen muscles to improve their figures and develop physical fitness, there are those who prefer to avoid looking "muscular." Since some women in athletics are very muscular, some people associate strength and muscular endurance development in women with bulging muscles. Research has shown that this association probably stems from the fact that muscular women are apt to be more successful in such sports as track and field. However, it has been shown that properly designed exercise programs contribute to attractive appearance, and because of a difference in hormones between males and females, there is very little likelihood that the average female will develop bulging muscles (Brown and Wilmore 1974; Mayhew and Gross 1974; Van Oteghen 1974).

Strength and muscular endurance aid sports performance (Clarke, D. H., 1961; Van Oteghen 1975).

Strength and muscular endurance exercises, whether isometric, isotonic, or isokinetic, have been shown to produce improvements in many motor performances. Exercise programs designed to strengthen and improve the endurance of muscles primarily involved in a particular sport can be used as supplements to regular practice for effectively improving one's skills and motor fitness.

If a person wants to develop strength or muscular endurance in a certain muscle, that specific muscle must be exercised.

You get what you train for. If you want to develop the arms, you must exercise the arms. If you want to develop the legs, you must exercise the legs. There are three important principles for developing strength and muscular endurance. The overload principle, which states that you must overload the muscles above the threshold of training and in the target zone for fitness; the principle of progression, which says that you should start slowly and progressively increase the amount of overload; and the principle of specificity, which says that you must work the specific muscle you want to develop (Gettman et al. 1978; Jackson and Frankiewicz 1975).

Anabolic steroids *cannot* produce important improvements in sports performance and can be dangerous (ACSM 1977; Lamb 1980).

Anabolic steroids are synthetic hormones. Their properties are similar to those of the male sex hormones. Some people feel that these drugs will produce great improvements in strength and sports performances. Research results show that important improvements in performance do *not* result for fully grown adults. Further, taking these drugs has been related to such health problems as liver disorders and cancer, and among women, growth of facial hair, menstrual difficulties, and lowering of the voice. Special growth problems may result from taking the drugs while still growing.

Suggested Readings

Clarke, H. H., ed. "Development of Muscular Strength and Endurance." *Physical Fitness Research Digest* 4 (January 1974): 1.

deVries, H. A. *Physiology of Exercise.* 3d ed., chaps. 17 and 18. Dubuque, Ia.: Wm. C. Brown Company Publishers, 1980.

Stone, W. A., and Kroll, W. A. *Sports Conditioning and Weight Training.* Boston: Allyn and Bacon, 1978.

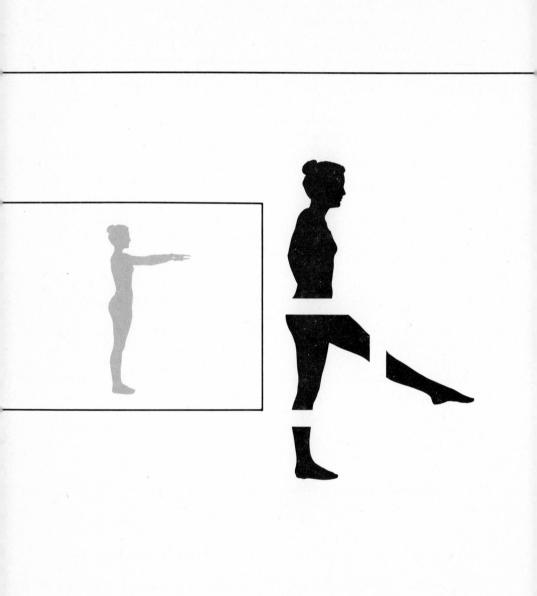

Flexibility

8

Concept 8

Adequate flexibility permits freedom of movement and may contribute to ease and economy of muscular effort, success in certain sports, and less susceptibility to some types of muscular injuries.

Introduction

Flexibility is a measure of the range of motion available at a joint or a group of joints. It is determined by the shape of the bones and cartilage involved in the joint and by the length and muscles that cross the joint. It is an often overlooked component of physical fitness that may become a concern of the average person only after the joints stiffen and muscles shorten from disuse, injury, or disease.

There is a wide range of flexibility possessed by different individuals. At one extreme is a significant lack of flexibility, which is evidenced by impaired and perhaps painful performance. At the other extreme is a high degree of flexibility (sometimes referred to erroneously as "double-jointedness") required for success by the acrobat, contortionist, gymnast, and dancer. Each person, depending on individual needs, must have a reasonable amount of flexibility to perform effectively for daily living.

Terms

Active Stretch (dynamic stretch)—Type of stretching exercise involving a bouncing or jerking motion to gain momentum in the body part in order to stretch farther. This type of stretching is sometimes called ballistic stretch.

Dysmenorrhea—Painful menstruation.

Elasticity—Property of tissue that allows it to regain its original length after being stretched.

Extensibility—Property of tissue that allows it to be stretched beyond its resting length.

Flexibility—Range of motion available in a joint or a group of joints: mobility.

Hamstrings—Muscles that cross the back of the hip joint and the back of the knee joint, causing hip extension and knee flexion.

Ligaments—Bands of connective tissue that connect bones to bones.

Lumbar Muscles—Erector spinae and other muscles of the lower back (lumbar) region of the spine.

Passive Stretch (static stretch)—Slow, sustained stretching exercise that places a muscle in a lengthened position and holds the position for a few seconds.

Reciprocal Innervation—When a muscle (agonist) contracts, its opposing muscle (antagonist) will reflexively relax.

Stretch Reflex—When a muscle is placed on sudden stretch, it will reflexively contract as a protective measure.

Tendons—Bands of connective tissue that attach muscles to bones.

The Facts

Flexibility is specific to each joint of the body.

No one flexibility test will give an indication of one's overall flexibility. For example, "tight hamstrings" might be revealed in a toe-touch test, but the range of motion in other joints may be quite different (Clarke 1975; Corbin and Noble 1980).

There are several effective methods of exercising to develop flexibility (Cooper and Fair 1977; Corbin and Noble 1980; de Vries 1980; Holt 1970).

Flexibility exercises can be classified into two different types, active (dynamic) and passive (static). Both are effective in developing flexibility.

Active stretching

Active stretching exercises, sometimes called dynamic or ballistic stretching exercises, involve bouncing or jerking to gain momentum in a body part to increase the amount of stretch that can be placed on a muscle. An example is an exercise called the hurdler's stride in which you place one foot up on an object such as a track hurdle and bounce your trunk forward to apply stretch to the muscles of the back of the leg.

Active stretching

Concept 8

Passive Stretching

Passive stretching exercises, also called static stretching exercises, involve slow, sustained stretching of a muscle. To do this type of exercise you slowly lengthen the muscle and hold it in the lenghtened position for several seconds. An example is the sit-and-reach exercise in which you sit with your legs straight in front of you and reach forward as far as you can to stretch the muscles in the back of the legs. You may have someone help you reach farther by gently pushing on your back or you may grasp and pull on the legs to provide greater muscle stretch. However, you do not bounce or jerk as you stretch.

Passive stretching

There is a minimum amount of exercise (threshold of training) and an optimal amount of exercise (target zone) necessary for developing flexibility (Corbin and Noble 1980).

Like other aspects of fitness, to develop flexibility the basic principles of exercise must be followed. For developing flexibility, the muscle must be stretched longer than its normal length (overload). Threshold of training and target zones for flexibility are presented in Table 8.1. Since thresholds and target zones are different for active and passive stretching exercises, each is discussed separately.

Each form of flexibility exercise has its advantages and disadvantages.

The advantages and disadvantages of active and passive flexibility exercises are presented in Table 8.2. While both are effective in developing flexibility, passive stretching is the preferred type of exercise for most people (Corbin and Noble 1980; deVries 1980; Schultz 1979). For persons training for involvement in sports, active stretching can be very effective but may be most effective if preceded by passive stretching.

Table 8.1 Flexibility Threshold of Training and Fitness Target Zones

| | Threshold of Training | | Target Zones | |
	Active	Passive	Active	Passive
Intensity	Stretch the muscle beyond its normal length. Gently bob or bounce against the muscle to produce stretch.	Stretch the muscle beyond its normal length. Gently reach as far as you can to stretch a muscle. If necessary, have a partner provide a gentle push to provide greater stretch. Hold the stretch.	For either type of stretching, the muscle must be stretched about 10 percent beyond its normal length. Some minimal pain may result, but excessive pain is not desirable and may even result in or be evidence of some sort of muscle or joint problem.	
Duration	Actively stretch the muscle 6 times.	Hold the stretch for 6 seconds.	Stretch 6 to 12 times. Repeat 1 to 3 times each day you exercise.	Hold the stretch for 6 to 15 seconds. Repeat 1 to 3 times each day you exercise.
Frequency	Stretch three days a week.	Stretch three days a week.	Stretch a minimum of three days up to 7 days a week.	Stretch a minimum of three days up to 7 days a week.

Table 8.2 Comparison of Advantages and Disadvantages of Passive vs. Active Stretching Exercises

Passive	Active
1. Safer; less apt to overstretch the muscle or cause muscle soreness.	1. More apt to cause injury by overstretch, especially in the presence of old injury where scar tissue is present. Contraindicated in presence of pathology.
2. Can be used to relieve some types of muscle soreness.	2. Utilizes momentum to provide the overload.
3. Is probably less effective on trunk and leg flexibility.	3. Is probably more effective on trunk and leg flexibility (although some research studies find no differences).
4. Will not elicit reflex contraction (stretch reflex) of the stretched muscle.	4. Will elicit the reflex contraction, but this is not detrimental to flexibility because the muscle will not be overloaded during contraction, since momentum has been spent.
5. Does not take advantage of the reciprocal innervation that would cause the stretched muscle to relax and be capable of greater extensibility. (Note: The individual can be taught to consciously contract the opposing muscle group to facilitate the reflex relaxation.)	5. Since the opposing muscle group usually produces the movement, the muscles being stretched will relax by virtue of reciprocal innervation, permitting greater stretch.
6. Requires use of a partner or ouside force greater than that which can be provided by contraction of opposing muscle group.	

There is some evidence to indicate that proprioceptive neuromuscular facilitation (PNF) techniques are useful in developing flexibility (Holt 1970; Rivera 1979; Rogers 1978).

One form of passive stretching exercise that is gaining in popularity is PNF. The technique, first developed as a physical therapy procedure for the rehabilitation of paralytic patients, has been shown to be an effective method of developing flexibility. To use the PNF technique, you first contract the muscle to be stretched. Then have a partner help you passively stretch it as you contract its antagonist. For example, to stretch the calf muscle, first contract the calf by pointing the toe; then contract the muscles of the front of the shin by voluntarily pulling your toes toward your shin while a partner assists by gently pushing your toes toward your shin. Similar PNF exercises can be used to stretch other muscles.

There is a proper way to perform flexibility exercises.

Guidelines are presented in Table 8.3.

Table 8.3 Guidelines for Performing Flexibility Exercises

1. Avoid active exercises on previously injured muscles.
2. Avoid active toe touches in the presence of backaches.
3. If active stretching is used, the bounces should be easy, gentle movements to avoid overstretching.
4. Exercises must be performed for each muscle group or joint in which increased flexibility is desired.
5. Exercises that do not cause a muscle to lengthen beyond normal may maintain flexibility but will not increase flexibility.
6. To increase flexibility, the muscle must be "overloaded" (i.e., stretched beyond normal length).

Lack of use, injury, and disease may cause a decrease in joint mobility.

Arthritis and calcium deposits may damage a joint, and inflammation may cause pain that prevents movement. Failure to regularly move a joint through its full range of motion may lead to a foreshortening of muscles and ligaments; static positions held for long periods of time, such as in poor posture or when a body part is immobilized in a cast, lead to shortened tissue and loss of mobility. Improper exercise that overdevelops one muscle group while neglecting the opposing group results in an imbalance that restricts flexibility (Holland 1968).

The length of body parts does not significantly affect flexibility.

Contrary to popular opinion, there is no relationship between leg length or trunk length and the scores made on flexibility tests.

Flexibility has been found to be influenced by age and sex.

As children grow older, they increase in flexibility until adolescence when they become progressively less flexible with age. As a general rule, girls tend to be more flexible than boys. This is probably attributable to anatomical differences in the joints as well as differences in the type and extent of activities the two sexes tend to choose (deVries 1980; Hupperick and Segerseth 1970).

Stretching exercises are useful in preventing and remediating dysmenorrhea.

Painful menstruation of some types can be prevented or reduced by stretching the pelvic and hip joint fascia.

Static muscle stretching appears to be effective in relieving muscle soreness and "shinsplints."

One theory suggests that local muscular soreness may be caused by slight reflex contractions. There is some evidence that static stretch of the affected muscle may relieve these slight contractions and thus relieve the pain. Even some cases of nonpathological shinsplints may be relieved by such exercise (deVries 1980).

Scores on flexibility tests may be affected by several factors other than joint structure.

Range of motion may vary considerably with effort, warm-up preparation prior to starting the test, presence of muscle soreness and tolerance for pain, room temperature, and the individual's ability to relax (Holland 1968).

Adequate flexibility may help prevent muscle strain and such orthopedic problems as backache.

Short, tight muscles are more apt to be injured by overstretching than are long muscles. One common cause of backache is shortened lumbar and hip flexor muscles. (A further discussion of back problems is presented in Concept 14.)

It is not necessary to sacrifice flexibility in order to develop strength.

A person with bulging muscles may be "muscle-bound" (lack of flexibility), but only if he or she has trained improperly. In any progressive resistance program both agonists and antagonists should receive equal attention and all movements should be carried through the full range of motion (Corbin and Noble 1980; deVries 1980).

Good flexibility may bring about improved athletic performance.

A hurdler must have good hip joint mobility to clear the hurdle. A swimmer requires shoulder and ankle flexibility for powerful strokes. A diver must be able to reach his or her toes in order to perform a good jackknife. Low back flexibility allows a runner to lengthen the stride. The fencer needs long hamstrings and hip adductors in order to lunge a long distance (Corbin and Noble 1980).

Too much flexibility in certain joints may make a person more susceptible to injury.

Muscles and tendons have both extensibility and elasticity. Ligaments are extensible but lack elasticity. When stretched, ligaments remain in a lengthened state. When this occurs, the joint lacks stability and may be susceptible to chronic dislocation or movement in an undesirable plane. This is particularly true of weight-bearing joints such as the knee joint. Loose ligaments may allow the knee to twist or move laterally, tearing the cartilage and damaging other soft tissue.

Exactly how much flexibility an individual should possess has not as yet been scientifically demonstrated.

There are test norms available that tell us how various subjects perform on flexibility tests, but we are not certain that the old adage "the more, the better" is true. Too much flexibility may be as detrimental as too little.

Suggested Readings

Corbin, C. B., and Noble, L. "Flexibility." *JOPER*, 1980.
Clarke, H. H., ed. "Joint and Body Range of Movement." *Physical Fitness Research Digest* 5 (October 1975):1.
Shultz, P. "Flexibility: Day of the Static Stretch." *The Physician and Sports Medicine* 7 (November 1979):109.

Body Composition/ Weight Control

9

Concept 9

Obesity is a significant health problem that can be controlled, in most cases, with a proper balance between caloric consumption (diet) and caloric expenditure (physical activity).

Introduction

Appearance is probably the major reason why most people are concerned about weight control. However, proper body composition is also very important to total health and fitness. It is the purpose of the following discussion to present facts about weight control, including information about diet and physical activity. Special consideration is given to the use of exercise as an effective means of maintaining ideal body weight.

Terms

Calorie—A unit of energy supplied by food; the quantity of heat necessary to raise the temperature of a kilogram of water one degree centigrade (actually a kilocalorie but usually called a calorie for weight control programs).

Caloric Balance—Consuming calories in amounts equal to the number of calories expended.

Diet—The usual food and drink for a person or animal.

M.E.T.—MET is an acronym for the basic amount of energy expended at rest. As you do work, your metabolism increases. Mets are multiples of the amount of energy expended at rest.

Obesity—Extreme weight, often considered as 20 to 30 percent above "normal"; probably best defined as an overfat condition.

Overfat—Having too much body composition as fat; for men, having more than 20 to 25 percent of the total body composition as fat; and for women, 25 to 30 percent.

Overweight—Having weight in excess of normal. Not necessarily harmful if weight is lean body tissue.

Somatotype—Inherent body build: ectomorph (thin); mesomorph (muscular); endomorph (fat).

The Facts

Overfatness rather than overweightness is more important in determining obesity.

Individuals who are interested in controlling their weight usually consult a height-weight chart to determine "desirable" weight. Being 20 percent or more above the ideal chart weight is the commonly accepted criterion of obesity. While proper chart weights are good general guidelines, it is now clear that for most people the height-weight chart is not as accurate an indication of obesity as is the percentage of body fat.

Underwater (hydrostatic) weighing and skinfold measurements now make it possible to estimate the percentage of the body that is comprised of fat. Some individuals who possess muscular body types have been shown to be overweight and even obese in terms of height-weight charts, yet they possess very little body fat. Since the amount of body fat, not the amount of weight, is the important factor in living a healthy life, it is wise to use "overfatness" rather than "overweightness" as the measure (Jette et al. 1979; Plowman and Falls 1978; 1979; Sinning 1980).

Obesity or overfatness contributes to many degenerative diseases and health problems.

Research evidence indicates that the . . . "complications associated with obesity are far-reaching, being associated with serious organic impairments and shortened life, with psychological maladjustments, with unfortunate peer relationships (especially among children); with inefficiency of physical movement, and with ineffectiveness in motor and athletic activities. Obesity is consistently encountered as a cause of physical unfitness among boys and girls, men and women. . ." (Clarke 1975). Fat people have a higher frequency of respiratory infections, a prevalence of high blood pressure and atherosclerosis, and are prone to disorders of the circulatory, respiratory, and kidney systems (Clarke 1975).

Overfatness or obesity may shorten life.

Results of several investigations indicate that people who are moderately overfat have a 40 percent higher than normal risk of shortened life, and more severe obesity yields a 70 percent higher than normal death rate (Clarke 1975). This fact is substantially reflected in the exorbitant life insurance premiums of obese individuals.

Obesity is a problem experienced by too many Americans.

Some experts indicate that as many as 60 million or half of all the adults in the United States are overweight (Katch and McArdle 1977). Others suggest that at least one-third of adult Americans are overfat. In addition to the problem of adult obesity, statistics indicate that as many as 10 million school children may be classified as overfat or obese (Katch and McArdle 1977).

In some cases, glandular problems may cause an obese condition. However, these conditions are quite rare. Obesity is usually a result of an imbalance between caloric intake and output. Crash diets, spot reducing, and passive exercise "gimmick" machines are *not* effective in producing lasting fat loss (Ribisl 1974).

To lose body fat, decreased caloric intake and increased caloric expenditure are necessary.

Determining the minimal and optimal amounts of exercise necessary to obtain a desirable body fatness level cannot be described using a threshold of training and a target zone for exercise alone. A combination of decreased caloric intake (dieting) and increased caloric output (exercise) is more effective than either one alone; therefore, it is most appropriate to talk of a threshold and target for both diet and exercise (Katch and McArdle 1977; Pollock and Jackson 1977; Pollock, Wilmore, and Fox 1978; Zuti and Golding 1976). Threshold and target zones are illustrated in Table 9.1.

Good exercise and diet habits can be useful in maintaining desirable body fat content and in gaining lean body weight (Clarke 1975; Noland and Kearney 1978).

Table 9.1 illustrates how body fat can be lost through regular exercise and proper dieting. However, not all people want to lose body fat. For those who wish to maintain their current body composition, keeping a balance between caloric intake and expenditure is effective. For those who wish to gain lean body mass, increased caloric intake with increased exercise can result in the desired changes, as shown by the illustration on page 63.

Exercise is one effective means of controlling body fat (Svoboda 1980; Zuti and Golding 1976).

Though physical activity or exercise will not result in immediate and large decreases in body fat levels, there is increasing evidence that fat loss resulting from exercise may be more lasting than fat loss from dieting. Vigorous exercise can increase the resting energy expenditure up to 13 times (13 METS).

If a person exercises moderately for fifteen minutes a day (all other things being equal), a loss of more than ten pounds in a year's time may be seen.

Table 9.1 Threshold of Training and Target Zones for Body Fat Reduction

	Threshold of Training* Exercise	Threshold of Training* Diet	Target Zones* Exercise	Target Zones* Diet
Intensity	To lose one pound of fat, you must expend 3,500 calories more than you normally expend.	To lose one pound of fat, you must eat 3,500 calories less than you normally eat.	Experts agree that crash exercise programs are *not* best. Slow, low intensity aerobic exercise that results in no more than 1 to 2 pounds of fat loss per week is best.	Experts agree that crash diets are *not* best. Modest caloric restriction resulting in no more than one to two pounds of fat loss per week is best.
Duration	To be effective, exercise must be sustained long enough to expend a considerable number of calories. At least 15 minutes per exercise bout is necessary to result in consistent fat loss.	Eating regular meals and restricting snacking is best. Skipping meals is *not* most effective.	Exercise durations similar to those for achieving aerobic cardiovascular fitness seem best. An exercise duration of 30 to 60 minutes is recommended.	Eating regular meals and restricting snacks is best. Skipping meals or fasting is *not* most effective.
Frequency	To be effective, exercise must be regular, preferably daily, though fat can be lost over the long haul with almost any frequency that results in increased caloric expenditure.	It is best to reduce caloric intake consistently and daily. To restrict calories only on certain days is *not* best, though fat can be lost over a period of time by reducing caloric intake at any time.	Daily moderate exercise is recommended. For those who do regular vigorous activity, five or six days per week may be best.	It is best to diet consistently and daily.

Note: It is best to combine exercise and diet to achieve the 3,500 caloric imbalance necessary to lose a pound of fat. Using both exercise and diet in the target zone is most effective.

Caloric input (diet)   Maintenance   Caloric output (exercise)

Weight gain   Fat loss

Regular walking, jogging, swimming, or any type of sustained exercise can be effective in producing losses in body fat (Clarke 1975; Pollock and Jackson 1977; Pollock, Wilmore, and Fox 1978). In fact, recent studies indicate that exercise combined with dietary restriction may be the *most* effective method of losing fat. One study of adult women indicated that diet alone resulted in loss of weight, but much of the weight was lean body tissue. For those dieting as well as exercising, there were similar weight losses, but there was a much greater loss in body fat. On the basis of this research, it was suggested that all weight loss programs should combine lowered caloric intake with a good physical exercise program (Zuti and Golding 1976).

Appetite is not necessarily increased through exercise.

The human animal was intended to be an active animal. For this reason, man's "appetite thermostat" (called the appestat by some) is set as if all people are active. Those who are inactive do not have a decreased appetite. Likewise, if one is sedentary and then begins regular exercise, the appetite does not necessarily increase because the "appetite thermostat" expects activity. Very vigorous activity does not necessarily cause an appetite increase that is proportional to the calories expended in the vigorous exercise (Mayer 1975).

Fat children may become fat adults.

Retention of "baby fat" is not a sign of good health. On the contrary, excess body fat in the early years is a health problem of considerable concern. As many as 25 percent of American school children are overfat. Of these children, four of five will become overfat adults. Twenty-eight of twenty-nine teenagers who are too fat will become overfat adults. There is evidence that children who are obese may actually increase the number as well as the size of their fat cells, thus making them predisposed to obesity in later life (Hirsch and Knittle 1970; Oscai 1973; 1974).

Inactivity contributes to childhood obesity.

Studies of fat children show that activity restriction is more often a cause of obesity than is overeating. Many fat children eat less but are considerably less active than their nonfat peers.

"Creeping obesity" often accompanies increase in age.

Many of the "too fat Americans" are between the ages of thirty and sixty. As one grows older, changes in metabolism cause a decrease in caloric expenditure necessary to sustain life. Unless activity is increased or diet is restricted, a gain in weight will occur. Activity usually decreases while eating habits remain fairly constant with age. Thus, obesity creeps up on an individual (Mayer 1975). To prevent "creeping obesity," it is suggested that the average person cut caloric intake 3 percent each decade after age twenty-five, so that by age sixty-five caloric intake is at least 10 percent less than it was at age twenty-five.

Suggested Readings

Clarke, H. H., ed. "Exercise and Fat Reduction." *Physical Fitness Research Digest* 5 (April 1975):1.
Katch, F. I., and McArdle, W. D. *Nutrition, Weight Control, and Exercise.* Boston: Houghton Mifflin Co., 1977.

Exercise and Nutrition

10

Concept 10

The basic nutritional needs of athletes and nonathletes do not differ except for caloric requirements. Although there are special considerations for athletes, many of their dietary practices are faddish, unsound, and even dangerous.

Introduction

In spite of the fact that nutrition is an advanced science, many myths and misconceptions prevail. These are propagated by commercial interests, which gain by the sale of their products through superstition and ignorance of the true facts by the public and even by physicians and educators. Superstition seems to thrive particularly among athletes and coaches. Such misconceptions can lead to imbalanced diets, high cost, and disappointment in its influence on performance.

Within this concept we will discuss some current theories and practices and attempt to dispel some myths about the feeding of athletes and others who engage in regular physical activity.

Because nutrition affects us all, it is important that we be knowledgeable about the subject. It is far too complicated to cover even the fundamentals in these pages; therefore, the reader is urged to enroll in a course on nutrition or study reliable books on the subject (see Recommended Readings at the end of this chapter).

Terms

Cellulose—Indigestible fiber (bulk) in foods.

Dehydration—Excessive loss of body fluids (e.g., through perspiration diarrhea, or urination).

Kilogram—A metric unit of weight equaling 2.2046 pounds.

"Making Weight"—Quick loss or gain in weight so an athlete (usually a wrestler) can compete in a given weight category.

The Facts

The amount and kind of food one eats affects one's size, strength, and fitness.

There are about forty to forty-five nutrients contained in food that are essential for the body's growth, maintenance, and repair. These are classified into carbohydrates, fats, proteins, vitamins, minerals, and water. The first three of these provide energy, which is measured in calories.

The Food and Nutrition Board of the National Academy of Sciences—National Research Council has established "recommended daily allowances" (RDA) of the nutrients. To help assure that we select foods containing the essential elements, they have classified foods into groups, each of which should be included in the daily diet. The quantity of nutrients recommended varies with age and other considerations; for example, a young growing child needs more calcium than an adult, and a pregnant woman needs more calcium than other women (Bailey 1978).

The specified number of servings from each of the food groups on a daily basis will provide a well-balanced diet (Bailey 1978).

See Table 10.1, "Recommended Food Selections for Good Health," for information on the four food groups and the recommended number of daily servings.

The number of calories needed per day depends on such factors as age, sex, size, muscle mass, glandular function, emotional state, climate, and exercise.

Table 10.1 Recommended Food Selections for Good Health

Food Group	Amount for Adults	Special Role in Diet
1. Milk, cheese, ice cream, and other dairy products	Two or more servings	Protein, calcium and other minerals, vitamins
2. Meat, poultry, fish, eggs (alternates: nuts, dried beans, peas)	Two or more servings	Protein, iron and other minerals, B vitamins
3. All vegetables and fruits, including potatoes		Minerals, vitamins, fiber
a. Green and yellow vegetables	Four or more servings	Iron, vitamin A, folacin
b. Citrus fruits, tomatoes, raw cabbage, etc.		Vitamin C
4. Grain products—bread, flour, cereals, baked goods (perferably whole-grain or enriched)	Four or more servings	Inexpensive source of energy, iron, vitamin B

A moderately active college-aged woman needs about 2,000 calories per day, while a moderately active man of the same age needs about 2,800 calories. A female athlete in training might burn 2,600-3,500; a male athlete in training may expend 3,500-5,500 (American Alliance for Health, Physical Education and Recreation 1971; Bailey 1978; Bogert et al. 1973; Mayer 1975). If weight remains at the optimum, the caloric content of the diet is correct. If weight varies from optimal, then the caloric content of the diet may need to be altered.

Athletes and active people do not need relatively more protein than nonathletes or inactive people.

Protein needs vary with age, size, and other factors such as pregnancy, but the well-balanced diet includes about sixty grams of protein per day. This is well over the minimum needed and is adequate for most people. The recommended protein intake is about one gram per kilogram of body weight or 11 to 16 percent of the total calories per day.

Athletes or active people frequently consume more calories than nonathletes or inactive people; and for this reason they consume more protein, assuming that they eat a balanced diet. Because protein is not used as an important source of energy, there is no need to supplement the athlete's or active person's diet with protein. For weight lifters, for example, excessive protein in the diet may have an unfavorable effect on the body. As the athlete's energy expenditure increases, he or she needs less protein and more carbohydrate; i.e., 13 percent protein when 4,500 Kcal are expended, 12 percent at 5,500 Kcal, and 11 percent at 8,000 Kcal (Parizkova and Rogozkin in 1978). High-quality protein is provided by all meats, milk, cheese, and eggs. Consequently, there is no reason for athletes to gorge themselves on beefsteak or to take supplemental proteins if they eat a balanced diet (American Alliance for Health, Physical Education and Recreation 1971; Bogert et al. 1973; Consolazio et al. 1975; Lewis and Gutin 1973; Mayer 1976).

Fat should be eaten only in moderate to low amounts.

Humans need some fat in their diet because fats are carriers of vitamins E, K, D, and A; are a source of essential linoleic acid; make food taste better; and provide a concentrated form of calories. Fat has twice the calories per gram of carbohydrates, but it does not provide twice the energy. High fat diets provide no special benefits for the athlete. Most popular weight loss diets are high in protein; unfortunately, that usually means lots of meat and, therefore, lots of fat. Most Americans consume about 40 percent of their calories in fats, but this amount should probably be reduced to about 25 percent to cut down on obesity and high blood fat levels in the population (American Alliance for Health, Physical Education and Recreation 1971; Bailey 1978; Mayer 1976).

Breakfast is an important meal.

Numerous studies have shown that omission of the breakfast meal results in poor performance because blood sugar drops in the long period between dinner the night before and lunch the following day. Persons on reducing diets probably eat more total calories when they omit breakfast because they tend to overeat at lunch and dinner. About one-fourth of the day's calories should be consumed at breakfast (Bogert et al. 1973; Mayer 1976).

Some dietary practices are detrimental to performance.

Skipping meals and dehydration are two practices that are detrimental to performance. Another practice that research has shown to adversely affect performance is vitamin deficiency. A reduced intake of vitamin B and thiamin are evident within a few days. A lack of minerals has a negative effect, but it does not become evident for a few weeks (with the exception of the electrolytes [e.g., sodium and potassium, where a deficiency occurs with dehydration]). Low carbohydrate diets are also detrimental to performance (Bogert et al. 1973).

There is *no* scientific basis for eliminating milk from the athlete's diet.

Milk does *not* cause "cotton mouth." Dryness of the mouth is due to decreased saliva flow caused by dehydration or an emotional state. Milk does *not* decrease speed, "cut wind," produce sour stomach, or interfere with performance unless the individual has an intolerance to milk (American Alliance for Health, Physical Education and Recreation 1971).

"Quick energy" foods eaten just before events of short duration do *not* enhance performance.

Ingesting honey, glucose, or other sweets just prior to short-term performance does not provide the athlete with a burst of energy. The body will use its own energy reserves. The carbohydrates eaten will go toward replacing the energy used in the performance (American Alliance for Health, Physical Education and Recreation 1971).

"Carbohydrate Loading" may improve performance in long endurance events, but it is not without hazard (Sheehan 1976).

Carbohydrates provide most of the energy used in heavy exercise and endurance events exceeding thirty to sixty minutes, such as in marathon runs. Several studies have supported the following dietary procedures for such events:

1. Approximately one week before the event, exhaust the muscles to be used in the event.

2. Four to six days before the event, eat a high protein, high fat, and low carbohydrate diet ("carbohydrate depletion").
3. One to three days before the event, add large quantities of carbohydrates to the diet ("carbohydrate loading") (American Alliance for Health, Physical Education and Recreation 1971; Bogert et al. 1973; Ledeux-Personnet 1979; Lewis and Gutin 1973).

The "loading" procedure has been shown to improve performance for some; however, serious side-effects have been reported (Mirken 1973; Sheehan 1976). It can cause cramps, kidney congestion, decreased running efficiency, and it may be especially hazardous to the older individual.

The timing may be more important than the makeup of the pre-event meal.

It is probably best to eat about three hours before competition or heavy exercise to allow time for digestion. Generally, the athlete can make his or her food selection on the basis of past experience. Tension, anxiety, and excitement are more apt to cause gastric distress than food selection. It is generally accepted that fat intake should be minimal because it digests more slowly; "gas formers" should probably be avoided; and proteins and high cellulose foods should be kept to a minimum prior to prolonged events to avoid urinary and bowel excretion. Two or three cups of liquid (avoid caffeine) should be taken to insure adequate hydration (American Alliance for Health, Physical Education and Recreation 1971; Bogert et al. 1973). It should be noted that the excitement associated with competition is probably the main reason for having a special diet before participation.

Since many people who exercise regularly do not compete during their exercise, there is little reason to alter their normal diet before their regular exercise. Likewise, there is no need to delay exercise for long periods after the meal if exercise is to be moderate and noncompetitive.

"Health foods," tonics, and supplements will not contribute to health, fitness, weight control, or athletic performance.

The Food and Drug Administration labels the health food racket as the most widespread quackery in the United States. Whether athletic or sedentary, the individual on a well-balanced diet does *not* benefit from special organic foods, additional vitamins (including vitamin E), choline, lecithin, wheat germ, brewer's yeast, gelatin, royal jelly, or any other supplement, unless specifically prescribed for a medical purpose by one's own physician (American Alliance for Health, Physical Education and Recreation 1971; Bogert et al. 1973; Bunnell 1975; Mayer 1976).

Fad diets are not a satisfactory means to long-term weight reduction and may adversely affect one's health.

There are hundreds of fad diets and diet books, but nutritionists warn that there is no scientific basis for drastic juggling of food constituents. Such diets are usually unbalanced and may result in serious illness or even death, especially for the obese person who is already apt to be suffering from a number of health disorders. Fad diets cannot be maintained for long periods of time; therefore, the individual usually regains any lost weight. Constant losing and gaining may be more harmful than the original obese condition.

Crash diets that bring about weight loss by dehydration of only 5 percent in forty-eight hours have been shown to reduce the individual's working capacity by as much as 40 percent. The practice of "making weight" in athletics, whether by dehydration, induced vomiting, or starvation diets is dangerous to health and should be condemned ("All the News That's Fit" 1971; American Alliance for Health, Physical Education and Recreation 1971; Mayer 1976).

Suggested Readings

American Association for Health, Physical Education and Recreation. *Nutrition for Athletes.* 1201 16th St., N.W., Washington, D.C. 20036, 1971.

Bogert, L. J., et al. *Nutrition and Physical Fitness*, 9th ed. Philadelphia: W. B. Saunders Co., 1973.

Chicago Nutrition Association. *Nutritional References and Book Reviews.* 8158 S. Kedzie Ave., Chicago, Illinois 60652, revised 1975.*

*This inexpensive paperback lists nutrition books by title, with brief abstracts, and categorizes them under four headings:
1. "Recommended"
2. "Recommended for Special Purposes"
3. "Recommended only with Reservations"
4. "*Not* Recommended"

Skill-Related Fitness

11

Concept 11

Skill-related fitness is essential to performance in games and sports as well as to working efficiency.

Introduction

Skill-related fitness consists of six different aspects: balance, agility, coordination, speed, power, and reaction time. Although these aspects of physical fitness do not necessarily make a person healthier, possessing these fitness aspects makes one better at games and sports as well as improving work efficiency. In a society that is becoming increasingly interested in leisure and recreation, skill-related physical fitness can be important to living a meaningful and enjoyable life.

The Facts

Good skill-related fitness may help an individual achieve good health-related fitness.

Individuals who achieve good skill-related fitness have the potential to succeed in sports and games. Regular participation in these activities can lead to improved health-related fitness throughout life. In addition, people who make an effort to learn activities involving skill-related fitness are more likely to be active in sports and games for a lifetime (Clarke 1974; Harris and assoc. 1979).

Skill-related fitness may improve one's ability to work efficiently (Corbin 1980; deVries 1980).

In manual labor, skillful performance improves efficiency. For example, a ditchdigger with great ditchdigging skill uses less energy than one who has not mastered the skill. Seemingly simple skills are often quite complex and may require some proficiency in each of the skill-related fitness aspects.

Skill-related fitness may improve one's ability to meet emergency situations.

Good agility would enable a person to dodge an oncoming car; good balance would lessen the likelihood of a fall; and good reaction time would decrease the chances of being hit by a flying object. Each aspect of skill-related fitness contributes in its own way to an individual's ability to avoid injury and meet emergencies.

Good skill-related fitness is beneficial to carrying out the normal daily routine and enjoying one's leisure time (Harris and assoc. 1979).

Walking, sitting, climbing, pushing, pulling, and other such tasks require varying degrees of skill-related fitness. Accordingly, improvement in these aspects resulting from regular practice may improve efficiency in performing daily activities and enjoying one's leisure or recreational time.

Potential for possessing outstanding skill-related fitness is based on hereditary predispositions, but all aspects of skill-related fitness can be improved through regular practice (Schmidt 1975).

In order for a skill to be improved, it must be repeated. Some skill-related fitness aspects such as power, agility, balance, and coordination can be enhanced greatly with practice. Others such as speed and reaction time can be improved somewhat but are determined to a greater extent by heredity.

Exceptional athletes tend to be outstanding in more than one aspect of skill-related fitness (Lawther 1977).

While people possess skill-related fitness in varying degrees, great athletes are likely to be above average in most if not all aspects. Indeed, exceptional athletes must be exceptional in many aspects of skill-related fitness. Different sports do require different specific fitness proficiencies.

Excellence in one skill-related fitness aspect may compensate for lack of another (Robb 1972).

Each individual possesses a specific level of each of the skill-related fitness aspects. The performer should learn his or her other strengths and weaknesses in order to produce optimal performances. For example, a tennis player may use superior shot placement to compensate for a lack of speed.

Excellence in skill-related fitness may compensate for lack of health-related fitness when playing sports and games.

As one grows older, health-related fitness potential declines. The individual may use superior skill-related fitness to compensate. For example, a baseball pitcher who lacks the strength and muscular endurance to overpower hitters may rely on knuckleball throwing skill to deceive the hitters.

Skills are specific in nature (Corbin 1980; Lawther 1977; Schmidt 1975).

An individual might possess ability in one area and not another. For this reason, "General Motor Ability" probably does not really exist. Individuals do not have one general capacity for performing skills. Rather, the ability to play games or sports is determined by combined abilities in each of the separate motor skill aspects of agility, coordination, balance, reaction time, speed, and power. It is, however, possible and even likely that some performers will have above-average skill in many areas.

Suggested Readings

Lawther, J. D. *The Learning and Performance of Physical Skills*. 2d ed. Englewood Cliffs, N.J.: Prentice-Hall, Inc., 1977.
Schmidt, R. A. *Motor Skills*. New York: Harper & Row, 1975.

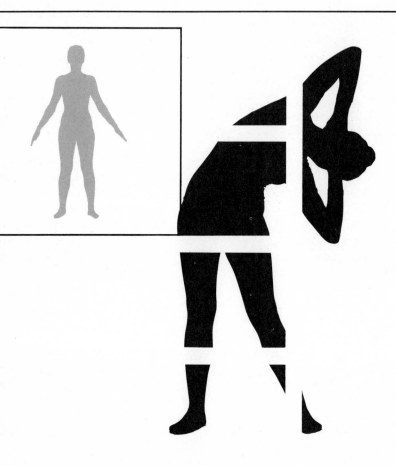

Learning Lifetime Sports and Physical Activities

12

Concept 12

Everyone, regardless of physical abilities, can find a sport or physical activity that can be enjoyed for a lifetime.

Introduction

The recent emphasis on "lifetime sports" has resulted in a considerable increase in participation by American adults. However, a recent survey indicates that 41 percent or roughly 64 million Americans over 18 years of age do not exercise on a regular basis (Harris and assoc. 1979). One of the reasons for nonparticipation is that too many adults were not successful in sports activities as children. It should be emphasized that there is some type of activity that will be meaningful to every person and that lack of competitive success does not mean that a person cannot be a regular participant in exercise for a lifetime.

Terms

Lifetime Physical Activity—An activity performed by adults on a regular basis after the school-age years. These activities include those not generally considered as sports, such as walking, jogging, bicycle riding, and calisthenics.

Lifetime Sports—Sports performed by adults on a regular basis after the school-age years. Among those of greatest current popularity are bowling, swimming, golf, and tennis.

Mental Practice—Imagining the performance of a skill without actually physically performing it.

Overlearning—Practicing a skill over and over many times in an attempt to make the skill a "habit."

"Paralysis by Analysis"—Overanalysis of skill behavior. This occurs when more information is supplied than the performer can really use or when concentration on too many details of a skill results in interference with performance.

Skill Analysis—Breaking the performance of a skill into component parts and critically evaluating each phase of the performance.

The Facts

There is no one best sport or physical activity for all people.

Some people would lead us to believe that "their" sport is the "best" or "only" sport. However, while each sport has its advantages in accomplishing certain objectives, there is no single best sport for all people. The best sport or physical activity for you depends on your abilities, interests, personality, and other personal factors.

A person does not have to be a "great" performer to enjoy sports and physical activity for a lifetime.

Evidence suggests that many Americans discontinue participation in physical activity as they get older because they "are not very good at sports." There are many different types of sports and activities and each requires different abilities. Failure in the past does not mean that one cannot find enjoyment in sports in the future. Some activities require coordination; some require agility and balance; while others may require health-related physical fitness, such as cardiovascular fitness, strength, and flexibility; and still others require daring or ability to use strategy (Corbin 1980).

Each person should analyze his or her own personal strengths to decide which is the best activity. Some may wish to choose activities that require relatively little skill but that can be very beneficial to health and can become a meaningful part of their lifestyle. Activities such as walking, jogging, bicycle riding, and calisthenics are among the most widely used by Americans today (Harris and assoc. 1979).

While most people learn recreational sports skills early in life, lifetime sports skills can be learned at any age.

Research evidence suggests that most skills are learned early in life. In fact, one study indicates that as many as 85 percent of all recreational skills are learned by the age of twelve (Nash 1960). This does not mean that "old dogs cannot learn new tricks," but it does suggest a need to teach skills to children at an early age.

Team and competitive sports provide enjoyment during our youth, but they are not activities that are likely to be engaged in as adults (Harris and Assoc. 1979).

A recent national survey indicates that of the ten most popular forms of physical activity, only three are sports. Of the top five, only one is a sport. The most popular activities include walking, jogging, bicycling, hiking, and other similar activities. The ten most popular sports including the three listed in the top ten of all activities are listed in Table 12.1.

Table 12.1 Achieving Fitness Through Sports

Sport	Participants (in millions)	Cardio-vascular	Muscular Endurance	Strength	Flexibility	Fat Control
Bowling	20.2	—	—	—	—	—
Tennis	14.0	**	**	*	*	*
Basketball	10.9	***	**	*	—	**
Softball	10.9	—	—	—	—	—
Baseball	9.3	—	—	—	—	—
Golf (walking)	7.8	*	*	—	*	*
Volleyball	7.8	*	**	*	*	*
Football	6.2	*	*	**	—	*
Frisbee	6.2	*	*	—	*	*
Table Tennis	6.2	—	—	—	*	—

***Very Good
**Good
*Minimum
—Low

Participation in a lifetime sport or physical activity does not insure good health-related physical fitness.

While there are many benefits to participation in lifetime physical activities, many are not of sufficient frequency, intensity, and duration to improve health-related physical fitness. For example, in most cases bowling would do little to improve cardiovascular fitness. The contribution of sports to the different aspects of fitness are illustrated in Table 12.1.

The way a person plays a sport has much to do with the amount of fitness it develops.

The way you play a sport will determine the fitness benefits derived from the activity. If you play basketball you may just shoot baskets, you may play on half the court, or you may play a vigorous full court competitive game. In tennis you may just hit the ball back and forth, you may play a recreational game, or you may play a vigorous competitive game. The benefits as illustrated in Table 12.1 are based on moderate recreational play. If you play less intensely or more vigorously the benefits will vary accordingly.

In many cases a person needs to exercise to get fit for sports rather than play sports to get fit.

Many sports require a considerable amount of fitness especially for those involving vigorous competition, yet the sport may do relatively little to develop fitness. For example, you need considerable strength, muscular endurance, and flexibility to play football; however, football is not a particularly good activity for developing these aspects of fitness.

Participation in lifetime sports can be a means of achieving physical fitness, but it can also provide other valuable benefits as well.

One of the real benefits of regular participation in lifetime physical activities can be improved health through improved cardiovascular fitness, muscular endurance, strength, and flexibility. However, the participants may also derive personal satisfaction and meaning from the participation and benefits from social interactions and the release of emotional tensions (Csikszentmihalyi 1977).

Skill proficiency in a sport and selection of a partner of similar ability are both important to enjoyment of the sporting experience.

It is true that people who have some skill in an activity are more likely to participate in that activity than those with little or no skill. For this reason it is advisable to practice and perhaps seek instruction to enhance enjoyment of a lifetime activity. People with greater skill are more likely to get involved because they are more likely to be successful. However, there is another way to increase the satisfaction gained from sports participation. Research indicates that you must be 65 to 75 percent as good as your partner if either of you are to enjoy the activity. For this reason it is not only advisable to improve your skills, but it is suggested that you find a playing partner or group of similar ability to your own (Cratty 1967).

There are certain guidelines that can be followed to help in effectively learning a lifetime sport or physical activity.

1. *When learning a new activity, concentrate on the "general idea" of the skill first; worry about details later.* For example, a diver who concentrates on pointing the toes and keeping the legs straight at the end of a "flip" may land flat on his or her back. To make it "all the way over," concentration should be on merely doing the flip. When the "general idea" is *mastered*, one can then concentrate on details (Lawther 1977).
2. *The beginner should be careful not to emphasize too many details at one time.* After the "general idea" of the skill is learned, the learner can begin to focus on the details, one or two at a time. Concentration on too many details at one time may result in "paralysis by analysis." For example, a golfer who is told to keep the head down, the left arm straight, the knees bent, etc., cannot possibly concentrate on all these details at once. As a result, neither the details nor the "general idea" of the golf swing are performed properly.

3. *In the early stages of learning a lifetime sport or physical activity, it is not wise to engage in competition.* Research indicates that beginners who compete are likely to concentrate on "beating their opponent" rather than learning a skill properly. For example, in bowling the beginner may abandon the newly learned hook ball in favor of the "sure thing" straight ball. This may make the person more successful immediately, but is not likely to improve the person's bowling skills for the future (Whiting 1971).

4. *To be performed well, lifetime sports skills must be "overlearned."* Oftentimes when we learn a new activity, we begin to "play the game" immediately. Evidence indicates that the best way to learn a skill is to "overlearn" it or practice it until it becomes "habit." Frequently game situations do not allow us to overlearn skills. For example, it is not a good time to learn the tennis serve during a game, since there may be only a few opportunities to serve. For the beginner it would be much more productive to hit many serves (overlearn) with a friend until at least the "general idea" of the serve is well learned. Further, the beginner *should not* sacrifice speed to concentrate on serving for accuracy. Accuracy will come with practice of a properly performed skill (Schmidt 1975).

5. *Once the "general idea" of a skill is learned, an analysis of the performance may be helpful.* Being careful not to overanalyze, it may be helpful to have someone who is knowledgeable about the sport help locate strengths and weaknesses. Movies and videotapes of performances have been shown to be of help to learners (Lawther 1977; Schmidt 1975).

6. *When "unlearning" an old (incorrect) skill and learning a new (correct) skill, performance may get worse before it gets better.* Frequently a performer hopes to unlearn a "bad habit" so as to be able to "relearn" the new or correct skill. For example, a golfer with a "baseball swing" may want to learn the correct golf swing. It is important for the learner to understand that the score may worsen during the relearning stage. As the new skill is overlearned, skill will improve, as will the golf score.

7. *Mental practice may aid skill learning.* Current research evidence suggests that mental practice may benefit performance of motor skills, especially if the performer has had previous experience in performing the skill. Mental practice might be used for golf, tennis, and other sports when the performer cannot participate regularly because of weather, business, or lack of time (Corbin 1972).

8. *For beginners, practicing in front of other people may be detrimental to learning a skill.* Research indicates that an audience may inhibit the learning of a new sports skill by the beginner. This is especially true if the learner feels that his or her performance is being evaluated by someone in the audience (Martens 1975).

Suggested Readings

Corbin, C. B., ed. *A Textbook of Motor Development*. 2d ed. Dubuque, Ia.: Wm. C. Brown Company Publishers, 1980.

Lawther, J. D. *The Learning and Performance of Physical Skills*. 2d ed. Englewood Cliffs, N. J.: Prentice-Hall, Inc., 1977.

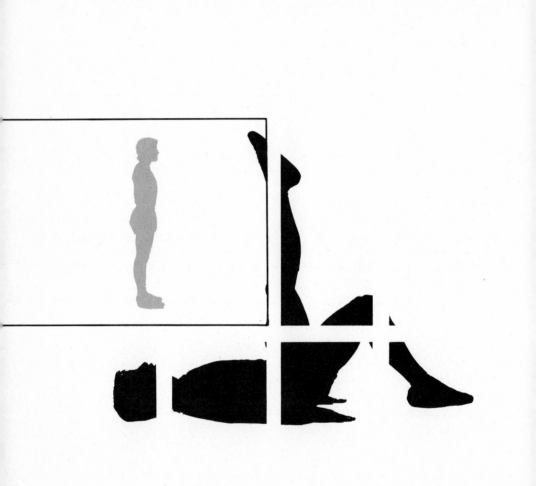

Body Mechanics

13

Concept 13

Since the human body is a system of weights and levers, its efficiency and effectiveness at rest or in motion can be improved by the application of sound mechanical and anatomical principles.

Introduction

"Body Mechanics" means the application of physical laws to the human body. The bones of the body act as levers or simple machines, with the muscles supplying the force to move them. Therefore, mechanical laws may be applied to the use of the body to aid in performing more and better work with less energy while avoiding strain or injury.

In the first half of this concept, discussion is centered on the daily activities of lifting, carrying, pushing, and pulling. The last part of this concept focuses on selected mechanical principles for the fundamental techniques employed in various sport activities.

Terms

Acceleration—The rate of change of velocity.
Center of Gravity—The center of the mass of an object.
Effectiveness—The degree to which the purpose is accomplished.
Efficiency—The relationship of the amount of energy used to the amount of work accomplished.
Linear Motion—Movement in a straight line.
Locomotor Movement—Movement from one place to another (i.e., running, walking, skipping).
Rotary Motion—Movement in an arc or circle around a center of rotation.
Stability—Degree of equilibrium; state of rest.
Velocity—Speed; rate of change of position.

Body Mechanics for Daily Living

Facts about Lifting and Carrying

The best method for lifting or carrying a given object depends upon its size, weight, shape, and position in space; however, there are some general principles that should be applicable in all situations (Broer 1973; Lindsey et al. 1979; Rasch and Burke 1978; Wells and Lutgens 1976).

1. *Stand close to the object and assume a wide base* (Rasch and Burke 1978; Wells and Lutgens 1976). Stand in a forward-backward stride position with the object at the side of the body, or assume a side-stride position with the object between the knees. The purpose of lifting from this position is that it allows one to lift straight upward from a stable position, utilizing the most efficient leverage.

2. *Keep the back straight and bend at the hips and knees. Squat, do not bend, regardless of how light the object may be.* The back was never meant to be used as a lever for lifting. Orthopedists constantly caution us against leaning forward to pick up objects without bending the knees because of the strain placed on the muscles and joints of the spine. This kind of back strain can occur when making a bed improperly or when lifting a child out of a crib. When bending from the waist, the body's center of gravity is higher than when squatting, thus the bending posture is less stable as well as more injurious than the squatting position (Hammond 1978; Lindsey et al. 1979; Tichauer 1978).

3. *Lower your body only as far as necessary, directly downward, keeping the hips tucked.* Squatting lower than is necessary is a waste of energy, but more importantly perhaps, deep knee bends can damage the structures of the knee joints. The deeper the flexion, the greater the twist on the joint and the greater the tension in the leg muscles (Klein and Allman n.d.).

4. *Grasp the object and lift with your leg muscles, keeping the object close to the center of gravity of the body.* The leg muscles are the strongest in the body, and if the back is kept erect, use of the legs for lifting allows a maximal force to be applied to the load, without wasting energy.

5. *Push or pull heavy objects if this can be done efficiently, rather than lifting them.* Theoretically, it takes about thirty-four times more force to lift than to slide an object across the floor. The size, shape, and friction of the object would determine whether or not it is feasible to push or pull it (Wells and Lutgens 1976).

6. *Carry the object close to the body's center of gravity and no higher than waist level (except when carrying on the shoulder, head, or back).* When objects are carried in front of the body above the level of the waist, one must lean backward to balance the load, producing an undesirable arch in the lower back. Carrying loads at the midline of the body such as in a knapsack or on the head or shoulders is effective in reducing the stress on the skeletal system (Grandjean 1969; 1974).

7. *Divide the load if possible, carrying half in each arm. If the load cannot be divided, alternate the load from one side of the body to the other.* When the weight is carried on one side of the body, the force on the opposite hip during walking is much greater than when the load is distributed on both sides. This is true even when the bilateral load is twice as great as the unilateral load (Greene and Bilger 1973). If the weight must be carried on only one side, the opposite arm should be raised to counterbalance the load and help keep the center of gravity over the base.

8. *Avoid arching the back when lifting and lowering an object from overhead. Any lift above waist level is inefficient* (Wells and Lutgens 1976). Occasionally, one must reach overhead to lift an object from a high shelf. To avoid back strain, climb a ladder or stand on a stool to prevent the necessity of raising the arms overhead. If this is not practical, reach for the object with your weight on the forward foot and then step backward on the rear foot as the object is lowered.

9. *Do not try to lift or carry burdens too heavy for you.* The most economical load for either a man or a woman is about thirty-five percent of his or her body weight. Obviously, with strength training, one can safely lift a greater load. (Refer to Table 13.1 for suggested maximum lifts for people of average strength.)

Table 13.1 Suggested Maximum Lifts for People of Average Strength (Grandjean 1974)

	Occasional Lifts	Frequent or Continuous Lifts
Men	50 kg or 110 lbs.	18 kg or 39.6 lbs.
Women	20 kg or 44 lbs.	12 kg or 26.4 lbs.
Boys	20 kg or 44 lbs.	15 kg or 33 lbs.
Girls	11-16 kg or 24-35 lbs.	7-11 kg or 15-24 lbs.

Facts about Pushing and Pulling

There is a controversy over whether pushing or pulling is easier; apparently it depends upon the nature of the task.

One must consider such factors as desired direction, type of movement, distance to be moved, and friction. If a downward force is desired, pushing would be best. If an upward force is desirable, pulling is probably better. Pushing tends to increase friction because of the downward force, but may offer better control since the object is closer to the person (Broer 1973; Kugelmass 1959; Rasch and Burke 1978; Shepard 1974).

Pushing and pulling are forms of lifting; therefore, the same mechanical principles may be applied.

When pushing or pulling, the back should be kept as straight as possible, a wide stance should be used, and the leg muscles should do the work rather than the back or arms. You may alternate the working muscles by changing positions occasionally, that is, face forward, then backward, then sideward (Lindsey et al. 1979).

Force should be applied as nearly as possible in the desired line of direction.

If linear motion is desired, you should apply force at the center of gravity of the object and push or pull in the desired direction by leaning from the hips, in that direction. To move an object horizontally, the upward and downward components of the push or pull should be reduced to a minimum. When pulling, increasing the length of the handle reduces the vertical component.

If there is a great deal of friction, the force should be applied below the object's center of gravity. Sufficient force should be applied continuously to keep the load moving, since it takes more force to start an object moving (overcoming inertia) than to keep it moving (Rasch and Burke 1978; Wells and Lutgens 1976).

When rotary motion is desired, apply force away from the center of gravity of the object.

Objects that are too heavy or too awkward to be moved as a whole, such as a refrigerator or couch, can be moved by applying force alternately at one end and then the other so that a pivoting or "walking" action is employed to rotate the object (Rasch and Burke 1978; Wells and Lutgens 1976).

Facts about Saving Energy during Work

When working with the arms in front of the body, a pulling motion is easier than a pushing motion because pulling uses the stronger flexor muscles of the arms.

To conserve energy and do a more effective job, try these suggestions (Kugelmass 1959):

1. *Painting*—Paint only a square foot at a time, pushing the brush lightly, but pulling it vigorously.
2. *Window Washing and Dishwashing*—Use a counterclockwise motion (if you are right-handed), since this puts the emphasis on the pull. It is more efficient and effective than up-and-down strokes.
3. *Floor Cleaning*—In mopping, washing, and vacuuming, put the pressure on the pull. The push takes twenty times more energy.
4. *Ironing*—Be sure the board is low enough and on a firm wide base; put the emphasis on the pull rather than the push to do a better job of ironing with less neck and shoulder strain.
5. *Bedmaking*—Tuck the sheet in on one side, walk around the bed and pull the sheet toward you. This is thirty times more efficient than pushing out the wrinkles.

Organize work to avoid stooping or unnatural positions (Grandjean 1969; 1974; Hammond 1978).

1. Sideward flexion of the trunk is more strenuous than forward trunk flexion.
2. Avoid constant arm extension, whether forward or sideward.
3. Try to sit while working but change to standing occasionally.
4. The arms should move either together or in opposite directions.
5. Tools most often used should be the closest to reach.
6. When working with the hands, the workbench or kitchen cabinet should be about 5-10 cm (2-4 inches) below the waist. The office desk should be about 74-78 cm (29-30 inches) high for the average man and about 70-74 cm (27-29 inches) high for the average woman.

Some types of arm movements are more accurate than others (Grandjean 1969; 1974).

Horizontal movements are more precise than vertical ones. Circular movements are better than zigzag ones. Movements toward the body are easier to control than those away from the body. Rhythmic movements are more accurate and less tiring than abrupt movements.

There is an optimum way to use tools (Grandjean 1969).

Shoveling—The best handle length is about 60-65 cm (23-25 inches). The best rate is twelve to fifteen shovelings per minute.
Sawing—For a two-man forest saw, the most efficient rate is forty-two double pulls per minute.
Hoeing—A swivel hoe is more efficient in soft soil. The grubbing hoe is best for hard soil.

Body Mechanics in Sports

The principles of body mechanics are the same for sports as for daily living. However, sports often require movements other than lifting, pushing, and pulling. For this reason, selected principles of body mechanics are presented with specific attention given to efficient sports participation.

Facts about Running and Other Locomotor Movements

There are many different ways to get from one place to another.

Regardless of the locomotor movement used, whether it be running in football, the shufflestep in boxing, or backward running as in defensive basketball, there are some general guidelines that apply to most sports situations.

1. To start quickly in a known direction, lean in the direction of the anticipated movement (Rasch and Burke 1978).
2. To stop quickly, lower the center of gravity by bending the legs, widen the base by spreading the feet, and lean in the direction opposite the movement (Rasch and Burke 1978; Wells and Lutgens 1976).
3. To move as fast as possible, do *not* leave the ground more than is necessary. The force necessary to move fast is provided by the feet or body part touching the ground. If the feet are off the ground they cannot push the body forward. (In swimming, if the hands or feet are out of the water, they cannot move the body forward) (Miller and Nelson 1973).
4. When moving in a circle or around a curve, centrifugal force can be counteracted by leaning into the curve, by slowing down, or by increasing the radius of the circle (Bunn 1972; Wells and Lutgens 1976).

Facts about Jumping and/or Moving the Body in Space

Whether it be performing the long jump, the front sommersault in diving, or a gymnastics maneuver, there are some basic guidelines for moving the entire body through space.

1. Once a person leaves the ground, the path of the center of gravity cannot be changed. However, the location of the center of gravity within the body can be changed. Raising the arms and legs raises the center of gravity and may make it appear that a jumper "hangs in the air"; for example, the jump shot in basketball may give the appearance of defying gravity (Bishop and Hay 1979; Northrip et al. 1979; Wells and Lutgens 1976).

2. When a person is unsupported in air, movement of one body part in one direction results in the rest of the body moving in the opposite direction; for example, in diving, if the head goes down, the feet go up. If the head and feet move down, the hips move up (Wells and Lutgens 1976).
3. Maximal jumping distance can be obtained by transferring momentum from body parts to the total body just before leaving the ground. For example, a swimmer can reach farther at the start by thrusting the arms forward before pushing off the starting block (Wells and Lutgens 1976).
4. When a fast turning motion (revolution) of the body or a limb is desired, the radius of rotation should be shortened. For example, in the somersault, the legs and arms should be tucked. When running, the leg can be swung faster if the hip and knee are bent and the foot is brought close to the buttocks.

Facts about Throwing an Object

There are some basic guidelines that should be considered for efficient throwing. Some of these guidelines also apply to jumping.

1. For maximal distance, an object such as a ball should be thrown at an upward angle at about 45 degrees. Because some objects tend to "sail" (lift) and then "stall," they should be thrown at a lesser angle. For example, a discus should be thrown at about 40 degrees. A long jumper is much like a thrown ball and in theory the jump should be as near 45 degrees as possible. However, in reality outstanding jumpers obtain the best distances at about 20 degrees (Bunn 1972; Ecker 1970, Hay 1978; Miller and Nelson 1973; Northrip et al. 1979; Terauds 1974).
2. To impart as much speed as possible to a thrown or struck object, the length of the lever (limbs and/or implement) imparting the force should be as long as possible at the moment of release or impact. For example, in a tennis forehand drive, the arm should be extended when the racket contacts the ball (Broer 1973; Wells and Lutgens 1976).
3. For maximum speed on a thrown or struck ball, the body levers should be added sequentially from inside to outside. For example, in an overhand throw, the forward motion should begin in the legs and trunk and then the upper arm should be added, then the elbow, the wrist, and finally the fingers. Each body part added should move faster than the preceding body parts (Broer 1973; Wells and Lutgens 1976).
4. Accelerate throughout as long a range of motion as possible, if speed is desired in a thrown or struck object. Take a long backswing and follow through so there is more time and distance to gain speed in the movement (Broer 1973; Wells and Lutgens 1976).

Facts about Catching or Receiving a Blow

Catching is basically receiving a blow from a thrown object. The following guidelines apply to catching a thrown object or receiving a blow of another type.

1. To avoid injury, a blow should be received over as large an area as possible. It hurts less to catch a ball on the palm of the hand than to catch it on the end of a finger. A fall on the elbow hurts more than a fall where the weight is received on the entire side of the arm (Wells and Lutgens 1976).
2. To avoid injury as well as to maintain control, "give" with the impact so the force is gradually reduced over a long distance. For example, when catching a ball, bend the arms and step back to lessen the force (Wells and Lutgens 1976).

Facts about Achieving Accuracy When Throwing or Striking an Object

One's ability to make an object "go where it is aimed" is referred to as accuracy. It requires coordination, balance, timing, and judgment of speed, distance, and force to project at the proper angle in order to hit a target.

1. Keep the movements of all body parts on line with the target as long as possible. For example, when bowling, the backswing, steps and follow-through should be straight and in line with the point of aim (Broer 1973).
2. The arc described by the arm during the swing can be "flattened" (straightened), so that it is in line with the target longer, if the performer steps toward the target and bends the forward knee. For example, in the underhand serve in volleyball, if the server fails to flatten the arc, there is a tendency for the ball to go too high (Broer 1973).

Suggested Readings

Bunn, W. *Scientific Principles of Coaching.* Englewood Cliffs, N.J.: Prentice-Hall, Inc., 1972.
Rasch, P. J., and Burke, R. K. *Kinesiology and Applied Anatomy.* 6th ed. Philadelphia: Lea and Febiger, 1978.
Wells, K., and Lutgens, K. *Kinesiology.* 6th ed. Philadelphia: W. B. Saunders Co., 1976.

Concept 13

Posture and Care of the Back

14

Concept 14

Good posture and sound care of the back can have positive effects on appearance, efficiency, effectiveness, and health.

Introduction

Good posture is something many Americans take for granted. Unless a posture problem is so severe that it causes deformity or pain, it may be ignored. Likewise, care of the back is often taken for granted until some type of problem presents itself.

When considering good posture and care of the back, the reader would do well to consider that early attention to good posture and care of the back can prevent problems later in life. Likewise, the reader should consider the fact that if a person already has a posture or back problem, other related problems may begin to present themselves.

Terms

Head Forward—The head is thrust forward in front of the gravity line; also called "poke neck."

Herniated Disc—The soft nucleus of the spinal disc protrudes through a small tear in the surrounding tissue; also called prolapse.

Hyperextended Knees—The knees are thrust backward in a locked position.

Kyphosis—Increased curvature (flexion) in the upper back; also called "hump back."

Lumbar Lordosis—Increased curvature (hyperextension) in the lower back (lumbar region) with a forward pelvic tilt; commonly known as "sway back."

Posture—The relationship of body parts, whether standing, lying, sitting, or moving. "Good posture" is the relationship of body parts that allows one to function most effectively, with the least expenditure of energy and with a minimum amount of strain on muscles, tendons, ligaments, and joints.

Referred Pain—Pain that appears to be located in one area, while in reality it originates in another area.

Round Shoulders—The tips of the shoulders are drawn forward in front of the gravity line.

Ruptured Disc—Spinal disc crushed from a severe blow or jolt.

Sciatica—Pain radiating down the sciatic nerve in the back of the hip and leg.

Scoliosis—A lateral curvature with some rotation of the spine—the most serious and deforming of all postural deviations.

Tension Myositis—Local disorder of the contractile state of the muscle. Symptoms include spasm, pain, and sometimes inflammation.

The Facts

Good posture has aesthetic benefits.

The first impression one person makes on another is usually a visual one. Good posture can help convey an impression of alertness, confidence, and attractiveness (Lindsey, Jones, and Whitley 1979).

There is probably no one best posture for all individuals, since body build affects the balance of body parts; but in general, certain relationships are desirable (Wells and Lutgens 1976).

In the standing position, the head should be centered over the trunk, the shoulders should be down and back, but relaxed, with the chest high and the abdomen flat. The spine should have gentle curves when viewed from the side, but should be straight as seen from the back. When the pelvis is tilted properly, the pubis falls directly underneath the lower tip of the sternum. The knees should be relaxed, with the kneecaps pointed straight ahead. The feet should point straight ahead and the weight should be borne over the heel, on the outside border of the sole, and across the ball of the foot and toes (Lindsey, Jones, and Whitley 1979).

Clinical evidence cited by physicians and opinions of educators indicate that poor posture can cause a number of health problems.

For example:

1. Protruding abdomen and lumbar lordosis may contribute to painful menstruation, susceptibility to back injury, and backache (Daniels and Worthingham 1977; Fait 1978; Lindsey, Jones, and Whitley 1979; Michele 1971; Wells and Lutgens 1976).
2. A forward position of the head can result in headache, dizziness, and neck, shoulder, and arm pain (Lindsey, Jones, and Whitley 1979).
3. Rounded shoulders may impair respiratory capacity (Daniels and Worthingham 1977; Lindsey, Jones, and Whitley 1979; Sherrill 1976).

Concept 14

4. Hyperextended knees may cause a predisposition to knee injury (Sherrill 1976).
5. Unbalanced postural lines can cause excessive tension in muscle groups, produce joint strain, stretch ligaments, damage joint cartilage, and become a factor in arthritic changes (Wells and Lutgens 1976).

Bad posture   Good posture

If one part of the body is out of line, other parts must move out of line to balance it, increasing the strain on muscles, ligaments, and joints.

The body is made in segments that are held balanced in a vertical column by muscles and ligaments. If gravity or a short muscle pulls one segment out of line, other portions of the body will move out of alignment to compensate, producing worse posture, more stress and strain, and possibly deformity in the musculoskeletal system (Lindsey, Jones, and Whitley 1979; Michele 1971; Sargent, Green, and Walters 1972).

There are many causes of poor posture, including hereditary, congenital and disease conditions, as well as certain environmental factors.

Some factors that may contribute to poor posture include: ill-fitting clothing, chronic fatigue, improperly fitting furniture (including poor beds and mattresses), emotional and personality problems, poor work habits, lack of physical fitness due to inactivity, and lack of knowledge regarding what constitutes good posture (Fait 1978; Lindsey, Jones, and Whitley 1979; Michele 1971).

Approximately 80 percent of the adult population suffers from acquired foot defects.

Most foot defects are acquired, and are preventable. They are most often caused by improperly fitting shoes and socks; excessive hard use (such as in athletics); long standing or walking on hard surfaces; obesity or rapid weight gain (as in pregnancy); and improper weight-bearing through poor foot and leg alignment (Lindsey, Jones, and Whitley 1979).

Exercises for the correction of postural deviations are generally based on the assumption that if it is a functional deformity, regardless of the factors causing the problem, muscular imbalance will be present.

If the muscles on one side of a joint are stronger than the muscles on the opposite side of that joint, then the body part is pulled in the direction of the stronger muscles. Corrective exercises are usually designed to strengthen the long, weak muscles and to stretch the short, strong ones in order to bring about an equal pull in both directions (Daniels and Worthingham 1977; Lindsey, Jones, and Whitley 1979).

Poor posture, especially lordosis, can cause back strain and pain and make the back more susceptible to injury.

The forward tilt of the pelvis may cause the sacral bone or one of the lumbar vertebrae to press on nerve roots with consequent low back pain and sciatica. To be on the safe side, some authorities advise the elimination of all exercises calling for the hyperextension of the spine for those who have lordosis and weak abdominals. Incidence of lordosis is about the same for men as it is for women, except for women there is added strain on the back during pregnancy; high heels may also contribute to spinal strain (Farfan 1973; Finneson 1973; Friedman and Galton 1973; Michele 1971; Sherrill 1976).

The neck is probably strained more frequently than the lower back.

The neck is constructed with the same curve and has the same mechanical problems as the lower back. The postural fault of "head forward" places a chronic strain on the posterior neck muscles. Tension in these muscles can lead to tension myositis and trigger points that may cause headache or be referred to as pain to the face, scalp, shoulder, arm, and chest (Lindsey, Jones, and Whitley 1979; Sargent, Green, and Walters 1972; Sarno 1978).

The overwhelming majority of back and neck aches are avoidable. A common cause of backache is muscular strain, frequently due to using the back improperly in daily activities or during exercise.

When lifting improperly, there is great pressure on the lumbar discs and severe stress on the lumbar muscles and ligaments. Many popular exercises place great strain on the back (see Concept 17). Sleeping flat on the back or abdomen on a soft mattress can also cause lower back strain (Daniels and Worthingham 1977; Finneson 1973; Ryan 1974).

Muscular fatigue and weak muscles are frequent causes of backache.

Backache has been referred to as a "hypokinetic disease," meaning that it is caused by insufficient exercise (Kraus 1972). Lack of exercise results in weak muscles that are easily strained and fatigued. Sedentary workers are particularly susceptible to spinal strain, and weak abdominal and back muscles are especially to blame. If the abdominals are weak, the pelvis is apt to tilt forward, causing lordosis (Finneson 1973; Friedman and Galton 1973; Ryan 1974).

Most people agree excessive muscle tension is a contributing factor in painful spines.

Some experts believe 95 percent of painful spines are caused by "tension myositis." Backaches may be precipitated by a minor injury or strain that sets off a muscle spasm; this causes pain, worry, excitement, fear, and stimulation of already hypersensitive muscular areas, referred to as "trigger points." These tender, painful spots occur frequently in the neck, shoulders, back, and hip as a result of constant tension, strain, or muscle spasm. When these tense muscles shorten, lose elasticity, and are weakened by lack of exercise, the "low back syndrome" occurs, as is illustrated in the following diagram. With a weak back, the mildest movement can trigger back pain. Back pains may result from "referred pain" from muscle tension in other areas. In some cases the pain is "referred" from the back of the legs if the hamstring muscles have been overstretched or injured (Sarno 1978).

Most of the treatment techniques for back pain caused by tension myositis can be done at home.

The most effective treatments usually include one or all of the following: massage or pressure on the trigger points; heat; ultrasound; electrical stimulation; strengthening exercises for the back, abdominal, neck and shoulder muscles; stretching of the low back muscles; and relaxation (Sarno 1978).

There is no such thing as a "slipped disc."

Laymen frequently misunderstand disc problems. Vertebral discs may herniate or rupture, but they do not slip. Pressure of disc material on nerves causes pain, and a protective reflex (muscle spasm) occurs to protect it. This causes more pain, thus a vicious cycle begins. The discs in the lumbar area are subjected to greater pressures, partly because they are at the bottom of the spine; therefore, they are more apt to be damaged by severe jolts or strains (Farfan 1973).

Most backaches can be prevented or alleviated by good sense, proper exercise, and relaxation.

Several "good sense" suggestions for taking care of the back are listed here (American Physical Therapy Assoc. 1980; Daniels and Worthingham 1977; Finneson 1973; Friedman and Galton 1973; Lindsey, Jones, and Whitley 1979; Ryan 1970; Sherrill 1976).

1. Avoid the swayback position at all times by taking such precautions as the following:
   a. To relieve back strain during prolonged standing, try to keep the lower back flat by propping one foot on a stool, bar, or rail; alternate feet occasionally.
   b. When sitting, use a hard chair with a straight back, placing the spine against it; keep one or both knees higher than the hips by crossing the legs (alternate sides) or by using a foot rest and keeping the knees bent.
   c. When driving a car, place a hard seat-and-backrest combination over the seat of the automobile; pull the seat forward so the legs are bent when operating the pedals.
   d. When lying, keep the knees and hips bent; avoid lying on the abdomen; when lying on the back, a pillow or lift should be placed under the knees.
   e. Avoid lifting and carrying improperly.
2. To prevent neck strain, avoid the head forward position. The forward thrust is apt to occur in such activities as card playing, sewing, studying, and watching television; sleeping on a high pillow may also cause back strain.

3. Do corrective exercises to strengthen the abdominal muscles and stretch the lower back muscles; avoid exercises that strain the lower back or cause it to arch.
4. General exercises, involving the entire body, are important in preventing weak muscles and lack of flexibility.
5. Warm up before engaging in strenuous activity.
6. Get adequate rest and sleep; avoid pushing yourself mentally or physically to the point of exhaustion.
7. Vary the working position by changing from one task to another before feeling fatigued; when doing desk work, get up and stretch occasionally to relieve tension.
8. Sleep on a firm mattress or place a three-fourths inch thick plywood board under the mattress.
9. Avoid sudden, jerky movements of the back.
10. The smaller the waistline, the lesser the strain on the lower back. Avoid being overweight.

Correct   Incorrect

Suggested Readings

Friedman, L. W., and Galton, L. *Freedom from Backaches*. New York: Simon & Schuster, 1973.
Michele, A. A. *Orthotherapy*. New York: M. Evans and Co., 1971.

Stress, Tension, and Relaxation

15

Concept 15

Mental and physical health are affected by an individual's ability to avoid or adapt to stress, emotional factors, and tension.

Introduction

Stress can trigger an emotional response that in turn evokes the autonomic nervous system to a "fight or flight" response. This adaptive and protective device stimulates the ductless glands to hypo- or hyperactivity in preparation for what is perceived as a threat or assault on the whole organism. In some instances, this "alarm reaction" of the body may be essential to survival, but when evoked inappropriately or excessively the adaptive reaction may be more harmful than the effects of the original stressor (Gunderson and Rahe 1974).

Terms

Adaptation—The body's efforts to restore normalcy.

Alarm Reaction—The body's warning signal that a stressor is present.

Anxiety—A state of apprehension with a compulsion to do something; excessive anxiety is a tension disorder with physiological characteristics (Dodge and Martin 1970).

Chronic Fatigue—Constant state of fatigue in the entire body.

Neuromuscular Hypertension—Unnecessary or exaggerated muscle contractions; excess tension beyond that needed to perform a given task; also called hypertonus.

Physiological Fatigue—A deterioration in the capacity of the neuromuscular system as the result of physical overwork and strain; also referred to as "true fatigue."

Psychological Fatigue—A feeling of fatigue usually caused by such things as lack of exercise, boredom, or mental stress resulting in lack of energy and depression; also referred to as "subjective" or "false" fatigue.

Relaxation—The release or reduction of tension in the neuromuscular system.

Stress—The nonspecific response of the body to any demand made upon it (Selye 1974).

Stressor—Anything that produces stress or increases the rate of wear and tear on the body.

The Facts

All living creatures are in a continual state of stress (some more; some less).

Stressors can be physical in nature or psychosocial. Physical stressors include heat, noise, overcrowding, malnutrition, climate, microorganisms, terrain, etc. Psychosocial stimuli are probably the most common stressors affecting humans. These include "life-change events," such as change in work hours or line of work, family illnesses, problems with superiors, deaths of relatives or friends, and increased responsibilities. In school, the pressures of grades, term papers, and oral presentations may induce stress (Gunderson and Rahe 1974; Selye 1974).

Too little stress is undesirable.

Stress is not always harmful. Moderate stress may enhance behavioral adaptation and is necessary for maturity and health. It stimulates psychological growth (Schontz 1975). It has been said that "freedom from stress is death" and "stress is the spice of life" (Selye 1974).

Too much stress or an inability to adapt appropriately to stress is harmful.

Cumulative clinical evidence has demonstrated the linkage between stress and disease and death (Benson 1975). Mental and physical conditions that can result from psychosomatic causes (Dodge and Martin 1970) include high blood pressure and heart disease (Benson 1975; Gunderson and Rahe 1974); psychiatric disorders such as depression and schizophrenia (Gunderson and Rahe 1974); indigestion; colitis; ulcers; headaches; insomnia; (Fisher 1978; Jacobson 1964); diarrhea; constipation; increased blood clotting time; increased cholesterol concentration; diuresis; edema; low back pain; and others.

Individuals react and adapt differently to different stressors.

What one person finds stressful may not be for others, and stress affects people differently. It mobilizes some to greater efficiency, while it confuses and disorganizes others. For example, skydiving or riding a roller coaster would be fun for some people, but for others it could be very stressful.

An individual's response to stress depends upon the intensity of the threat, the type of situation in which it occurs, and such personal variables as cultural background, tolerance levels, and past experience (Glass and Singer 1972; Gunderson and Rahe 1974; Schontz 1975). The capacity of the individual to adapt is not a static function but fluctuates with energy, drive, and courage.

Individuals tend to adapt best to moderate stress.

One would expect mild stress to produce mild adaptations, and strong stress to produce strong adaptive responses, but this is not so. High levels of threat tend to evoke ineffective, disorganized behavior (Schontz 1975). The following graph shows this relationship between stress and adaptive responses.

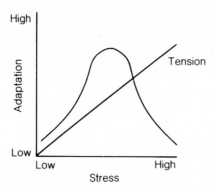

Stress can be self-induced and pleasurable or unpleasurable.

Some people may deliberately place themselves in stressful situations; for example, athletes place themselves under maximum strain; lawyers and surgeons are challenged by difficulties; pregnancy imposes psychological and physiological stress on a woman. Self-induced stress may also be an unpleasant but necessary interlude that cannot be avoided. For example, there is a risk of falling that is necessary in learning to ride a bicycle (Schontz 1975).

Neuromuscular hypertension may be both a cause and an effect of stress.

Tension is a primary index of stress (Schontz 1975). Anxiety is an emotional response caused by stressors that can be seen in the form of muscular tension (Dodge and Martin 1970). Muscular tension may also be physical in origin, resulting from overuse of a muscle group. This tension can cause muscle spasms and pain that in turn become additional stressors. Trigger points and the myofascial pain syndrome that lead to backache and headache are good examples of this (Schontz 1975; Woodworth and Schlosberg 1972).

Excessive tension can cause psychophysical disorders.

One physician claims 50 percent of his patients have tension disorders. These disorders are of three types: (a) primary—those caused by tension (irritable colon, spastic esophagus, nervousness, emotional imbalance, fatigue, insomnia, etc.); (b) mixed—those that probably would not have occurred in the absence of hypertonus (high blood pressure, peptic ulcers, angina, etc.); and (c) secondary—those in which tension is the result of pain and discomfort from other conditions, such as fractures and tumors (Jacobson 1970).

Some tension is normally present in muscles and contributes to the adjustment of the individual to the environment.

We need some tension to remain awake, alert, and ready to respond—a certain degree aids some types of mental activity. There appears to be an optimum level of tension for each individual to facilitate the thought process. However, too much tension can inhibit some types of mental activity and physical skills (such as those requiring accuracy and steadiness in held postures) (Lindsey et al. 1979; Woodworth and Schlosberg 1972).

Fatigue and neuromuscular hypertension are closely related.

High levels of tension are a source of fatigue. Fatigue from lack of rest, sleep, emotional strain, pain, disease, and muscular work may produce too much muscle tension. Fatigue may be either psychological or physiological in origin, but both can result in a state of exhaustion or chronic fatigue with muscle tenseness (Jacobson 1964; 1970).

Excessive tension can be avoided or relieved by proper planning of our daily lives.

"Moderation in all things" may still be a helpful adage. Work must be balanced with rest. Provision should be made for recreational activities and diversions. Diversions may be even more important than rest, since stress on one system helps to relax another. This may range from a temporary change from one task to another (e.g., from studying to lawn mowing) or a change of scene, a change in job, a vacation, or even retirement (Selye 1974). We may even need to change our approach to life.

Some methods of relieving tension are less desirable or not recommended.

There is no magic cure for stress or tension, but there are a variety of therapeutic approaches. Some treatments are less desirable than others because they act only as "crutches" or "fire extinguishers" and do not get at the root of the cause. Hypnosis may lead to fantasy and dependency. Alcoholic beverages, tranquilizers, and painkillers may give temporary relief and may be prescribed by the physician as part of the treatment, but they do not relieve the cause of the problem and may even mask the symptoms or cause further problems. Drugs do not provide a long-term solution to chronic tension; neither does another treatment: the drastic surgery called frontal lobotomy.

Mild rhythmic exercise, stretching exercises, heat, and massage are beneficial in relaxing "tight" muscles. In some cases, group therapy and counseling have been used successfully in alleviating the causes of anxiety and tension. Acupressure and shiatsu may also be helpful (Fisher 1978; Jacobson 1964; 1970).

There are several satisfactory methods of releasing tension through techniques of conscious relaxation.

In some way not fully understood, certain involuntary bodily functions can be controlled by an act of will (voluntarily). Relaxation of the muscles is a skill that can be learned through practice just as other muscle skills are learned (Benson 1975; Jacobson 1964; 1970).

Conscious relaxation techniques usually employ the "Three Rs" of relaxation: (1) reduce mental activity, (2) recognize tension, and (3) reduce respiration.

Some examples of these systems are described below:

1. *Jacobson's Progressive Relaxation Method*—One must recognize how a tense muscle feels before one can voluntarily release the tension. In this technique, the individual contracts the muscles strongly and then relaxes. Each of the large muscles is relaxed first and later the small ones. The contractions are gradually reduced in intensity until no movement is visible. Always, the emphasis is placed on detecting the feeling of tension as the first step in "letting go," or "going negative." Jacobson emphasizes the importance of relaxing eye muscles and speech muscles, since he believes these muscles trigger reactions of the total organism more than other muscles (Jacobson 1964; 1970).

2. *Autogenic (self-generated) Relaxation Training*—Relaxation is brought about by passive concentration upon phrases of preselected words. This practice is done several times daily, lying down in a quiet room with eyes closed. This technique has been used to focus on heaviness of limbs, warmth of limbs, heart regulation, breathing regulation, and coolness in the forehead. It evokes changes opposite to those produced by stress.
   Transcendental Meditation (TM) as used by the Eastern religions falls into this category. The individual sits quietly and attempts to block out distracting thoughts by mentally repeating a personal secret word or phrase. Research has shown that those who are skilled in this technique can decrease their oxygen consumption, change the electrical activity of the brain, slow the metabolism, decrease blood lactate, lower body temperature, and slow the heart rate (Barber et al. 1971; Benson 1975; Carr 1974; Sargent, Green, and Walters 1972).

3. *Biofeedback-Autogenic Relaxation Training*—Biofeedback training utilizes machines that monitor certain physiological processes of the body and provide visual or auditory evidence of what is happening to normally unconscious bodily functions. When combined with autogenic phrases, subjects have learned to relax and reduce the electrical activity in their muscles, lower blood pressure by increasing the temperature of their hands, decrease heart rate, change their brain waves, and decrease headaches, asthma attacks, and other psychosomatic disorders (Barber et al. 1971; Fried 1974; Riss 1973; Sargent, Green, and Walters 1972).

4. *Imagery*—Thinking autogenic phrases, one can visualize such feelings as "sinking into a mattress or pillow" or can think of being a "limp, loose-jointed puppet with no one to hold the strings." One can imagine being a "half-filled sack of flour resting on an uneven surface" or pretend to be "a sack of granulated salt left out in the rain, melting away."

Some people seem to respond better to the concept of "floating" than to feeling "heavy," but whatever the image one wishes to conjure, it is a form of self-hypnosis that helps to take the mind off anxieties and distractions and at the same time allows the release of unwanted tensions in the muscles through "mind over matter" (Lindsey et al. 1979).

5. *Tension Relieving Exercises*—Some specific but simple tension relieving exercises that can be used with little previous "muscle relaxing" experience are presented in Lab 24. Some Yoga exercises are useful for relaxation purposes. Usually exercises that are rhythmical or involve stretching are useful for relaxation.

Suggested Readings

Benson, H. *The Relaxation Response.* New York: William Morrow and Co., 1975.
Fisher, D. D. *I Know You Hurt But There's Nothing to Bandage.* Beaverton, Oregon: Touchstone Press, 1978.
Fried, J. "Biofeedback: Teaching Your Body to Heal Itself." *Family Health,* February 1974; and *Reader's Digest,* May 1974, p. 110.
Jacobson, E. *Anxiety and Tension Control.* Philadelphia: J. B. Lippincott Co., 1964.

Psychosocial Considerations

Concept 16

Physical education is more than just physical fitness and health.

Introduction

Much has been said in recent years about the psychosocial "values" of physical activity and sports. In fact, many claims have been made that are difficult to verify. It is not the purpose of this unit to review these "marginal" claims but to present some facts that might be helpful to people interested in continuing physical activity throughout life. While basic social and psychological patterns are almost entirely established by the college or adult years, there are some psychosocial considerations concerning physical activity that should be meaningful to people of all ages. This unit is designed to present some of these facts.

Terms

Aesthetics—The theory, study, or appreciation of beautiful things.
Catharsis—The release or purifying of one's emotions; for the purposes of this book, the release of stress and tension.
Movement Personality—An individual's characteristic way of moving.
Psychosocial—In this book the term is used to characterize factors related to the individual's behavior (alone or as a member of a group) specifically with reference to sport and physical activity.

The Facts

Movement has meaning (Csikszentmihalyi 1977).

As discussed in previous chapters, movement is a means to many ends. Through movement one performs work, achieves health and physical fitness, and accomplishes other useful objectives. However, movement can be an end in itself. Those who have performed a dance, played a game, or jogged a mile realize that the mere performance of any of these tasks is an accomplishment in itself. Movement and physical activity does not always have to be purposeful; satisfaction can be derived from the mere involvement in a movement experience.

There are at least seven major reasons why people participate in regular physical activity (Corbin 1976; Ellis 1973; Kenyon 1968).

People participate in activity for different reasons. Some of these reasons are listed here.

1. *Physical Activity for Social Purposes*—People may choose activity for their own social enjoyment or as a means of advancing socially.
2. *Physical Activity for Thrills and Excitement*—People seek excitement and certain types of activities can fulfill this need for excitement.
3. *Physical Activity for Aesthetic Experience*—Some forms of activity are more aesthetic or beautiful than others. Participation in dance or an individual sport such as gymnastics can be a beautiful experience both for the participant and the observer.
4. *Physical Activity for Recreation and Relaxation*—In an age of stress and tension, some people choose to be active as a means of relaxing and relieving tensions. Various activities can provide a means of getting away from it all, blowing off steam, or venting frustrations in a socially acceptable manner.
5. *Physical Activity to Meet a Challenge*—Some people enjoy the challenge of vigorous training and physical accomplishments. Marathon runners reap satisfaction from completing the race, football players enjoy contact, and race drivers relish the danger of racing. Meeting a challenge is one reason why people engage in regular physical activity.
6. *Physical Activity as Games of Chance*—There are some who participate in activity, though not commonly of a vigorous nature, to determine their ability to pick a winner. For these people, chance or the luck involved in the activity is the major reason for their participation. Dice and horse racing are examples of this type of activity.
7. *Physical Activity as a Means of Achieving Health and Physical Fitness*—The most common reason why people participate in physical activity is to improve their physical fitness and health.

People choose recreational activities in which they succeed (Harris and assoc. 1979).

Most men and women will choose leisure activities in which they enjoy success. Every individual should develop skills in "lifetime" sports and activities to insure success in recreational pursuits later in life.

Success in lifetime sports need not be equated with "winning" (Fisher 1976).

Sport psychologists agree that one problem experienced by many Americans in sports is that they cannot enjoy sports unless they "win." The chances of success and enjoyment of sports, especially of the competitive variety increases with the realization that success is not necessarily equated with winning. Though most people who play sports enjoy winning, it must be realized that only 50 percent of the participants can win a given contest. Suggestions for finding success and enjoyment in sports are as follows:

1. Set realistic goals for yourself. To play well against someone better than yourself should be considered a successful experience.
2. Consider a handicap system such as that used in golf or bowling.
3. In team sports or doubles games, change partners frequently to make competition more balanced.
4. Consider, before you play, the benefits you expect to get from participation—social contact, release of tension, physical fitness; if these are accomplished you have been successful.
5. Consider your improvement over a period of time as a successful accomplishment.
6. Consider the fun of playing as your success, and don't allow a "poor score" (compared to an opponent's) to take away the fun.
7. If you cannot have fun unless you win the game, consider noncompetitive activities such as jogging, swimming, and bicycling.

Involvement in regular physical activity can benefit a person socially and emotionally.

Although some recent studies have indicated that participation in highly competitive athletics may not contribute to character development (Ogilvie and Tutko 1971) or good sportsmanship (Corbin 1971), there is evidence that those people involved in regular exercise throughout life reap both social and emotional benefits.

1. Participation in physical activity can provide a "catharsis" or emotional release from the pent-up tensions of regular daily activity (Kenyon 1968).
2. Physically fit individuals are more likely to try new leisure-time activities, which can provide for a meaningful social life (Harris and assoc. 1979).
3. People who exercise regularly are more likely to have good physical health, which is a contributor to good total health which includes good mental health. For more details, see Table 2.2, page 10.
4. There is evidence that people who suffer from psychological depression can benefit from regular exercise. Regular exercise can be an effective means of reducing depression for many people (Brown 1978; Greist 1978; Kostrubala 1977).

5. Evidence suggests that regular exercise and fitness are associated with a sense of well being. Also, people who exercise regularly develop what some call a "positive addiction" to exercise. A positive addiction is a need to do something for which the consequences are positive, in this case exercise (Carmack and Martens 1979; Glasser 1976).

Whatever psychosocial benefits sports and physical activity have for men, they also have for women (Herkowitz 1980).

In the past, sport was the domain of men, with women relegated to the role of spectator. Much of the reason for this was related to the ideas that women were "too emotional" to participate in competitive activities and such activity was unfeminine. There is no research to indicate that sports programs with good leadership are harmful to women. In fact, women can and do benefit from regular physical activity in the same ways as male participants, and it is now a culturally acceptable and popular program for women.

Overemphasis in sports and physical activity can detract from enjoyment of the activity and can create anxiety in the performer (Eitzen and Sage 1978).

Whatever the benefits of regular physical activity or sports, none should be exaggerated to the point of detracting from a fuller life. There is evidence that overemphasis on sports can cause anxiety and even a type of neurosis (Little 1969). In fact, people who create stress for themselves by being excessively competitive may increase their chances of getting stress-related diseases (Friedman and Rosenman 1974).

To be a spectator at a sports event is *not necessarily* bad.

There is little doubt that in our society there is a danger of watching rather than doing. This is especially dangerous if an individual is *always* a spectator and never a participant. However, to enjoy watching sports could be compared to enjoying a form of art. Steinhaus (1963) likens the performance of a sports team to "creating a picture of the highest form of art." He believes that sport and art can bring to a person "a satisfying experience" and be a "transmitter of culture."

Just as each person has an individual personality, one also has a unique movement personality (Fast 1971).

No two people move in the same way. Given similar circumstances, different people react with different movement patterns according to their personalities. One's movement can convey his or her personality and communicate his or her feelings. Because movement personalities differ, there is wide variety in the leisure activities selected by different individuals. People should try to select leisure activities that are compatible with their own movement personalities.

Concept 16

Suggested Readings

Glasser, W. *Positive Addiction*. New York: Harper & Row, 1976.

Eitzen, D. S., and Sage, G. H. *Sociology of American Sport*. Dubuque, Ia.: Wm. C. Brown Company Publishers, 1978.

Journal of Sport Psychology, published four times a year by Human Kinetics Publishers, Champaign, Ill.

Exercise Cautions and Fallacies

Concept 17

There are correct and incorrect ways to exercise. **For maximum benefits, one should know the difference between the facts and the fallacies.**

Introduction

Mankind has always searched for the "easy," the "quick," and the "miraculous" route to health and happiness. This search has included the areas of physical fitness, especially exercise and weight loss. Because of the popularity of these two subjects, the mass media have made it possible to convey as much *mis*information as information. Everyone should seek the truth. This chapter attempts to expose some myths and separate fact from fallacy.

Terms

Hyperventilation— "Over-breathing"; forced, rapid, or deep breathing.
I.U.D.—Intrauterine device for birth control.
Lumbar—Lower back region.
Synnovial Membrane—The membrane surrounding the freely movable joints in the body.
Valsalva Maneuver—Exerting force with the glottis closed, increasing intrathoracic pressure, and raising arterial pressure. When released, arterial pressure drops rapidly, blood vessels expand and are then filled, causing a lag in blood flow to the left ventricle; thus, peripheral arterial blood pressure drops.

The Facts

Exercise has many benefits, but it is not a panacea.

There are many benefits of exercise described throughout this book, but for those who contemplate beginning a fitness or reducing program, these reminders are included: (a) the most satisfactory way to lose weight is a combination of caloric reduction and exercise; (b) exercise will **not** change the size of boney structures (e.g., ankles); (c) exercise will **not** change the size of glands (e.g., women's breasts are glands; bust *girth* may be increased by developing chest *muscles*); (d) exercise does **not** "break-up" fatty deposits, but it does burn calories and thus, eventually, fat; (e) exercise does **not** *insure* good posture or good health, but it does help to attain and maintain it; and (f) there is **no** such thing as effortless exercise (Lindsey, Jones, and Whitley 1979).

Passive exercise is *not* effective in weight reduction, spot reduction, increasing strength, or increasing endurance (Lindsey 1971).

Passive exercises come in a variety of forms, some of which are described below:

1. *Rolling Machines*—These **ineffective** wooden or metal rollers, operated by an electric motor, roll up and down the body part to which they are applied. They do **not** remove or redistribute fat.
2. *Vibrating Belts*—These wide canvas or leather belts may be designed for the chin or for the hips, thighs, and abdomen. Driven by an electric motor, they jerk back and forth causing loose tissue of the body part to shake. They do **not** "break down" fat nor are they effective in weight loss or reduction of girth (Hernlund and Steinhaus 1957). These devices may cause a temporary increase in local circulation, but they may also be potentially harmful if used on the abdomen, especially if used by women during pregnancy, menstruation, or while an I.U.D. is in place (Lindsey 1971).
3. *Vibrating Tables and Pillows*—Contrary to advertisements, these passive devices will **not** improve posture, trim the figure, reduce the weight, or develop muscle tonus. They may be useful in inducing relaxation.
4. *Motor-Driven Cycles and Rowing Machines*—Like all mechanical devices that "do the work" for the individual, these machines are **not** effective in weight reduction, figure improvement, or development of physical fitness. They may help increase circulation and flexibility. Only if the rider exerts his or her own effort against the machine by opposing or hurrying its rhythm could some beneficial strengthening be expected to occur (Lindsey 1971).
5. *Massage*—Whether done by a masseur or by a mechanical device, massage is passive, requiring no effort on the part of the individual. It can help increase circulation, prevent or loosen adhesions, and induce relaxation, but it has **no** value in developing physical fitness or in removing fatty tissue (Lindsey 1971).
6. *Electric Muscle Stimulators*—These devices when applied to a muscle, cause the muscle to contract involuntarily. They are dangerous in that they may induce heart attacks; complicate gastrointestinal, orthopedic, kidney, and other disorders; and possibly aggravate epilepsy, hernia, and

varicose veins. In the hands of qualified medical personnel, muscle stimulators are valuable therapeutic devices. They should never be used by the layman and have **no** place in a reducing or fitness program (Sherrill 1971).

7. *Weighted Belts*—These belts are claimed to reduce waists, thighs, and hips when worn for several hours under one's clothing. In reality, they do **none** of these things and have been reported to cause actual physical harm (Sherrill 1971).

8. *Inflated, Constricting or Nonporous Garments*—These include rubberized inflated devices, sometimes referred to as "Sauna Belts or Shorts," and garments that are air-tight plastic or rubberized. Evidence indicates that their claims of girth reducing are **unwarranted.** If one performs exercise in conjunction with the wearing of such garments, the exercise, **not** the garment, may have beneficial effects (Sherrill 1971).

9. *Figure Wrapping*—Some reducing salons advertise that wrapping the body in bandages soaked in a "magic solution" will cause a permanent reduction in body girth. This so-called "treatment" is pure quackery. There is **no** magic solution to make fat disappear and the pressure of the bandages can at best have only a very temporary shrinking effect (the way one's watchband may temporarily indent the arm) (Lindsey 1972). It may be dangerous to your health.

Some active exercises should be used with caution or not used at all by some individuals, and some popular exercises do not have the benefits commonly ascribed to them (Ryan September-October 1970).

A few such exercises are described here.

1. *Double Leg Lifts*—Raising and lowering both legs simultaneously from the back-lying position is a potentially dangerous exercise for the person with weak abdominals. This exercise is often mistakenly prescribed for strengthening the abdominals, but it is in reality a hip flexor exercise. If the abdominals are not well developed, the pull of the hip flexor muscles on the pelvis and lumbar spine will cause the back to arch during the exercise. This may result in serious injury to the back. In addition, it will further stretch the already weakened abdominals and possibly cause an abdominal hernia (Almekinder 1976; Kuntzleman 1971; Lindsey, Jones, and Whitley 1979).

2. *Sit-ups with Straight Legs*—This exercise has the same effect as double leg-lifts in terms of the anatomical and mechanical stresses involved. It is primarily an exercise for the muscles that flex the hip joint. If weak abdominals are present and the lower back is permitted to hyperextend, injury may result. Sit-ups are best performed with the knees bent and the feet unstabilized; the spine should "curl" up and "curl" down.

3. *Deep Knee Bends*—Deep squatting exercises may be harmful to the knee joint, causing a stretching of the ligaments and an irritation to the synovial membrane (Almekinder and La Point 1976; Kuntzleman 1971). If one desires to strengthen the legs by knee bends, the half-squat (with a 90° angle of knee flexion) is a satisfactory substitute.
4. *Backbends*—The acrobatic backbend and other exercises, such as the "swan" position and backward trunk circling, that require arching the lower back are designed to increase the strength of the lumbar muscles or increase trunk flexibility. For the individual who has weak abdominals and/or "sway back," such exercises further aggravate these conditions (Almekinder and La Point 1976; Ryan May-June 1970).
5. *Standing Toe Touches*—Some people, because of body build may never be able to touch their toes, but they have strived mightily by vigorous "bounces" of up to 100 repetitions! The use of this exercise is controversial, but because of the potential for abuse and the possibility of gravity-assisted momentum causing injury to the back or to the muscles and ligaments that cross the back of the knee joint, some authorities recommend avoiding this exercise in favor of sitting toe touches. If one chooses to "bounce," this should be done gently (Almekinder and La Point 1976; Kuntzleman 1971; Ryan 1971).
6. *Rising on the Toes and Heels*—This "tiptoeing" exercise will develop the calf muscles, but at the same time it stretches the muscles and ligaments that help support the long arch of the foot. "Heel-walking" may have the same effect—that is, develop already strong muscles while further weakening the arch of the foot. The potential harm is lessened if these exercises are performed with the toes turned in slightly ("All the News That's Fit" 1971).
7. *Isometric Exercises*—As previously pointed out, this type of exercise develops strength but does not contribute to cardiovascular fitness or flexibility. One study has shown such a program to be more dangerous to heart patients than isotonic exercises, since twice as many patients developed irregular heart beats during isometric testing than they did on the bicycle exerciser ("All the News That's Fit" 1971).
8. *"Slimming Wheels"*—This popular device is a small wheel with a handle passing through its center. It is used in a push-up type exercise, advertised for back and abdominal strengthening. Little research has been done to prove its value, but one hospital has reported a case of abdominal muscle hemorrhaging resulting from the use of the wheel ("All the News That's Fit" 1971). One should not strive for that "familiar soreness" in the exercise of the abdominals, but rather should discontinue exercise when a feeling of discomfort occurs (Lindsey, Jones, and Whitley 1979).

Exercise, even of an active nature, is *not* effective in promoting physical fitness unless the exercise meets the appropriate threshold of training.

Some popular literature suggests that only a few minutes of exercise a day is necessary to develop total physical fitness (Morehouse and Gross 1975). Research evidence indicates that total fitness (cardiovascular fitness, strength, muscular endurance, flexibility, and desirable body composition) can be attained only through considerable effort. As mentioned previously in this text, exercise must be of sufficient intensity, frequency (daily or every other day), and duration (at least fifteen to thirty minutes *each* day you exercise) for it to be effective. Programs that "promise" complete fitness but do not meet the necessary levels for intensity, frequency, and duration of exercise should be strongly questioned.

Sauna, steam, and whirlpool baths are *not* effective in weight reduction nor in the prevention and cure of colds, arthritis, bursitis, backaches, sprains, and bruises.

The effect of such baths is largely psychological, although some temporary relief from aches and pains may result from the heat. The same effect can be had by sitting in a tub of hot water at home (Lindsey 1972). Sauna and steam baths are potentially dangerous for the elderly and persons suffering from diabetes, heart disease, or high blood pressure. They should not be used within an hour of eating or while under the influence of alcohol or drugs such as anticoagulants, stimulants, hypnotics, narcotics, or tranquilizers (Federal Trade Commission News 1970).

Health clubs and/or reducing salons may lack qualified personnel for advising or prescribing exercise programs or diets (Lindsey 1971).

Studies indicate that the majority of the salons or clubs lack personnel with special training or education in such recognized fields as physical therapy, corrective therapy, or physical education. The employees had not taken such courses as anatomy, physiology, kinesiology, exercise therapy, or nutrition. Most of their training had consisted of two or three weeks of on-the-job experience. Out of a survey of thirty health clubs in Los Angeles, only two claimed to do cardiovascular testing and only two others listed aerobic programs. The remainder gave "body building" exercises. Only two claimed to have professionally qualified personnel (Smith, M. 1980).

Exercise tests are necessary to determine physical fitness, but certain cautions should be observed.

No exercise program should be undertaken without the approval of a physician. Sedentary individuals need a thorough physical exam and a stress test to detect ischemic heart disease and to evaluate cardiac fitness. These tests should be administered by trained individuals with resuscitation equipment easily available, but the risk is very low in normal subjects (no greater than a number of medical procedures such as coronary angiography) (Rochmis and Blackburn 1971; Schlesinger 1973; Stanton 1974).

Jogging is an excellent exercise for cardiovascular conditioning, weight control, and improvement of a variety of conditions; however, reasonable cautions should be observed.

Jogging has been used successfully in rehabilitating cardiac patients and people with pulmonary emphysema; reducing diabetics; relaxing insomniacs, the emotionally disturbed, and migraine patients; overcoming incontinence after pregnancy; and reducing the discomfort accompanying arthritis in the legs and back. A regular program will also decrease the risk of coronary artery disease. Specific guidelines for postcoronary joggers have been outlined recently (Kavanaugh 1976). Jogging should not be undertaken without a physician's approval, especially for those with osteoporosis and heart and circulatory diseases.

Jogging *can cause* shin splints, blisters, and foot, ankle, and hip problems. Using the proper footwear and learning how to jog correctly will minimize these hazards.

Dehydration, a hazard in certain sports and exercise situations, is a serious medical problem.

Excessive loss of body fluids and an accompanying loss of electrolytes can impair performance and lead to illness or even death. Weight losing gimmicks (including high protein/low carbohydrate diets) that cause dehydration are dangerous, especially for athletes (e.g., wrestlers trying to "make weight").

Athletes subjected to heat stress should weigh before and after practice and replace water loss; water intake should *not* be restricted during practice. It is doubtful that any beneficial effects accrue from adding electrolytes to water ingested after dehydration. The person regularly exposed to vigorous physical activity with heat stress may benefit from drinking a quart of milk and two eight-ounce glasses of orange juice per day (American College of Sports Medicine 1978; Costill et al. 1975; Smith 1976).

The hazards of drugs far outweigh any improvement in athletic performance that might result from their use.

Authorities disagree on whether drugs can enhance athletic performance. Examples of research studies include evidence suggesting that increased intake of vitamin E does not improve endurance (Lawrence et al. 1975). Anabolic steroids have been shown to temporarily increase strength when combined with a high protein diet and exercise, but possible side effects make them inadvisable (Freed et al. 1975). "Doping" of athletes has included the use of drugs ranging from caffeine and vitamins to cocaine, strychnine, adrenalin, tranquilizers, and narcotics.

Drugs can make a person feel like he or she has performed well whether or not he or she has; they also tend to mask symptoms that are important in knowing when the body is being taxed beyond safe limits; almost all drugs have side effects, which can sometimes be dangerous; drugs can be addictive. When sports are conducted on the basis of pharmacological expertise rather than on athletic competence, the traditional philosophy and spirit of competition is lost (Cooper 1972; Kournakis 1972; Lamb 1975).

There are certain hazards inherent in exercise that should be minimized by proper technique, knowledgeable instructors, proper equipment and apparel, and judicious practice schedules.

Some examples of exercise hazards are included here.

Weight-lifters may be subject to inguinal hernias and blackouts as a result of the Valsalva maneuver. This can be prevented by avoiding hyperventilation, squatting as briefly as possible, and raising the weight as rapidly as possible to a position in which it can be supported while normal breathing is resumed (Compton et al. 1973).

Excess activity during the adolescent stage may result in a degeneration of the hip joint and knee joints, especially among boys, and especially in the presence of growing pains (Murray and Duncan 1971). This suggests parents and coaches should examine all the evidence related to athletics during this so-called "dangerous age." The merit of long-distance runs, particularly on hard surfaces, as a form of athletic training should also be examined.

Most runners and occasionally joggers at some time complain of shin splints. This usually disappears within a few weeks and often can be prevented by proper technique, but one form of the injury may require surgery. For most individuals the exercises presented in this text will be of benefit; however, if pain persists or is unusually severe, a physician should be consulted (Puranen 1974).

Suggested Readings

Cooper, D. "Drugs and the Athlete." *Journal of the American Medical Association* 221 (August 28, 1972): 107.

Kuntzleman, C. "Dangerous Exercises: Which, When, Why." *Fitness for Living,* January-February 1971, pp. 25–29.

Lamb, L. E. "Those Exercise Deaths"; "Exercise and Heart Irregularities"; "Dangerous Health Food"; "Modified Deep Knee Bends." *Health Newsletter,* 10 (August 26, 1977): 4.

"What You Should Know Before Joining a Health Club," *Today's Health,* February, 1971, p. 17.

Programs of Exercise 18

Concept 18

There are many different exercises, both formal and informal, that can be adapted to the needs of individuals.

Introduction

Over the years many different types of exercise programs have been developed with the intent of meeting the needs of people of diverse interests and needs. Among the more popular and well-known exercise programs are: The Aerobics Program, the President's Council on Physical Fitness and Sports Adult Fitness Program, the Royal Canadian XBX and 5BX Programs, Continuous Rhythmical Exercise, Circuit Training, Speed Play or Fartlek, Interval Training, Jogging, Aerobic Dance, Weight Training, Calisthenics, and Sports Exercise Programs. Each of these programs is described briefly and a brief analysis of the strengths and weaknesses of each is presented so that the reader can consider the possibility of using one of these plans as part of a personal physical activity program.

Terms

Formal Exercise Program—A program that is preplanned and done to predetermined specifications.

Informal Exercise Program—Informal exercise is done without a formalized plan and is frequently done "on one's own" as opposed to being part of a class or group.

Programs of Exercise

Aerobics

Based on the needs of military personnel, Dr. Kenneth Cooper developed a program of physical fitness that he called aerobics. Aerobics means "with oxygen." Basically, exercises are of two types: aerobic—those that can be performed with the amount of oxygen the body can supply; and anaerobic—those that are so vigorous that the body does not supply the muscles with enough oxygen to continue work. In anaerobic exercise, the body incurs an oxygen "debt" as exercise continues. The "debt" is paid back after exercise. For example, the 100-yard dash is anaerobic. During the run the body requires more oxygen than is supplied. After the run the heart rate and rate of breathing remain high to pay back the "debt." Cooper suggests that physical fitness is best developed in aerobic activities or those activities that can be continued for a long time without building up an oxygen debt.

In the aerobics program several activities are suggested as methods for developing physical fitness. Each activity is selected according to the amount of oxygen required to perform the activity. The more oxygen a person uses to perform the activity, the greater the likelihood that the activity will actually contribute to physical fitness. Each of the activities is assigned a point value on the basis of its oxygen consumption and its ability to produce physical fitness.

In order to reap the cardiovascular benefits of the aerobics program, an individual must earn thirty points a week by performing any combination of the activities suggested. Details of the program are outlined in Appendix C.

Although the program of aerobics was developed for use by air force personnel, it has received wide recognition as a method of physical fitness development for the average American. (For complete details on the program refer to the Suggested Readings.)

Adult Physical Fitness Program

The President's Council on Physical Fitness and Sports, because of its concern for the total physical fitness of every American, has developed a program of progressive exercise that can be adapted to the specific needs of the individual. A sample program is presented in Appendix D. (For more details refer to the Suggested Readings.)

Royal Canadian XBX and 5BX Programs

The XBX program and the 5BX program are programs of progressive exercise designed to build total physical fitness. These plans, originally developed for use by The Royal Canadian Air Force, require eleven to twelve minutes a day. They were, like the Aerobics Program, originally designed as programs for developing and maintaining the physical fitness of military personnel. However, the programs have been widely received by the public. The exercises are progressive in nature and the intensity of exercise is graduated according to the fitness level of the individual performing them. A sample program is presented in Appendix E. (For more details refer to the Suggested Readings.)

Continuous Rhythmical Exercise

This type of exercise program was pioneered by Dr. Thomas Cureton at the University of Illinois. Each person progresses at his or her own rate or ability from low intensity exercise to exercise of higher intensity. Cureton labeled the different stages low gear, middle gear, and high gear. Every lesson begins with an introduction, followed by a warm-up period, the main exercises, and a tapering off period involving deep breathing, stretching, massage, and rest. Work is continuous with a build-up of speed and exertion during each lesson. The low-gear program emphasizes flexibility and endurance exercises conducted at a slow pace. The middle-gear exercises are more difficult exercises performed at a faster pace and for a longer period of time. Emphasis is on flexibility, strength, and endurance. The high-gear program consists of high speed exercises designed to place greater demands on the body in terms of strength, endurance, flexibility, balance, speed, and power. A modified continuous rhythmical endurance program is presented in Appendix F. (For further details, refer to the readings by Corbin and Cureton in the Suggested Readings.)

Circuit Training

This is a physical training program of timed exercises at several stations. Each day a participant is to complete the series of exercise stations (placed around a gymnasium or field) in progressively shorter periods of time. Each station may require several repetitions of an activity such as pull-ups, squat thrusts, push-ups, medicine ball put, agility run, and sit-ups. The circuit may consist of an obstacle course of various activities including climbing, crawling, running, and lifting. After correctly completing each exercise the performer moves on to the next station attempting to complete the circuit as quickly as possible. The objective is to complete the circuit in less time on each successive day. At intervals the number of repetitions or the difficulty of the activities is increased. (For more information, refer to the reading by Morgan and Adamson in the Suggested Readings.)

Speed Play or Fartlek

Fartlek is a Swedish word for speed play. This type of exercise was developed in Scandinavia where pinewood paths follow curves of lakes, up and down many hills where the scenery takes one's mind off the task at hand. The idea is to get away from the regimen of running on a track and enjoy the woods, lakes, and mountains. Because of the terrain the pace is never constant, since the uphill path requires a slowing down while a straight stretch or downhill trail allows for speed. In the speed play or fartlek system one runs easily for a time, a steady hard speed for a while, rapid walking, easy running broken with wind sprints, full speed uphill, and a fast pace for a while. A sample program is presented in Appendix G. (For more information, refer to the reading by Wilt in the Suggested Readings.)

Interval Training Program

An interval training program is a program of repeated anaerobic running or swimming for short periods of time separated by measured intervals of recovery jogging or stroking. (As developed by Gerschler of Germany, the stress of anaerobic running raises the heart rate to near maximal from which it drops to 110–120 during recovery.) This program is controlled in terms of distance, pace, number of repetitions, and recovery interval, allowing for a wide variety of programs at various intensities. Guidelines for this type of intermittent training are presented in Table 5.2 on page 27. (The reader is referred to the Suggested Readings by Wilt and Astrand for further details.) A sample program is presented in Appendix H.

Jogging Program

It is generally recommended that a jogging program begin slowly, alternating walking and jogging for a quarter-mile, and gradually building up to a mile or more at such a speed that you can talk easily to another person as you run. Intensity, frequency, and duration of jogging can be varied according to needs of specific individuals. The heart rate can be used to determine the desired intensity of exercise for a jogging program. The reader is referred to the aerobic exercise guidelines in Table 5.1 on page 26 for details. A sample jogging plan is presented in Appendix I. (Additional information on jogging can be found by referring to the readings by Clarke, Fixx, and Sheehan in the Suggested Readings.)

Aerobic Dance

Aerobic dance is a modification of aerobics that includes some calisthenics and some basic dance or rhythmical steps. Developed by Jackie Sorenson, aerobic dance was designed to increase cardiovascular fitness through sustained aerobic exercise, but it was also designed to create interest for those people who enjoy dancing and moving to music as opposed to running or jogging. In aerobic dance the participant alternately performs dance steps, jogging in place, and calisthenics. (For further details refer to the reading by Sorenson in the Suggested Readings.)

Weight Training

Weight training is performed using barbells, dumbbells, pulleys, or other types of weight machines. Generally, weight training is performed isotonically. However, it can be modified to include isometric contractions. Weight "lifting" is *not* the same thing as weight "training." Weight training is exercising to improve your fitness level while weight lifting is an international sport that involves competition in three basic lifts. Information relating to weight training (isotonic and isometric exercise) is presented in Concept 7, pages 45 and 46. In addition the reader is referred to Appendix J and Appendix K. (For additional information refer to the reading by Stone and Kroll in the Suggested Readings.)

Calisthenics

Calisthenics are programs consisting of a series of formal exercises. Actually, the adult fitness programs, the XBX, and the 5BX programs are calisthenic programs. A calisthenic program can be adapted to individual needs by selecting the exercises of your choice. The reader could develop a program of calisthenics by selecting exercises from Lab 22 and the appendixes.

Sports Exercise Programs

Because sports and games are often fun and enjoyable, many people choose them as their form of regular exercise. While some sports require considerable activity and are quite good for developing physical fitness, not all sports and games are active enough to promote physical fitness. Activities such as bowling, softball, and even golf are often not vigorous enough to build or maintain reasonable levels of physical fitness in young adults (See Table 12.1, p. 79). Sports do have many advantages, but one should consider supplementing a sports exercise program with some other more vigorous type of activity if physical fitness is the goal. An advantage of sports and games as a regular form of exercise is the wide variety of activities from which the participant can select.

There are advantages and disadvantages of each of the various types of exercise programs.

Since the needs and interests of each individual are unique, it is obvious that no single exercise program is best suited for all individuals. One should study each of the different programs and select the program (or combination of programs) that is best for that individual. Some of the advantages and disadvantages of each of the programs are presented in Table 18.1. It should be emphasized that the advantages or disadvantages of any specific program depend on the needs and interests of a given individual. For this reason, the information presented in Table 18.1 may not be entirely accurate for all individuals. The table attempts to summarize the information based on the needs and interests of the "typical American."

Suggested Readings

Astrand, P. O., and K. Rodahl. *Textbook of Work Physiology.* New York: McGraw-Hill Book Company, 1970.

Clarke, H. H., ed. "Jogging." *Physical Fitness Research Digest* 7, no. 1 (1977): 1–23.

Cooper, K. H. *The New Aerobics.* New York: M. Evans and Co., 1970.

———. "Key to Fitness at Any Age—The New Aerobics." *The Reader's Digest,* March 1970, pp. 213–30.

Cooper, K. H., and Cooper, M. *Aerobics for Women.* New York: M. Evans and Co., 1972.

Corbin, C. B. "An Exercise Program for Large Groups," *The Physical Educator* 30 (March 1973): 46.

Cureton, T. K. *Physical Fitness and Dynamic Health.* New York: Dial Press, 1965.

Fixx, J. *Complete Book of Running.* New York: Random House, 1977.

Fox, E. L., and Mathews, D. K. *Interval Training.* Philadelphia: W. B. Saunders Co., 1974.

Morgan, R., and Adamson, G. T. *Circuit Training.* New Rochelle, N.Y.: Sportshelf and Soccer Associates, 1961.

President's Council on Physical Fitness. *Adult Physical Fitness.* Washington, D.C.: U.S. Government Printing Office, publication no. 20402. Copies available from Superintendent of Documents.

Royal Canadian Air Force. *Exercise Plans for Physical Fitness.* Queen's Printer, Ottawa, Canada; Revised U.S. Edition, published by Simon and Schuster, Inc., by special arrangement with *This Week Magazine.* Copies available from *This Week Magazine,* P.O. Box 77-E, Mount Vernon, N.Y.

Sheehan, George A. *Dr. Sheehan on Running.* Mountain View, Calif.: World Publications, 1975.

Sorensen, J. *Have Fun! Keep Fit!* LP1120 Booklet, available from Educational Activities Inc., Box 392, Freeport, N.Y.

Stone, W. J., and Kroll, W. A. *Sports Conditioning and Weight Training.* Boston: Allyn and Bacon, 1978.

Wilt, F. "Training for Competitive Running." In *Exercise Physiology,* chap. 14. Edited by H. B. Falls. New York: Academic Press, 1968.

Table 18.1 Strengths and Weaknesses of Various Exercise Programs (++ = Good; + = Fair; − = Poor)

Program Type	Cardiovascular Fitness	Strength and Muscular Endurance	Flexibility	Body and Fat Control	Skill-Related Fitness	Enjoyment or Fun*
Aerobics	++	−	−	++	−	+
Adult fitness program	−	++	++	+	−	−
XBX-5BX	−	++	++	+	−	−
Rhythmical endurance	++	++	++	++	−	+
Circuit training	++	++	++	++	−	+
Speed play or fartlek	++	+	−	++	−	+
Interval training	++	+	−	++	−	+
Jogging	++	+	−	++	−	+
Aerobic dance	++	+	++	++	+	++
Weight training	−	++	+	+	−	+
Calisthenics	−	++	++	+	−	−

*Enjoyment and fun are relative and for this reason it is impossible to classify activities accurately. However, for the average person some activities seem to be more enjoyable than others. The above listed classifications reflect the opinions of the typical person. *Any of the activities listed above can be fun and enjoyable for a given person in the right circumstances.*

Programs of Exercise

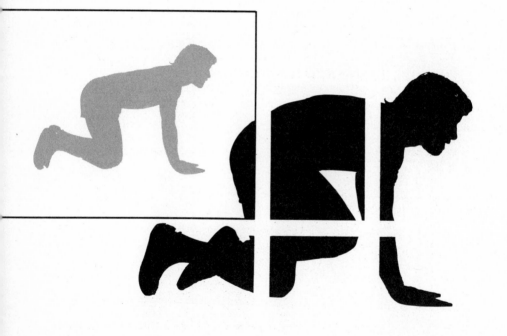

Planning Your Exercise Program

19

Concept 19

In order to attain maximal benefits from exercise it is essential that a regular progressive program be planned to meet the specific needs of the individual.

Introduction

There is no single exercise program best suited to all people. In planning an exercise program it is important to consider your own unique needs and interests.

Five steps to fitness program development are presented within this concept to aid you in your planning.

The Facts

There are five steps that should be considered in planning your personal exercise program.

Step 1—Identify your personal fitness needs. To identify your personal fitness needs, you should first get a medical examination and then test yourself for each of the different fitness aspects. Information concerning fitness self-testing and standards for rating your physical fitness are presented in Labs 5, 6, 7 (cardiovascular fitness); 8, 9 (strength); 10 (muscular endurance); 11 (flexibility); 12, 13 (fatness); 21, 22 (posture and back care); 15, 16, 17, 18 (skill-related fitness); and 19, 20 (body mechanics).

Step 2—Learn the value of different exercises and physical activities. Exercise is an excellent way to achieve fitness and one means of attaining good health. However, all exercise is not necessarily good. Once you know what your exercise needs are, make sure you are aware of the facts about exercise.

Be sure the exercises you select are safe and that they get you above the threshold of training and in the fitness target zone. Information concerning the facts about exercise and the best way to exercise for each aspect of fitness are presented in the preceding sections of this book. Labs 25 to 37 and Appendixes A to M present samples of various types of exercises and discuss the strengths and weaknesses of each.

Step 3—Make sure that you are meeting all of your exercise and fitness needs. Once you have determined what your exercise needs are and which exercises do what, it is important to make sure that you are exercising to meet all of your exercise needs. No single exercise can meet all of your needs. Make sure you have selected exercises for all aspects of physical fitness and especially make sure that you have selected a program that you enjoy. The best program in the world is not good unless you do it. If you don't enjoy it, you may not do it.

Step 4—Plan your program and then *write it down*. You are more likely to do your exercise program if you write it down. Lab 38 provides a place to record your exercise program.

Step 5—Select a regular time and place for your exercise. Regularity is one of the keys to the success of your exercise program. The "hit or miss" program is likely to evolve into no program at all. From the beginning set a time and a place for your activity. Place a high priority on your exercise time. *Don't allow just anything to interrupt your exercise.* Build your exercise program into your daily routine; make it as much a habit as taking a bath or eating regular meals. It is recommended that some form of exercise be done daily; three days a week should be the minimum.

There are some important *guidelines* for carrying out the well-planned exercise program.

1. *An exercise program should be started gradually to avoid soreness or injury.* Begin with a minimum of repetitions (or load) and gradually increase them over a period of time. It is better to "underexercise" than to "overexercise" initially. Some muscle soreness can be expected if you are unaccustomed to activity, but repeating the exercises the next day will alleviate it. Much soreness and possible strain can be avoided by progressing gradually, by warming up with a few mild stretching and circulatory exercises, and by performing the exercises slowly and deliberately with no quick jerky movements. To avoid injury to the abdominals, start slow, avoid soreness in those muscles, and do not hold your breath during exertion. Breathe normally or try to inhale during the recovery phase and exhale during the effort phase of an exercise.
2. *Periodically vary your exercise program.* Repeating the same program over a long period of time may result in loss of interest. Since there are many types of physical activity that can result in similar types of fitness improvement, consider changing your program from time to time.
3. *Avoid those exercises that are termed "questionable."* Certain exercises have dangers to the typical person and may result in injury. These exercises should be avoided (see Concept 17). Also be sure to exercise

through the full range of joint movement. Do not hurry through your exercises, especially weight training and calisthenics.

4. *Make exercise fun.* Wear appropriate clothing and keep the exercise period short and well organized. To make the session more interesting and provide more motivation, exercise with a partner or a group. To help break the monotony of a routine, vary the program by changing exercises and by performing to musical accompaniment or while watching T.V. When doing calisthenics on the floor, use padding to avoid pressure on bony areas that might become bruised.

5. *Set realistic goals and measure your progress.* Set goals that you have a reasonable chance of attaining and do not expect miracles. Since you did not become "unfit" overnight, do not expect to become "fit" in a day. It is a slow process, but periodic reevaluation will boost your morale by revealing progress. When your initial goals are met, you may wish to set higher goals. Some of the same tests for assessing your exercise needs can be used to measure your progress.

6. *Warm up and cool down before and after moderate to vigorous physical activity.* Recent research indicates that in addition to warming up the skeletal muscles before exercise, the heart muscle should be warmed up. Research results indicate that approximately two minutes of easy jogging should precede moderate to vigorous activity to improve blood flow to the heart. This is necessary since, for many adults, blood flow to the heart does not increase instantly at the beginning of work by the heart (Barnard 1976).

There are those who believe that a warm-up is also advised for the skeletal muscles. Those who hold this position feel that passive stretching of the muscles prior to moderate or vigorous exercise can reduce muscle soreness and possible muscle injury. Others, most notably Dr. A. J. Ryan, feel that similar stretching exercises may be most beneficial following activity (Ryan 1974).

"Cooling down" or tapering off after exercise is also important. After moderate to vigorous activity it is wise to gradually decrease the amount of activity performed, as opposed to stopping abruptly. After a jog or a bout of exercise, you should continue to walk and move around; particularly the legs should continue to move.

During exercise much blood is pumped to the large muscles of the legs. If you stop exercising abruptly much of the blood pumped to the leg muscles is left there with no quick way provided for that blood to return to the heart. If you walk around, the massaging action of the muscles will move the blood out of the legs and back to the heart. If too much blood is pumped to the legs and not back to the heart muscle it could cause a person to "pass out" after exercise.

Suggested Readings

Cooper, K. H. *The Aerobics Way*. New York: M. Evans and Co., 1977.
Pollock, M. L.; Wilmore, J. H.; and Fox, S. M. *Health and Fitness Through Physical Activity*. New York: John Wiley and Sons, 1978.

Exercise for a Lifetime

20

Concept 20

Physical activity and exercise can contribute to physical fitness, good health, and an improved quality of life for people of all ages.

Introduction

In our culture, activity is often for the older child, the adolescent, and the young adult. Yet research evidence indicates that *all people,* including young children and older people, can benefit from regular physical activity.

Terms

Acquired Aging—The acquisition of characteristics commonly associated with aging but that are in fact caused by immobility or inactivity.

Time Dependent Aging—The loss of function resulting from growing older.

The Facts

Physical Activity for Children

Children, even very young children, are quite capable of vigorous physical activity. However, the optimal time for development of high levels of health-related fitness occurs after the beginning of adolescence.

Children can exercise regularly. The typical child needs several hours of large muscle activity daily. For their body size children can perform equal to young adults, but should not (because of their smaller size and because they are not mature emotionally) be expected to compete with adolescents and young adults (Corbin 1980).

A healthy child cannot physiologically injure his or her heart through physical exercise (Corbin 1976).

Parents should not be concerned about the old wives' tale that suggests that exercise for children will result in damage to the heart. Research dispells this myth. At the same time, children are not miniature adults and programs of exercise for health-related fitness, including cardiovascular fitness, should be designed to meet both the physical and psycholgical needs and interests of children. Too much too soon may breed dislike for any type of physical activity.

Children should be exposed to a wide variety of physical activity experiences in order to establish a basis for a lifetime of activity (Corbin 1976).

Recent research indicates that nearly all Americans have had some physical education during their school years. Nevertheless, only 40 percent of all school children have physical education in the elementary school (Clarke 1974). Evidence indicates that most skills are learned by age twelve or by the end of the sixth grade (Nash 1960). For this reason, it is important that children not specialize in one activity too early, thus allowing more time to concentrate on learning as many activities as possible during the school years. Just as a child learning to read must first learn the alphabet and grammar, the child in physical activity should be exposed to many fundamental activities early in life so that he or she can take advantage of more than one lifetime activity in adulthood.

Physical Activity for the Adolescent

It is during adolescence that exercise contributes the most dramatic improvements in health-related physical fitness (deVries 1980).

During adolescence hormonal changes occur that promote dramatic increases in cardiovascular fitness and strength with regular exercise. Both boys and girls can improve significantly in fitness at this age with regular exercise.

Adolescence is a time when the social aspects of sports competition and participation can provide great satisfaction to both the participant and the spectator.

Because adolescence is a social age and because sports and sporting events provide social experiences, sports can be a significant part of the life of the adolescent. However, for a lifetime of exercise the adolescent should be encouraged to become involved in sports as a participant, as opposed to becoming only a spectator.

Adolescence is a good time to refine lifetime sports skills.

Though most skills are learned early in life it is during adolescence that lifetime sports skills are refined. Adolescents acquire the health-related, as well as the skill-related, fitness necessary to refine and become efficient in sports skills. Adolescents should be exposed to a variety of skills that can be used for a lifetime.

Physical Activity for Adults (Age 17 Plus)

Most of the limitations of adults in exercise are self-imposed (deVries 1980).

Approximately 64 million adult American men and women do not engage in physical activity for the purpose of exercise (Harris and assoc. 1979). Of those who do not exercise regularly it is their own lack of fitness resulting from years of inactivity that makes them feel unable to participate. While one of five American adults has been told by a physician to exercise, rarely does a physician suggest inactivity except for short periods of time for a specific ailment.

The "weekend" adult athlete may create rather than solve exercise problems.

A "weekend athlete" is one who exercises, sometimes vigorously, only on the weekend. This person may avoid exercise during the "busy" weekdays and attempt to "make up" for a week of inactivity on Saturday or Sunday. To be effective, exercise must be regular (at least three times a week). Vigorous exercise done only one day a week can be dangerous because the weekly exercise is not sufficient to produce improvements in fitness. Thus, the unfit person may be exposing himself or herself to exercise for which the body is not prepared.

Being "too busy" is not a good excuse for inactivity.

The most common reason for inactivity among adults is, "I can't take the time." If business or other obligations make it such that weekday activities in golf or tennis are impossible, then walking, jogging, or calisthenics are appropriate. These activities take relatively little time and if planned properly can provide important fitness and health benefits. After the inactive person has had a heart attack or some other hypokinetic disease, he or she will have more free time than he or she really wants. Exercise may be as important as food and, like meals, should be scheduled on a regular basis.

Physical Activity for Older Adults

Adults are never "too old" to begin exercising (deVries 1975).

Physical fitness for old age should begin in the early years in order for maximum benefits to come to each individual. If this does not occur for one reason or another, one is never too old to begin exercising (deVries 1975). Studies conducted over a period of years indicate that properly planned exercise for older people is not only safe but that older men and women are *not* significantly different from youth (in a relative sense) when it comes to improving fitness through exercise (deVries 1975).

Regular exercise can have a significant delaying effect on the aging process (deVries 1975; Elrich 1975; Pollock 1978; Rosentswieg 1980).

One researcher suggests that "exercise is the closest thing to an antiaging pill now available" (Butler 1975, p. 67). Another indicates that continued mental and physical activity is ". . . the only antidote for aging that I know" (Klump 1975, p. 93).

There is a difference between "acquired aging" and "time-dependent aging" (Lamb 1975).

Forced inactivity in young adults has been shown to cause losses in function (acquired aging) that are very much like those that we generally consider to occur with aging (time-dependent aging). Recent studies conducted on older adults over a long period of time suggest that aging appears to be more a product of a sedentary life-style than of aging (Radd 1975). Studies in Africa, Asia, and South America, where older adults (age 65 and older) maintain an active life-style, show that these individuals do not "acquire" many of the characteristics commonly associated with aging (Elrich 1975).

In our culture middle-aged and older people are encouraged (and sometimes compelled) to reduce their physical activity to the extent that they cannot continue to function on their own (Klump 1976).

In our society the attitude toward older people is often one of overprotection, placing the person in a position of being dependent. A spokesperson for the President's Council for Physical Fitness and Sports suggests that ". . . a state of physical fitness enhances the quality of life for the elderly by increasing independence. The ability to 'go places and do things' without being dependent on others provides a strong psychological lift which is conducive to good mental health" (Conrad 1975, p. 83).

One famous active American, H. G. "Dad" Miller, a one-hundred-year-old golfer who recently made a hole-in-one, suggests "we don't stop exercising because we get old—we get old because we stop exercising."

Participation in regular activity has benefits other than improved physical health and fitness.

A general feeling of "well-being" is frequently reported to be one of the real benefits of regular fitness for older people. Nervous tension, which detracts from the feeling of well-being, is a problem of many older adults. One recent study showed that exercise can be more effective than tranquilizers in the treatment of nervous tension in older people (deVries 1975).

Participation in regular physical activity has many physical health benefits for the older adult.

In addition to the health benefits of exercise already presented in this book, there are other benefits to older adults that result from regular physical activity.

1. "The syndrome of shaky hand and tottery gait is responsible in a large degree for much of the dependency of the aged. The treatment (of this condition) is physical exercise" (Swartz 1975, p. 7). Merely fifteen minutes of exercise a day will not do it, rather there must be a shift from a sedentary to an active life-style.
2. Studies at Duke University Center for the Study of Aging indicate that active older people have fewer illnesses and fewer early deaths than do those who are inactive (Radd 1975).
3. Studies show that reductions in physical working capacity, which is the most obvious result of aging, do not occur in older men who engage in regular exercise. Researchers indicate that regular exercise prevents the expected decline in physical working capacity (Kasch 1976; Pollock 1978).
4. Regular exercise can help older adults in the "War with Gravity." Gravity has its effect on the human body. With time, if muscles are not kept fit, gravity can cause "Bay Window" or protruding abdomen, sagging shoulders, poor posture, and joint immobility. All of these "gravity" problems result from lack of strength, muscular endurance, and flexibility, and can be forestalled with regular activity (Lamb 1975).
5. Bones that are not used tend to decalcify. Regular exercise for older adults can delay decalcification of bones (Lamb 1975).
6. With age the ability of the heart to function effectively as a pump decreases for the typical adult. This decrease is at the rate of 1 percent per year after adulthood. Regular exercise can forestall the decline in circulatory function. In addition, normal increases in atherosclerosis, blood pressure, and EKG abnormalities that occur with age can be prevented with appropriate regular exercise (deVries 1975).
7. Other changes in function that occur in "normal" adults with age include decreased skeletal muscle, gain in body fat, decrease in oxygen-use capacity, and decreased respiratory function. These changes in function can be postponed with regular exercise (deVries 1975; Rosentswieg 1980).

Older adults can participate in a wide variety of sports and physical activity.

It has been shown that with appropriate progressively maintained exercise older adults can participate in most sports for a lifetime. For example, one man of age eighty-five regularly plays handball (Klump 1976; Kuland 1979; Fardy 1978) and the increased participation in masters (over 50) classifications in track and field, swimming, and tennis are well documented. Bowling is the leading participant sport in the United States and is well suited for older people. Golf is another activity well suited for older Americans. For those who do not wish to choose a sport, walking, jogging, bicycle riding, swimming, and calisthenics are forms of physical activity that are widely used by people of all ages.

Older adults should be especially careful to follow the exercise guidelines presented in Concept 19.

Suggested Readings

"Testimony on Physical Fitness for Older Persons." Washington, D.C.: National Association for Human Development, 1975. Reprinted and available from the President's Council on Physical Fitness and Sports, Washington, D.C. 20201.

Concept 20

The Values of Physical Activity

Name_____ Section_____ Date_____

Purpose

The purpose of this laboratory session is to evaluate individual attitudes about the value of physical activity.

Procedures

Read each of the sixteen items in Chart 1.1 and check "strongly agree," "agree," "undecided," "disagree," or "strongly disagree." Give only one answer that best indicates the way *you* feel. Try not to use the response "undecided" unless absolutely necessary. Score the sixteen items using the scoring method on page 150.

Expected Results

People participate in sports, physical activity, and exercise for different reasons. Before you answer the questions in Chart 1.1, indicate your reasons for either choosing to exercise or choosing not to exercise. Check the box or boxes that apply to you.

I exercise for physical fitness. ☐
I exercise for social reasons. ☐
I exercise to relax. ☐
I exercise because I think I should. ☐
If other reasons—list them here:

I choose not to exercise regularly. ☐

Results

The sixteen-item questionnaire is designed to help you determine your attitude toward physical activity. There are different reasons for participation, and your scores will help you to better understand your reasons for choosing to exercise or not to exercise. How did you score on each of the scales?

	Ex.	Good	N	Poor	VP
Health and Physical Fitness	☐	☐	☐	☐	☐
Social	☐	☐	☐	☐	☐
Recreation-Relaxation	☐	☐	☐	☐	☐
General	☐	☐	☐	☐	☐

Conclusions

Did you score as you expected? Yes ☐ No ☐
Why or why not?

Implications

Of what significance is your attitude toward physical activity with reference to your future participation in sports and activity?

Could anything be done to change your attitude?

When did you establish your basic attitude toward activity, sports, and exercise?

Read each of the statements listed on the following page, and check the box that best represents your feeling about the statement.

Chart 1.1   Attitude Test

	Strongly Agree	Agree	Un-decided	Disagree	Strongly Disagree	SCORE
1. Physical education is all right for those who like sports but is not for me.	☐	☐	☐	☐	☐	_____
2. Physical exercise and activity are as dangerous to health as they are valuable.	☐	☐	☐	☐	☐	_____
3. I enjoy taking part in a sport just to get away from it all.	☐	☐	☐	☐	☐	_____
4. I like to participate best in those games that involve working as a team.	☐	☐	☐	☐	☐	_____
5. Physical activity is one way to rid yourself of the worries and tensions of everyday life.	☐	☐	☐	☐	☐	_____
6. Probably one of the main values of sports is to fill leisure time in our automated society.	☐	☐	☐	☐	☐	_____
7. I would only enroll in physical education if it were a graduation requirement.	☐	☐	☐	☐	☐	_____
8. The time some people spend exercising could probably be better spent in other ways.	☐	☐	☐	☐	☐	_____
9. Sports and games build social confidence.	☐	☐	☐	☐	☐	_____
10. Industry might be wise to substitute exercise breaks for coffee breaks.	☐	☐	☐	☐	☐	_____
11. Competition in sports is often a way to destroy good friendships.	☐	☐	☐	☐	☐	_____
12. Most jobs provide all the exercise and activity a person needs.	☐	☐	☐	☐	☐	_____
13. Everyone should have skill in several sports that can be used later in life.	☐	☐	☐	☐	☐	_____
14. Social dancing and other similar forms of activity are a waste of time.	☐	☐	☐	☐	☐	_____
15. Health and physical fitness are basic to all of life's activities.	☐	☐	☐	☐	☐	_____
16. I would recommend that everyone take physical education because of the important nature of the subject.	☐	☐	☐	☐	☐	_____

Score the attitude test as follows:

1. For items 1, 2, 7, 8, 11, 12, and 14 give one point for *strongly agree,* two for *agree,* three for *undecided,* four for *disagree,* and five for *strongly disagree.* Put the correct number on the blank to the right of these statements.
2. For items 3, 4, 5, 6, 9, 10, 13, 15, and 16 give five points for *strongly agree,* four for *agree,* three for *undecided,* two for *disagree,* and one for *strongly disagree.* Put the correct number on the blank to the right of these statements.
3. Add the scores for items 2, 8, 12, and 15. This total represents your health and fitness attitude score.
4. Add the scores for items 4, 9, 11, and 14. This total represents your social attitude score.
5. Add the scores for items 3, 5, 6, and 13. This total represents your recreation-relaxation attitude score.
6. Add the scores for items 1, 7, 10, and 16. This total represents your general attitude score.
7. Circle your scores on Chart 1.2 and record them in the "results" section.

Chart 1.2   Attitude Rating Scale

Attitude Scale
First Test

Classification	HF Scale	Social	Recreational Relaxational	General	Total
Excellent (Ex)	18	18	18	18	69–72
Good	15–17	15–17	15–17	15–17	57–68
Marginal (M)	8–14	8–14	8–14	8–14	32–56
Poor	6–7	6–7	6–7	6–7	21–31
Very poor (VP)	0–5	0–5	0–5	0–5	0–20

Physical Fitness

Name   Section   Date

Purpose

The purposes of this laboratory session are:

1. To help you identify different aspects of physical fitness. It is hoped that through participation you can begin to see the differences between the various aspects of physical fitness, especially the differences between health-related and skill-related physical fitness aspects.
2. To help you to gain insight into the importance of various aspects of physical fitness and to help you evaluate these aspects.

Procedures

Perform all of the physical fitness stunts described in Chart 2.1. Record your results in the appropriate blank opposite each item.

Expected Results

Check the aspect of fitness on which you expect to score the best, poorest.

	Best	Poorest		Best	Poorest
Agility	☐	☐	Muscular	☐	☐
Balance	☐	☐	endurance		
Cardiovascular	☐	☐	Power	☐	☐
fitness			Strength	☐	☐
Flexibility	☐	☐			

Results

The stunts you tried are not good tests of fitness but attempting the stunts may help you see that fitness is not just one thing; it is many different things. Based on the readings in Concepts 2 and 3, circle the numbers of the items you think are skill related and the numbers of the items you think are health related.

Skill-Related   1 2 3 4 5 6 7 8 9

Health-Related   1 2 3 4 5 6 7 8 9

Conclusions and Implications

To really test your fitness you will need to do many of the tests presented later in this text. Therefore, you may be especially interested in testing yourself in those areas in which you did not do well on various stunts.

For your own well being you should want to do well in health-related fitness. How many of the five health-related stunts did you pass? Circle the number.

1   2   3   4   5

Were you surprised at your performance? Were you disappointed? Explain.

To perform sports well you need skill-related fitness. How many of the three skill-related fitness stunts did you pass? Circle the number.

1   2   3

Were you surprised at your performance? Were you disappointed? Explain.

Chart 2.1 Physical Fitness Stunts

	Item	Fitness Aspect	Pass	% Men Passing	% Women Passing
1.	*One Foot Balance.* Stand on one foot, press up so that the weight is on the ball of the foot with the heel off the floor. Hold the hands out in front and the other leg straight.	Balance (10 sec.)	Yes ☐ No ☐	80	80 *No*
2.	*Long Jump.* Stand with the toes behind a line; use no run or hop step; and jump as far as possible. To pass, men must jump their height plus six inches. Women must jump their height only.	Power	Yes ☐ No ☐	95	70 *Yes*
3.	*Toe Touch.* With the feet together and knees straight, bend forward at the hips and touch the thumbs to the floor. Do not bounce, bend slowly.	Flexibility	Yes ☐ No ☐	90	90 *Yes ½*
4.	*Jack Spring.* From a standing position, jump into the air, kick the legs up and out and touch the feet with the hands. Repeat 5 times, touching the floor once between jumps.	Agility and power	Yes ☐ No ☐	70	50 *No*
5.	*Back Hyperextension.* Lie face down on the floor. Have a partner hold the back of the thighs. With the hands behind the head lift the chin off the floor the length of a forearm.	Flexibility and back strength	Yes ☐ No ☐	90	70 *Yes*
6.	*Lower the Legs.* Lie on the back with the feet lifted in the air at 90 degrees. With the legs straight, lower the feet. Keep the back on the floor. To pass you must lower the feet to within two fists of the floor without allowing the back to arch higher than the thickness of a partner's hand. Breathe normally. Caution: people with known back problems should not do this test.	Strength	Yes ☐ No ☐	76	60 *No*
7.	*High Leg Press Up (women).* Start in the push-up position with a partner holding the legs off the ground, keep the body straight, press off the floor until the arms are fully extended.	Strength	Yes ☐ No ☐		64 *No*

Chart 2.1   Physical Fitness Stunts (Cont.)

	Item	Fitness Aspect	Pass	% Men Passing	% Women Passing
	Hand Stand Push-up (men). Do a handstand against the wall. Lower body and touch the chin. Push back to the handstand position.		Yes ☐ No ☐	53	
8.	*Run in Place.* Run in place for 1 and ½ minutes. (120 steps per minute.) Rest for 1 minute and count the heart rate for 30 seconds. A heart rate of 60 or lower passes.	Cardio-vascular fitness	Yes ☐ No ☐	68	55 rate 68
9.	*Four-Minute Hop Test.* With the hands behind the head, pogo hop over a line as many times as possible in four minutes. 500 jumps over the line passes.	Cardio-vascular fitness and muscular endurance	Yes ☐ No ☐	77	65 No

Exercise and the Heart

Purpose

The purposes of this laboratory session are:

1. To discover which physical activities allow the heart to slow down and rest.
2. To discover which physical activities cause greatest overload on the heart muscle.
3. To discover which physical activities allow the quickest and most efficient recovery from exercise overload.

Procedures

1. Practice taking your carotid pulse for several thirty-second periods. The instructor will show you how and will signal by saying "Start" and "Stop" before and after several thirty-second periods at rest.
2. Take your thirty-second pulse after each of the following:
   a. standing at attention for one minute
   b. performing three minutes of a vigorous exercise of your choice (running, sit-ups, rope jumping, etc.)
   c. one minute of recovery from the exercise above (take a sitting position to aid the heart in returning to normal)
   d. two minutes of recovery from the exercise above
   e. three minutes of recovery from the exercise above
   f. four minutes of recovery from the exercise above
3. Record results on the graph in the results section by filling in the bars to the appropriate level.

Expected Results

Read the procedures and estimate:

How high do you expect your heart rate to go after three minutes of exercise?

_____beats per min.

How long do you think it will take for your heart rate to return to normal?

_____

Results

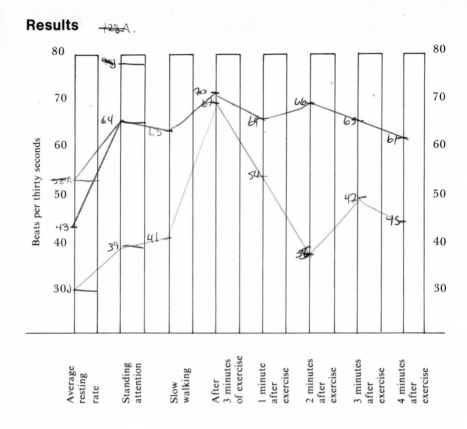

Beats per thirty seconds

| | Average resting rate | Standing attention | Slow walking | After 3 minutes of exercise | 1 minute after exercise | 2 minutes after exercise | 3 minutes after exercise | 4 minutes after exercise |

It can be said that the "normal" resting heart rate is about 70 beats per minute for adults. However, it is not abnormal to have heart rates from 40 to 80. People who exercise regularly may have lower resting heart rates than others. After exercise, heart rates return to normal quite quickly. Within 1½ to 2 minutes after most exercise, your heart rate should return to near normal. (It may stay 10 to 20 percent above normal for a considerably longer period.)

What is your normal heart rate? _____ beats per min?
Did your heart rate return to normal at any time after the beginning of the lab session? Yes ☐ No ☐

Conclusions and Implications

What practical implications can you draw from this experiment?

The Cardiovascular Threshold of Training

Lab 4

Name   Section   Date

Mild exercise will not produce increases in cardiovascular fitness. Researchers suggest that exercise must be vigorous enough to elevate the heart rate to a "minimum threshold" value if the exercise is to be effective in producing fitness. For optimal benefits you should elevate the heart rate into the cardio-vascular fitness target zone.

Those just beginning exercise are encouraged to start with threshold values and gradually work up into the target zone. Once exceptionally high levels of cardiovascular fitness have been attained, a new target zone higher than those listed in Chart 4.1 may need to be used. However, for most people the values presented in the chart will be best.

Purpose

The purpose of this laboratory session is to help you discover how much exercise is necessary to elevate the heart rate to threshold and target levels, and more specifically to help each individual:

1. Understand the threshold of training and target zone concepts.
2. Establish a personal minimal cardiovascular threshold of training.
3. Establish a personal target zone for cardiovascular fitness.
4. Determine the specific speed of jogging necessary to elevate the heart rate to threshold of training and target zones.

Procedures

To determine your cardiovascular fitness threshold and target heart rates you will use your age and your resting heart rate. Use Chart 4.1 to determine your threshold of cardiovascular training and your target zone.

1. Find your threshold of training and target zone on Chart 4.1.
2. Select a partner.
3. One partner should run a quarter mile, the other partner should count her or his (use carotid pulse) heart rate at the end of the run. Try to run at a rate that you think will keep the rate of the heart above the threshold of training and in the target zone.

4. Repeat, alternating roles, one running, one counting heart rate.
5. Repeat the test so each person runs twice.
6. Record heart rates in the "results" section of this experiment.

Expected Results

Read the procedures and guess whether you can stay in the target zone. First trial, Yes ☐ No ☐ Second trial, Yes ☐ No ☐.

Results

What is your threshold of training (from Chart 4.1)? _____ BPM

What is your target zone (from Chart 4.1)? _____ to _____BPM

What was your heart rate for the first run? _____ BPM

What was your heart rate for the second run? _____ BPM

How fast do you have to run to get your heart rate above threshold and into the target zone? Check below.

First run speed just right	☐
Faster than the first run	☐
Slower than the first run	☐
Faster than the second run	☐
Slower than the second run	☐
Second run speed just right	☐

Conclusions and Implications

Do you think the average American achieves the cardiovascular threshold of training in the course of a normal day? Yes ☐ No ☐

Do you achieve the cardiovascular threshold in the course of a normal day? Yes ☐ No ☐

What would you suggest for yourself as a regular daily cardiovascular exercise program?

Chart 4.1 Threshold of Training and Target Zone Heart Rates (Heart rates necessary to produce improved cardiovascular fitness)

Resting Heart Rate		Age Less than 25	25-29	30-34	35-39	40-44	45-49	50-54	55-59	60-64	Over 65
below 50	Threshold	136	133	130	127	124	121	118	115	112	109
	Target zone	136-156	133-164	130-160	127-156	124-152	121-148	118-144	115-140	112-136	109-134
50-54	Threshold	138	135	132	129	126	123	120	117	114	111
	Target zone	138-167	135-165	132-161	129-157	126-153	123-149	120-145	117-141	114-137	111-135
55-59	Threshold	140	137	134	131	128	125	122	119	116	113
	Target zone	140-168	137-166	134-162	131-158	128-154	125-150	122-146	119-142	116-138	113-136
60-64	Threshold	142	139	136	133	130	127	124	121	118	115
	Target zone	142-169	139-167	136-163	133-159	130-155	127-151	124-147	121-143	118-139	115-137
65-69	Threshold	144	141	138	135	132	129	126	123	120	117
	Target zone	144-170	141-168	138-164	135-160	132-156	129-152	126-148	123-144	120-140	117-138
70-74	Threshold	146	143	140	137	134	131	128	125	122	119
	Target zone	146-171	143-169	140-165	137-161	134-157	131-153	128-149	125-145	122-141	119-139
75-79	Threshold	148	145	142	139	136	133	130	127	124	121
	Target zone	148-172	145-170	142-166	139-162	136-158	133-154	130-150	127-146	124-142	121-140
80-85	Threshold	150	147	144	141	138	135	132	129	126	123
	Target zone	150-173	147-171	144-167	141-163	138-159	135-155	132-151	129-147	126-143	123-141
85 and over	Threshold	152	149	146	143	140	137	134	131	128	125
	Target zone	152-174	149-172	146-168	143-164	140-160	137-156	134-152	131-148	128-144	125-142

Evaluating Cardiovascular Fitness—
The Twelve-Minute Run

Name _____ Section _____ Date _____

When you engage in a regular exercise program you need some type of evaluation to determine your progress. One of the best methods of evaluating cardiovascular fitness is a test called Maximal Oxygen Uptake. It is an all-out test that takes several hours to complete. A more practical test is the Twelve-Minute Run, which requires very little equipment. The Twelve-Minute Run test was developed by Dr. Kenneth Cooper and is considered to be better than runs of other lengths for assessing cardiovascular fitness.

Purpose

The purpose of this laboratory session is to evaluate your cardiovascular fitness and to acquaint you with an effective means of evaluating cardiovascular fitness throughout life.

Procedures

Perform the Twelve-Minute Run and record your score in the result section of this report. To perform the test you should run as far as possible during the twelve-minute period. The further the distance the better the score. Attempt to establish a steady pace that can be maintained for the full twelve-minute period.

Expected Results

Check the classification you expect to achieve on this test of cardiovascular fitness.

Excellent	☐
Very good	☐
Marginal	☐
Poor	☐
Very poor	☐

How far do you expect to run on this test? _____

Results

What distance did you cover in twelve minutes? _____

What is your rating? _____ (See Charts 5.1, 5.2, and 5.3.)

Conclusions and Implications

Did you score as well as you thought you would? Yes □ No □
Did you score better than you thought? Yes □ No □
Does this test indicate your fitness level? Yes □ No □
What do the results of this test imply to you about your exercise needs?

Find the distance that you ran in 12 minutes on the appropriate chart to determine your fitness. Chart 5.1 is for people seventeen to twenty-five years of age. Older people should use Charts 5.2 or 5.3.

Chart 5.1 Twelve-Minute Test for Ages 17–25

Classification	Men	Women
Excellent	1.9 miles	1.5 miles
Very good	1.8–1.89 miles _ J.	1.4–1.49 miles
Marginal	1.6–1.79 miles	1.1–1.39 miles
Poor	1.5–1.59 miles	1.0–1.09 miles
Very poor	1.4–1.49 miles	below .9 miles — A.

J. 1.84
A. .82

*Adapted from K. H. Cooper. *The New Aerobics*. New York: M. Evans & Co., 1972.

The following charts are provided to help you evaluate your fitness as you get older. You may wish to make these charts available to an older friend or relative.

Chart 5.2 Twelve-Minute Test for Adult Men

	Age		
Classification	26–39	40–49	50+
Very poor	<.95 miles	<.85 miles	<.80 miles
Poor	.95–1.14 miles	.85–1.04 miles	.80–.99 miles
Fair	1.15–1.39 miles	1.05–1.29 miles	1.0–1.24 miles
Good	1.40–1.64 miles	1.30–1.54 miles	1.25–1.49 miles
Excellent	1.65+ miles	1.55+ miles	1.50+ miles

Adapted from K. H. Cooper, *The New Aerobics*. New York: M. Evans & Co., 1972.

Chart 5.3 Twelve-Minute Test for Adult Women

	Age		
Classification	26–39	40–49	50+
Very poor	<.85 miles	<.75 miles	<.65 miles
Poor	.85–1.04 miles	.75–.94 miles	.65–.84 miles
Fair	1.05–1.24 miles	.95–1.14 miles	.85–1.04 miles
Good	1.25–1.54 miles	1.15–1.44 miles	1.05–1.34 miles
Excellent	1.55+ miles	1.45+ miles	1.35+ miles

Adapted from K. H. Cooper, *The New Aerobics*. New York: M. Evans & Co., 1972.

Evaluating Cardiovascular Fitness— The Step Test

Name   Section   Date

When you engage in a regular exercise program you need some type of evaluation to determine your progress. Laboratory 5 explains one practical test for measuring cardiovascular fitness—the "Twelve-Minute Run." This lab explains the "Step Test," another practical test that requires very little equipment. There are several modifications of the "Step Test." The Kasch Three-Minute Step Test* is used for this laboratory session because it can be performed by all age groups and by both sexes. Only extremely unfit or ill persons would find the test too strenuous.

Purpose

The purpose of this laboratory session is to evaluate your cardiovascular fitness and to acquaint you with an effective means of evaluating cardiovascular fitness throughout life.

Procedures

1. Choose a partner. After you exercise, your partner will count your pulse.
2. Step up and down on a twelve-inch bench for three minutes at a rate of twenty-four steps a minute.**
3. Immediately after exercise sit down on the bench and relax. Don't talk.
4. Your partner will locate your carotid pulse. Five seconds after exercise your partner will count your pulse for sixty seconds.
5. Your score is the sixty-second pulse rate. Find your score in Chart 6.1 to determine your cardiovascular fitness rating.
6. Record your rating in the results section of the lab.
7. Now count for your partner after he/she does three minutes of stepping.

---

*Adapted from Kasch, F. W., and Boyer, J. L. *Adult Fitness: Principles and Practices.* Palo Alto, Calif.: Mayfield Publishers, 1968.
**"One step" consists of: up with the right foot, up with the left foot, down with the right foot, and down with the left foot. Completely straighten the legs as you step up on the bench.

Expected Results

How do you expect to perform on the Step Test?

Excellent ☐   Poor ☐
Very good ☐   Very poor ☐
Marginal ☐

Results

What was your heart rate at the end of the test? _____ What was your rating (see Chart 6.1)?

Excellent ☐   Poor ☐
Very good ☐   Very poor ☐
Marginal ☐

Chart 6.1   Step Test Rating Chart

Classification	Sixty-second Heart Rate	
Excellent	84 or less	
Very good	85–94	
Marginal	95–114	
Poor	115–124	↲ /2)
Very poor	125 and above	4 - /44)

As you grow older you would want to continue to score well on this rating chart. Because your maximal heart rate decreases as you grow older you should be able to score well if you exercise regularly.

Conclusions and Implications

Did you score as well as you thought you would? Yes ☐ No ☐
Did you score better than you thought you would? Yes ☐ No ☐
Do you think this test is a true measure of your cardiovascular fitness? Yes ☐ No ☐
What do the results of this test imply regarding your need for exercise?

Evaluating Cardiovascular Fitness— The Astrand-Ryhming Bicycle Test

Name   Section   Date

When you engage in a regular exercise program you need some type of evaluation to determine your progress. The Step Test and the Twelve-Minute Run are good substitutes for the more scientific Maximal Oxygen Uptake Test because they require very little equipment. However, if the equipment is available the Astrand-Ryhming Bicycle Test is probably a better substitute predictor of maximal oxygen uptake than either of the tests used in Labs 5 or 6.

Purpose

The purpose of this laboratory session is to evaluate the individual's cardiovascular fitness and to acquaint the student with an effective means of evaluating cardiovascular fitness.

Procedures

1. Ride a stationary bicycle ergometer for six minutes at a rate of fifty pedal cycles per minute (one push with each foot per cycle).
2. Your instructor will set the work load of the bicycle depending on an estimation of your current exercise regularity. (Usually 300 to 900 KPM for women and 450 to 1,200 for men).
3. During the sixth minute of the ride your heart rate will be determined (the carotid pulse or the stethoscope will be used). For the test to be valid your heart rate must be in the range between 125 and 170 beats per minute.
4. Use the nomogram on page 169 to determine your predicted oxygen uptake score. Connect the point that represents your heart rate with the point on the right-hand scale that represents the work load you used in riding the bicycle (use the ♂ scale for men and the ♀ scale for women). Read your score at the point where a straight line connecting the two points crosses the Max VO$_2$ line. For example, the sample score for the woman represented by the dotted line is 2.55 or nearly 2.6. She had a heart rate of 150 and worked at a load of 600 KPM.

5. Check Chart 7.1 to determine your cardiovascular fitness rating for the Max : VO_2 (Maximum Oxygen Uptake) score obtained from the nomogram.
6. Determine your VO_2 per kilogram of body weight. Divide your body weight by 2.2. (This figure represents kilograms.) Divide this amount into your Max VO_2 score as determined from the nomogram. Locate your rating on Chart 7.1. This score will adjust your Max VO_2 for body weight and is a more accurate rating for people other than those of average weight.

Expected Results

Do you think you can easily ride a stationary bicycle against resistance for six minutes? Yes ☐ No ☐
Check your expected score on this cardiovascular fitness test.

Excellent ☐   Poor ☐
Very good ☐   Very poor ☐
Marginal ☐

Results

At what work load did you ride the bicycle? _____ KPM

What was your heart rate during the last minute of the ride? _____ BPM

What was your score on the test? _____ liters of O_2

What was your score when corrected for body weight? _____ ml/O_2/kg

What is your cardiovascular fitness rating on the bicycle test?

_____ without weight adjustment

_____ with weight adjustment

Conclusions and Implications

Did you score as well as you thought you would? Yes ☐ No ☐
Do you think this test indicates your true level of cardiovascular fitness? Yes ☐ No ☐
Are the ratings corrected for body weight different from the uncorrected rating? Yes ☐ No ☐
Explain.

What do the test results imply to you about your need for exercise?

Nomogram

Chart 7.1 Bicycle Test Rating Scale

Classification	Men O₂ in Liters	Men ML/O₂/KG	Women O₂ in Liters	Women ML/O₂/KG
Excellent	4.1+	54+	3.1+	47+
Very good	3.3–4.0	46–53	2.6–3.0	42–46
Marginal	2.7–3.2	37–45	2.0–2.5	36–41
Poor	2.2–2.6	34–36	1.7–1.9	30–35
Very poor	2.1 or below	33 or below	1.6 or below	29 or below

You can continue to use this rating scale as you grow older.

Evaluating Isotonic Strength

Lab **8**

Name   Section   Date

Isotonic exercises are those in which a muscle changes its length. There are two types of isotonic contractions: concentric and eccentric; both involve movement of a body part. Concentric contractions involve the shortening of a muscle such as in the contraction of the biceps when the elbow is bent. Eccentric contractions are lengthening contractions such as in the contraction of the biceps while lowering the body to the hanging position after performing a chin-up.

Purpose

The purpose of this laboratory session is to evaluate the isotonic strength of four muscle groups.

Procedures

You will be tested on four isotonic (concentric) strength tests. These tests are *minimal* strength measures. All young adults should be able to pass all of these tests. Tests to determine maximal or high levels of strength can be done with barbells or more sophisticated testing devices. Details of the four tests—the bent knee sit-up, the hanging leg-lift, the upper trunk-lift, and the lower trunk-lift—are presented on pages 173–4. Scores should be recorded in the results section of this report. When not being tested, perform the isotonic strength exercises in Appendix L.

Expected Results

Do you expect to pass the tests of minimal isotonic strength? Yes ☐ No ☐

Results

	Pass	Fail
Bent knee sit-up	☐	☐
Hanging leg-lift	☐	☐
Lower trunk-lift	☐	☐
Upper trunk-lift	☐	☐

Check one below:

☐ Minimal strength = All four tests passed

☐ Less than minimal strength = One or more tests failed

Conclusions and Inplications

Did you score as expected on minimal isotonic strength? Yes ☐ No ☐
Why or why not?

Even if you passed all four strength tests, is it possible you might need even more strength for your daily needs? Yes ☐ No ☐
Explain.

Do you need to perform regular strength exercises? Yes ☐ No ☐
What isotonic strength exercises would you suggest?

Tests

Perform the four tests indicated below:

1. *The Bent Knee Sit-Up*—Lie on your back with the hands behind your head. Bend the knees at a 90° angle and hold your feet flat on the floor. Sit up, keeping the knees bent (see illustration). Lower the body to the starting position. You pass if you can do one!

2. *Hanging Leg-Lift*—Hang from a horizontal bar. Without swinging, *keeping the knees straight*, lift both legs until they touch the bar (see illustration). Lower the legs to the starting position. You pass if you can do one!

3. *Lower Trunk-Lift*—Lie prone on bench or table with legs hanging over the edge. Have a partner stabilize the upper back or grasp the edges of the table with the hands. Raise the legs parallel to the floor and lower them. Do *not raise past the horizontal or arch the back.* You pass if you can do one!

4. *Upper Trunk-Lift*—Lie on a table or bench with the upper half of the body hanging over the edge. Have a partner stabilize the feet while the trunk is raised parallel to the floor, then lower the trunk to the starting position. Place hands behind neck. *Do not raise past the horizontal or arch the back.* You pass if you can do one!

Record your results. To have *minimal* muscular strength, you should pass *all* four tests.

Evaluating Isometric Strength

Name _____ Section _____ Date _____

Isometric exercises are those in which the muscles do not change in length. Examples include pushing against an immovable object or contracting antagonistic muscles equally so that no movement results. The easiest method for measuring isometric strength is through the use of the strength dynamometer.

Purpose

The purpose of this laboratory session is to evaluate the isometric strength of three muscle groups.

Procedures

All individuals will be tested on four isometric strength tests: right-hand grip strength, left-hand grip strength, back strength, and leg strength. Measurements are made on a dynamometer. Scores should be recorded in the results section of this report.

1. *Grip Strength*—Using a grip dynamometer, adjust the dynamometer to fit your hand. Squeeze as hard as possible keeping the hand and arm away from the body. Perform with both right and left hands.
2. *Leg Strength*—Using a back and leg dynamometer, pull the handle of the dynamometer while keeping the back erect. Begin with the knees bent at approximately 120 degrees.
3. *Back Strength*—Using the back and leg dynamometer, pull the handle of the dynamometer while keeping the legs straight and the low back erect. Roll the shoulders back as you pull.

When not being tested, perform the isometric strength exercises in Appendix K.

Expected Results

Check the rating you expect on these tests of isometric strength.

Excellent ☐   Poor ☐

Very good ☐   Very poor ☐

Marginal ☐

Results

Isometric strength scores:

Grip strength   Grip strength   Back strength   Leg strength

right _____   left _____   _____   _____

Total strength = _____

(Sum of above four figures)

To determine strength per pound of body weight, divide *Total Strength* by the body weight.

Strength per/lb./wt. _____

Check your rating on isometric strength using Chart 9.1. Note that there are different charts for men and women.

	Excellent	Very good	Marginal	Poor	Very poor
Right grip	☐	☐	☐	☐	☐
Left grip	☐	☐	☐	☐	☐
Back strength	☐	☐	☐	☐	☐
Leg strength	☐	☐	☐	☐	☐
Total strength	☐	☐	☐	☐	☐
Per/lb./wt.	☐	☐	☐	☐	☐

Conclusions and Implications

Did you score well on isometric strength? Yes ☐ No ☐

Are you as strong as you thought you were? Yes ☐ No ☐

Are you strong enough? Yes ☐ No ☐

Why or why not?

Do you need to perform strength exercises (regularly)? Yes ☐ No ☐
What isometric exercises would you choose?

Chart 9.1 Isometric Strength Rating Scales

Classifica-tion	Strength Rating Scale for Women					
	Left Grip	Right Grip	Back Strength	Leg Strength	Total Strength	Strength per/lb/wt
Excellent	77+	86+	241+	261+	665+	5.30+
Very good	71–76	76–85	215–240	226–260	588–664	4.60–5.29
Marginal	48–70	56–75	125–214	145–225	370–587	2.90–4.59
Poor	40–47	49–55	95–124	105–144	280–369	2.20–2.89
Very poor	below 39	below 48	below 94	below 104	below 279	below 2.19

Classifica-tion	Strength Rating Scale for Men					
	Left Grip	Right Grip	Back Strength	Leg Strength	Total Strength	Strength per/lb/wt
Excellent	131+	141+	460	476+	1200	7.26+
Very good	111–130	126–140	390–459	421–475	1050–1201	6.96–7.25
Marginal	95–110	105–125	277–389	352–420	826–1049	4.82–6.95
Poor	86–94	91–104	201–276	301–351	676–825	4.81–5.20
Very poor	below 85	below 90	below 200	below300	below 675	below 4.80

Because there is typically some loss of muscle tissue as you grow older, persons older than age 50 may wish to make an approximately 10 percent adjustment in the scores presented above.

Evaluating Muscular Endurance

Name   Section   Date

Muscular endurance is the ability of muscles to exert repeated effort. Although chin-ups and the bent arm hang are measures of strength, the repetition of these tasks also requires muscular endurance.

Purpose

The purpose of this laboratory session is to evaluate the muscular endurance of two muscle groups.

Procedures

1. *Sitting Tucks*—Sit on the floor so that the back and feet are off the floor. Interlock the fingers behind the head. Alternately draw the legs to the chest and extend them away from the body. Keep the feet and back off the floor. Repeat as many times as possible up to thirty-five.
2. *Chins or Bent Arm Hang*
   a. *Chins*—Pull the body weight above the horizontal bar, gripping the bar with palms facing the bar. Repeat as many times as possible.
   b. *Bent Arm Hang*—(For men and women who cannot perform one chin). Hang from a horizontal bar with palms facing the bar. Count the number of seconds that the chin can be held above the bar. *This test is only for people who cannot do one chin.* A separate rating chart is provided for this measure of muscular endurance.
3. When not being tested, perform muscular endurance exercises in Appendix L using a light weight and many repetitions.
4. Record your test scores in the results section. Determine your rating from Chart 10.1.

Expected Results

Check your expected score on the tests of muscular endurance.

Excellent   ☐   Poor   ☐
Very good   ☐   Very poor   ☐
Marginal   ☐

Results

Record your scores below.

Sitting tucks _____ Chins _____ Hang _____ seconds
Check your rating using Chart 10.1.

	Excellent	Very good	Marginal	Poor	Very poor
Sitting tucks	☐	☐	☐	☐	☐
Chins	☐	☐	☐	☐	☐

Hang ☐ Making progress toward a chin ☐ Poor ☐ Very good

Conclusions and Implications

Did you score well on muscular endurance? Yes ☐ No ☐
Did you have as much muscular endurance as you thought? Yes ☐ No ☐
Do you have enough muscular endurance? Yes ☐ No ☐
Why or why not?

Do you need to regularly perform muscular endurance exercises?
Yes ☐ No ☐
If no, why not?

What muscular endurance exercises do you think you need to perform regularly?

Chart 10.1 Rating Scale for Muscular Endurance

Classification	Men		Women	
	Sitting Tuck	Chins	Sitting tuck	Chins
Excellent	35+	15+	22	2
Very good	25–34	11–14	16–21	1
Adequate	12–24	7–10	8–15	—
Poor	7–11	4–6	5–7	—
Very poor	6 or less	3 or less	4 or less	—

Adjust scores downward by 10 percent after age fifty.

Chart 10.2 Rating Scale for Flexed Arm Hang
(for people who cannot do one chin)

Classification	Score in Seconds
Making progress toward chin-up	25
Poor	12
Very poor	8 or less

Evaluating Flexibility

Lab **11**

Name _____ Section _____ Date _____

Flexibility is one of many important aspects of physical fitness. It is now clear that flexibility is specific to each body joint. For this reason it is important to perform exercises for each joint and muscle group if you want to develop flexibility in all areas. To test the flexibility of many areas of the body you need different tests. Two of the flexibility tests are presented in this lab. These are *static* flexibility tests. If you want to test total body flexibility you will need to do additional tests of both static and dynamic flexibility.

Purpose

The purpose of this laboratory session is to evaluate the flexibility of several body parts.

Procedures

1. Take the two flexibility tests as outlined on page 185.
2. Record your scores in the results section.
3. Use Chart 11.1 to determine your rating on both of the flexibility tests and record your rating in the results section.

Expected Results

How do you expect to score on the flexibility tests?

Excellent ☐   Poor ☐
Very good ☐   Very poor ☐
Marginal ☐

Results

	Test 1	Test 2	
		Right up	Left up
What were your flexibility scores?	_____	_____	_____
Record your flexibility rating.	_____	_____	_____
(Use Chart 11.1.)			

Conclusions and Implications

Did you score well on flexibility? Yes □ No □
Are you as flexible as you thought you were? Yes □ No □
On Test 2, did you score better with one arm up than with the other arm up?
Yes □ No □
Do you need to perform flexibility exercises regularly? Yes □ No □
What flexibility exercises do you think you need to perform regularly?
(See appendix M for suggestions)

Flexibility Tests

Since it is impractical to test the flexibility of all joints, perform these tests for the joints used most frequently in movement performance.

1. *Flexibility Test of Lower Back and Hamstrings*
    a. Sit on the floor with the knees together and the feet flat against a bench turned on its side.
    b. With a partner holding the knees straight, reach forward with the arms fully extended.
    c. Measure the distance the fingertips reach on the yardstick fixed on the bench.

Note: Ruler extends six inches over the end of the bench

2. *Shoulder Flexibility*
    a. Stand with your nose, chest, and abdomen against a projecting corner or a vertical pole.
    b. Raise the right arm, bend the elbow, and reach down across the back as far as possible.
    c. At the same time, extend the left arm down and behind the back, bend the elbow up across the back and try to cross the fingers over those of the right hand as shown in the accompanying illustration.
    d. Measure the distance to the nearest half-inch. If fingers overlap, score as a plus; if they fail to meet, score as a minus; use a zero if the fingertips just touch.
    e. Repeat with the arms crossed in the opposite direction (left arm up). Most people will find that they are more flexible on one side than the other.

Chart 11.1   Flexibility Rating Scale

Classification	Men					Women			
	Test 1	Test 2				Test 1	Test 2		
			R up	L up				R up	L up
Excellent	29+	14+	7+	7+		28+	15+	8+	8+
Very good	21–28	11–13	6	3–6		25–27	12–14	7	6–7
Marginal	14–20	7–10	4–5	0–2		18–24	7–11	5–6	0–5
Poor	12–13	4–6	1–3	–2–1		13–17	4–6	1–4	–2–1
Very poor	11 or less	3 or less	less than 0	–3 or less		11–12	3 or less	less than 0	–3 or less

Though many people become less flexible as they grow older, for optimal health, it is recommended that you attempt to maintain adequate levels of flexibility on the above chart throughout life.

Evaluating Body Fatness

Name _____ Section _____ Date _____

The critical factor in determining if a person is obese is whether the person has too much body fat rather than too much body weight. Unfortunately, the method most often used in determining obesity is the height-weight chart. In many cases this type of measure is inadequate. Thus, a height-weight chart might indicate that a highly muscular person is overweight. It is also possible for a "thin looking" person who possesses too much fat to be judged "normal" weight on a height-weight chart. The most practical method for determining body fatness is by using calipers for measuring skinfold thickness.

Purpose

The purpose of this laboratory session is to determine the percent of body fat possessed by each individual.

Procedures

1. Have your skinfold thicknesses measured as outlined on page 189.
2. Use nomogram 1 (women) or nomogram 2 (men) to determine the percent of body fat from your skinfold thickness scores. For women, locate your two skinfold scores on the appropriate scales of the nomogram. Read your percent of fat on the center scale. For men, follow the procedure located in the center of the nomogram.
3. Rate your "fatness" using Chart 12.1. Record your percent of body fat and your body fat rating in the "results" section.

Results

What are your skinfold measurements?

Women			**Men**		
Iliac crest	_____	mm	Abdomen	_____	mm
Triceps	_____	mm	Chest	_____	mm
			Triceps	_____	mm

What is your percent of body fat? _____ (Use nomogram 1 or 2)
What is your fatness rating?

Very lean ☐   Fat   ☐
Lean   ☐   Obese   ☐
Marginal   ☐

Conclusions and Implications

Does your percent of body fat rating show you to be too fat? Yes ☐ No ☐
How do you account for your current body composition, and what do the
results imply for you in the future?

Skinfold Tests

1. Take the following measures for women using a skinfold caliper. (See diagram.)
   a. Triceps.
   b. Illiac crest.
2. Take the following measures for men using a skinfold caliper. (See diagram.)
   a. To right of navel.
   b. Chest, above and to the right of the right nipple.
   c. Triceps.

Note: All measurements are taken on the right side.

Chart 12.1 Fatness Rating Scale

Classification	Men	Women
Very lean	10 or less	15 or less
Lean	11–14	16–17
Marginal	15–17	18–22
Fat	18–19	23–27
Obese	20 plus	28 plus

Though many people allow themselves to become fatter as they grow older, for optimal health, it is recommended that you attempt to maintain lean ratings of fatness throughout life.

Nomogram 1

Nomogram 1 is for conversion of skinfold thickness to specific gravity and percent of fat in young women.

Example:

Given: Iliac skinfold of 24 mm and tricep of 19 mm.

1. With a straight-edge, align iliac value (24) with tricep value (19).
2. Read specific density (1.046) and percent fat (23) from the scale in the middle.

Adapted from a nomogram by Irene Paul.

Nomogram 2

Nomogram 2 is for conversion of skinfold thickness to specific gravity and percent of fat in young men.

Example:
Given: abdominal skinfold 10 mm, chest skinfold 15 mm, and arm skinfold 20 mm

1. With a straight-edge, align abdominal value (10 mm) in column A with chest value (15 mm) in column B.
2. Place pin at point where straightedge crosses reference line C.
3. Pivot straightedge on pin to arm skinfold value (20 mm) in column D.
4. Read specific gravity (1.061) and percent body fat (18.5) where straightedge crosses column E.

Nomogram adapted from Consolazio, C. F., et al. *Physical Measurements of Metabolic Function in Man.* New York: McGraw-Hill, 1963 by permission.

Determining "Desirable" Body Weight

Lab 13

Name _____ Section _____ Date _____

Purpose

The purposes of this laboratory session are:

1. To determine "desirable" weight.
2. To compare two different methods for determining "desirable" body weight.

Procedures

1. Measure percent of body fat (see Lab 12), height (without shoes), and weight (with indoor clothing).
2. Determine your frame size (small, medium, or large) using the following procedure. With a tape, measure the smallest girth of your wrist just above the styloid process (boney bump on wrist). Pull the tape snugly (but not tight enough to indent the skin) around the wrist as you measure. Look up your frame size on Chart 13.1.
3. Determine your "desirable" weight. Locate your height in inches on the left and your frame size across the top. Find the "desirable" weight for your height and frame size. Men are to use Chart 13.2; women are to use Chart 13.3.
4. Determine your "desirable" weight using a different procedure. Locate your actual body weight on the left and your percent body fat (from Lab 12) across the top. Find the "desirable" weight for your weight and body fat percent. Men are to use Chart 13.4; women are to use Chart 13.5.

Results

Record your scores below:

Percent body fat _____ Weight (indoor clothes) _____ lbs.

Height (without shoes) _____ inches

Frame size small ☐ medium ☐ large ☐

"Desirable" weight (Chart 13.1 or 13.2) _____ lbs.

"Desirable" weight (Chart 13.3 or 13.4) _____ lbs.

Conclusions and Implications

Is your "desirable" weight as determined from the height-weight chart what it should be? Yes ☐ No ☐
Is your "desirable" weight as determined from percent body fat what it should be? Yes ☐ No ☐
Is there a discrepancy between your answers? Yes ☐ No ☐
If yes, why?

Using both "desirable" weights, what body weight do you feel you should maintain for the rest of your life? _____ lbs. Explain.

Chart 13.1 Determining Frame Size Using Wrist Size in Inches

	Men	Women
Small Frame	6½″ or less	5½″ or less
Medium Frame	6¾″–7¼″	5¾″
Large Frame	7½″ or more	6″ or more

Chart 13.2 Determination of "Desirable" Weight for Men

Height (without shoes)		Weight in Pounds According to Frame (in Indoor Clothing)		
Feet	Inches	Small Frame	Medium Frame	Large Frame
5	1	112–120	118–129	126–141
5	2	115–123	121–133	129–144
5	3	118–126	124–136	132–148
5	4	121–129	127–139	135–152
5	5	124–133	130–143	138–156
5	6	128–137	134–147	142–161
5	7	132–141	138–152	147–166
5	8	136–145	142–156	151–170
5	9	140–150	146–160	155–174
5	10	144–154	150–165	159–179
5	11	148–158	154–170	164–184
6	0	152–162	158–175	168–189
6	1	156–167	162–180	173–194
6	2	160–171	167–185	178–199
6	3	164–175	172–190	182–204

Adapted from tables provided as a courtesy of the Metropolitan Life Insurance Co.

Chart 13.3 Determination of "Desirable" Weight for Women

Height (without shoes)		Weight in Pounds According to Frame (in Indoor Clothing)		
Feet	Inches	Small Frame	Medium Frame	Large Frame
4	8	92– 98	96–107	104–119
4	9	94–101	98–110	106–122
4	10	96–104	101–113	109–125
4	11	99–107	104–116	112–128
5	0	102–-110	107–119	115–131
5	1	105–113	110–122	118–134
5	2	108–116	113–126	121–138
5	3	111–119	116–130	125–142
5	4	114–123	120–135	129–146
5	5	118–127	124–139	133–150
5	6	122–131	128–143	137–154
5	7	126–135	132–147	141–158
5	8	130–140	136–161	145–163
5	9	134–144	140–155	149–168
5	10	138–148	144–159	153–173

Adapted from tables provided as a courtesy of the Metropolitan Life Insurance Co.

Chart 13.4 Determination of Desirable Body Weight for Men

Actual Body Weight	Percent Fat																	
	6	8	10	12	14	16	18	20	22	24	26	28	30	32	34	36	38	40
240	263	258	254	249	244	240	234	230	225	220	215	210	206	201	196	191	186	182
235	257	253	248	243	239	235	266	225	220	215	210	206	201	196	192	187	182	178
230	252	247	243	238	233	230	224	220	215	210	206	201	197	192	187	183	178	174
225	247	243	238	234	229	225	220	216	211	207	202	198	193	189	184	180	175	171
220	241	237	233	228	223	221	215	211	206	202	197	193	189	184	180	175	171	167
215	236	231	227	223	218	215	210	206	201	197	193	188	184	180	175	171	167	163
210	230	226	222	217	215	210	205	202	200	192	188	184	180	175	171	167	163	159
205	224	220	216	212	208	205	200	197	191	187	183	179	175	171	167	163	159	155
200	220	216	212	208	204	200	196	192	188	184	180	176	172	168	164	160	156	152
195	214	210	206	202	198	195	190	187	183	179	175	171	167	163	159	155	151	148
190	208	204	201	197	193	190	185	182	178	174	170	166	163	159	155	151	147	144
185	202	199	195	191	187	185	180	177	173	169	165	162	158	154	151	147	143	140
180	197	193	190	186	182	180	175	172	168	164	161	157	154	150	146	143	139	136
175	192	189	185	182	178	175	171	168	164	161	157	154	150	147	143	140	136	133
170	186	183	180	176	173	170	166	163	159	156	152	149	146	142	139	135	132	129
165	181	177	174	171	167	165	161	158	154	151	148	144	141	138	134	131	128	125
160	175	172	169	165	162	160	157	153	149	146	143	140	137	133	130	127	124	121
155	169	166	163	160	157	155	151	148	144	141	138	135	132	129	126	123	120	117
150	165	162	159	156	153	150	147	144	141	138	135	132	129	126	123	120	117	114
145	159	156	153	150	147	145	141	139	136	133	130	127	124	121	118	115	112	110
140	153	150	148	145	142	140	136	134	131	128	125	122	120	117	114	111	108	100
135	147	145	142	139	137	135	131	129	126	123	120	118	115	112	110	107	104	102
130	142	139	137	134	131	130	126	124	121	118	116	113	111	108	105	103	102	98
125	137	135	132	130	127	125	122	120	117	115	112	110	107	105	102	100	97	95
120	131	129	121	129	122	120	117	115	112	110	107	105	103	100	98	95	93	91

Along the side locate your actual body weight and across the top locate your estimated percent fat. The intersection of the two entries is your desirable weight (fat-free body weight plus 16 percent fat). Example: 175 pounds is the desirable weight for a man who weighs 195 pounds and currently has a body fat amount of 26 percent.

Chart 13.5 Determination of Desirable Body Weight for Women

	Percent Fat																	
	6	**8**	**10**	**12**	**14**	**16**	**18**	**20**	**22**	**24**	**26**	**28**	**30**	**32**	**34**	**36**	**38**	**40**
200	228	224	220	216	212	208	204	200	196	192	188	184	180	176	172	168	164	160
195	222	218	214	210	206	202	198	195	191	187	183	179	175	171	167	163	159	156
190	216	212	209	205	201	197	193	190	186	182	178	174	171	167	163	159	155	152
185	210	207	203	199	196	192	188	185	181	177	173	170	166	162	159	155	151	148
180	205	201	198	194	190	187	183	180	176	172	169	165	162	158	154	151	147	144
175	199	196	192	189	185	182	178	175	171	168	164	161	157	154	150	147	143	140
170	193	180	177	173	170	166	163	170	166	163	159	156	153	149	146	142	139	136
165	188	184	181	178	174	171	168	165	161	158	155	151	148	145	141	138	135	132
160	182	179	176	172	169	166	163	160	156	153	150	147	144	140	137	134	131	128
155	176	173	170	167	164	161	158	155	151	148	145	142	139	136	133	130	127	124
150	171	168	165	162	159	156	153	150	147	144	141	138	135	132	129	126	123	120
145	165	162	159	156	153	150	147	145	142	139	136	133	130	127	124	121	118	116
140	159	156	154	151	148	145	142	140	137	134	131	128	126	123	120	117	114	112
135	153	151	148	145	143	140	137	135	132	129	126	124	121	118	116	113	110	108
130	148	145	143	140	137	135	132	130	127	124	122	119	117	114	111	109	106	104
125	142	140	137	135	132	130	127	125	122	120	117	115	112	110	107	105	102	100
120	136	134	132	129	127	124	122	120	117	115	112	110	108	105	103	100	98	96
115	131	128	126	124	121	119	117	115	112	110	108	105	103	101	98	96	94	92
110	125	123	121	118	116	114	112	110	107	105	103	101	99	96	94	92	90	88
105	119	117	115	113	111	109	107	105	102	100	98	96	94	92	90	88	86	84
100	114	112	110	108	106	104	102	100	98	96	94	92	90	88	86	84	82	80
95	108	106	104	102	100	98	96	95	93	91	89	87	85	83	81	79	77	76
90	102	100	99	97	95	93	91	90	88	86	84	82	81	79	77	75	73	72

Actual Body Weight (row labels)

Along the side locate your actual body weight and across the top locate your estimated percent fat. The intersection of the two entries is your desirable weight (fat-free body weight plus 20 percent fat). Example: 150 pounds is the desirable weight for a woman who weighs 160 pounds and currently has a body fat amount of 26 percent.

Exercise and Nutrition

Name _____ Section _____ Date _____

Purpose

The purposes of this laboratory session are:

1. To determine your caloric consumption at a typical lunch.
2. To experience an exercise period that will expend as many calories as are consumed at a typical lunch.
3. To relate caloric consumption (eating) to caloric expenditure (exercise).

Procedures

1. From Chart 14.1, choose several foods that you might choose if you were to eat out at lunch. Pick the foods you think you would really eat if you had the choice. Record the foods you chose on the blanks provided on the next page.
2. Using Chart 14.1, determine the calories you would consume if you actually ate the foods you selected. Write the calories on the blanks on the next page.
3. Walk, run, or swim until you have expended enough calories to equal the lunch item with the fewest calories. Check that item off the list in the results section. Continue this procedure until all the lunch items are checked off or until the period is over.

Expected Results

Do you think you can expend the calories consumed at lunch during one period? Yes ☐ No ☐

Results

List the lunch items you chose. Determine their calorie content from Chart 14.1 and record the calories next to the food. Check off each food as you exercise to expend enough calories.

Lunch Items	Calories	Expended by Exercise
_____	_____	_____
_____	_____	_____
_____	_____	_____
_____	_____	_____
_____	_____	_____

Conclusions and Implications

Did you think it would take more or less exercise to expend the calories in your lunch? More ☐ Less ☐ Explain.

Do you feel that you exercise enough each day to expend the calories you eat? Yes ☐ No ☐

Do you feel that exercise alone is the method you could use to balance the calories you eat? Yes ☐ No ☐ Explain.

Chart 14.1 Minutes of Activity Necessary to Burn Off Lunch Foods

Lunch Food	Calories	Minutes of Activity Required to Burn Off Food			
		Walking	Swimming	Running	Sitting
Apple (raw)	70	13.3	6.3	3.5	53.9
Cheeseburger					
Plain	425	80.8	38.3	21.3	327.3
Catsup	440	83.6	39.6	22.0	338.8
Pickle and onion	445	84.6	40.1	22.3	342.7
Everything	460	87.4	41.4	23.0	354.2
Cake (two layer white with icing)	250	47.5	22.5	12.5	192.5
Chili with beans (one cup)	335	63.7	30.2	16.8	258.0
Drinks					
Soft drink 12 oz.	145	27.6	13.1	7.3	111.7
Soft drink 16 oz.	195	37.1	17.6	9.8	150.2
Apple juice 8 oz.	120	22.8	10.8	6.0	92.4
Lemonade 8 oz.	110	20.9	9.9	5.5	84.7
Fries					
Small	225	42.8	20.3	11.3	173.3
Large	450	85.5	40.5	22.5	346.5
Hamburger					
Plain	320	60.8	28.8	16.0	246.4
Catsup	335	63.7	30.2	16.8	257.9
Pickle and onion	340	64.6	30.6	17.0	261.8
Everything	355	67.5	32.0	17.8	273.4
Hot dog					
Plain	270	51.3	24.3	13.5	207.9
Catsup	285	54.2	25.7	14.3	219.5
Pickle and onion	290	55.1	26.1	14.5	223.3
Everything	305	58.0	27.5	15.3	234.9
Ice cream (cup)	255	48.5	23.0	12.8	196.4
Pie (fruit)	325	61.8	29.3	16.3	250.3
Pizza (cheese, one slice from 14 in. pizza)	185	35.2	16.7	9.3	142.5

Exercise and Nutrition

Evaluating Balance Performance— ^{Lab} 15
The Bass Test of Dynamic Balance

Name_____ Section_____ Date_____

The possession of motor skills is desirable. Although the possession of skills contributes less directly to physical health than do other aspects of physical fitness; the possession of skill can contribute to a rich life. One who possesses skills can work more efficiently, enjoy leisure time through sports and games, and react positively to emergency situations. Some may choose to develop and maintain physical fitness through sports. One aspect of skill-related fitness is balance. For most people dynamic balance is the most important type of balance. Though the Bass Test is an old test, it is still considered a good test of dynamic balance.

Purpose

The purpose of this laboratory session is to evaluate your dynamic balance.

Procedures

1. Perform the Bass Test of Dynamic Balance as outlined on page 205.
2. Record your score in the results section.
3. Determine your balance rating from Chart 15.1 and record your rating in the results section.

Expected Results

How do you expect to score on this test of dynamic balance?

Excellent ☐   Poor ☐
Very good ☐   Very poor ☐
Marginal ☐

Results

What is your balance score? _____

What is your balance rating? _____ (see Chart 15.1)

Conclusions and Implications

Did you perform as expected? Yes ☐ No ☐
Did you score well? Yes ☐ No ☐
Explain the reason for your test results.

What do the results imply to you for your daily life and recreational activities?

The Bass Test of Dynamic Balance

Eleven circles (9½-inch) are drawn on the floor as shown in the illustration. The test is performed as follows:

Circles 9 1/2 inches in diameter
X = starting circle
18" from X to 1
33" between other circles

1. Stand on the right foot in circle X. *Leap* forward to circle one, then circle two . . . through 10, alternating feet with each leap.
2. The feet must leave the floor on each leap and the heel may not touch. Only the ball of the foot may land on the floor.
3. Remain in each circle for five seconds before leaping to the next circle. (A count of five will be made for you, aloud).
4. Practice trials are allowed.
5. The score is fifty, plus the number of seconds taken to complete the test, minus the number of errors.
6. *All* errors are deducted at the rate of three points each. Errors include: touching the heel, moving the supporting foot, touching outside a circle, or touching any body part to the floor other than the supporting foot.
7. Scores should be plotted on the appropriate rating scales.

From McCloy, C. H. *Tests and Measurements in Health and Physical Education.* New York: Appleton-Century-Crofts, 1954, p. 106.

Chart 15.1 Bass Test Rating Scale

Rating	Score
Excellent	90–100
Very good	80– 89
Marginal	60– 79
Poor	30– 59
Very poor	0– 29

Evaluating Agility Performance— The Illinois Agility Run Test

Name _____ Section _____ Date _____

An important aspect of skill performance is agility—that is, the ability to change body positions quickly and accurately. The Illinois Agility Run is one method of testing agility.

Purpose

The purpose of this laboratory session is to evaluate your agility performance.

Procedures

1. Perform the Illinois Agility Run as outlined on page 209.
2. Record your running time in the results section.
3. Determine your agility rating from Chart 16.1, and record it in the results section.

Expected Results

How do you expect to score on this test of agility?

Excellent ☐   Poor ☐
Very good ☐   Very poor ☐
Marginal ☐

Results

What is your agility run time? _____ seconds

What is your agility rating? _____ (see Chart 16.1)

Conclusions and Implications

Did you perform as expected? Yes ☐ No ☐
Did you score well? Yes ☐ No ☐
Explain the reason for your test results.

What do the results imply to you for your daily life and recreational activities?

The Illinois Agility Run*

An agility course using four chairs and a thirty-foot running area will be set up as depicted in the illustration.

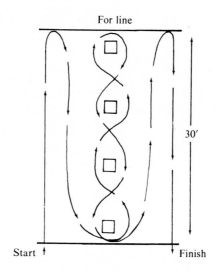

The test is performed as follows:

1. Lie prone with the hands by the shoulders and with the head at the starting line. On the signal to begin, the performer will run the course as fast as possible.
2. The performer's score is the time required to complete the course.

Chart 16.1   Agility Rating Scale

Classification	Men	Women
Excellent	15.8 or faster	17.4 or faster
Very good	16.7–15.9	18.6–17.5
Marginal	18.6–16.8	22.3–18.7
Poor	18.8–18.7	23.4–22.4
Very poor	18.0 or slower	23.5 or slower

J. 15.5
A. 18.9

---

*Adams, et al. *Foundations of Physical Activity* (Champaign, Ill.: Stipes and Co., 1965), p. 111.

Evaluating Explosive Power— The Standing Long Jump

Name _____ Section _____ Date _____

Explosive power is an aspect of fitness that is defined as strength times speed— in other words, strength feats that are performed explosively or quickly. An example of explosive power is the standing long jump.

Purpose

The purpose of this laboratory session is to evaluate your explosive power.

Procedures

1. Perform the Standing Long Jump Test as outlined on page 212.
2. Record your distance score in the results section.
3. Determine your explosive power rating from Chart 17.1 and record it in the results section.

Expected Results

How do you expect to score on this test of explosive power?

Excellent	☐		Poor	☐
Very good	☐		Very poor	☐
Marginal	☐			

Results

Record your standing long jump score. _____ inches

What is your explosive power rating? _____ (see Chart 17.1)

Conclusions and Implications

Did you perform as expected? Yes ☐ No ☐
Did you score well? Yes ☐ No ☐
Explain the reason for your test results.

What do the results imply for your daily life and recreational activities?

The Standing Long Jump Test

The test is performed as follows:

1. Stand with both feet behind a starting line.
2. Jump forward with both feet as far as possible.
3. Measure the jump distance to the point where the body touched nearest the take-off line.
4. Your score is the best of three jumps.

Chart 17.1 Power Rating Scale

Classification	Men	Women
Excellent	8'6" +	6'8" +
Very good	7'9"–8'5"	5'10"–6'7"
Marginal	6'4"–7'8"	4'8"–5'9"
Poor	5'10"–6'3"	4'2"–4'7"
Very poor	Below 5'9"	Below 4'1"

Evaluating Coordination—
The Stick Test of Coordination

Name _____ Section _____ Date _____

Coordination is the ability to use the senses together with the body parts. The stick test is one method of evaluating hand-eye coordination.

Purpose

The purpose of this laboratory session is to evaluate your coordination.

Procedures

1. Perform the Stick Test of Coordination as outlined on page 215.
2. Record your score in the results section.
3. Determine your coordination rating from Chart 18.1, and record it in the results section.

Expected Results

How do you expect to score on this test of coordination?

Excellent	☐	Poor	☐
Very good	☐	Very poor	☐
Marginal	☐		

Results

Record your coordination score. _____

What is your coordination rating? _____ (see Chart 18.1)

Conclusions and Implications

Did you perform as well as expected? Yes ☐ No ☐
Did you score well? Yes ☐ No ☐
Explain the reason for your test results.

What do the results imply to you for your daily life and recreational activities?

Do you think you could improve your coordination with practice?
Yes ☐ No ☐
How much improvement would you expect? Discuss.

The Stick Test of Coordination

The Stick Test of Coordination requires you to juggle with three wooden wands. The wands are used to perform a one half flip and a full flip as shown in the illustrations.

1. *One Half Flip*—Hold two twenty-four inch (one-half inch in diameter) dowel rods, one in each hand. Support a third rod of the same size across the other two. Toss the supported rod in the air so that it makes a half turn. Catch the thrown rod with the two held rods.
2. *Full Flip*—Perform the above task letting the supported rod turn a full flip.

One half flip   Full flip

Hand position

The test is performed as follows:

1. Practice the half flip and the full flip several times before taking the test.
2. When you are ready, attempt a half flip five times. Score one point for each successful attempt.
3. When you are ready, attempt the full flip five times. Score two points for each successful attempt.

Chart 18.1 Coordination Rating Scale

Classification	Men	Women
Excellent	14–15	13–15
Very good	11–13	10–12
Marginal	5–10	4– 9
Poor	3– 4	2– 3
Very poor	0– 2	0– 1

Body Mechanics

<u>Name</u>   Section   Date

There are some general principles of good body mechanics that should be observed when giving and receiving force, but within that framework, there are a variety of correct methods. There is no one best method that applies in every situation. One must consider all of the factors involved in a specific problem and choose the procedure that best accomplishes the job. Remember the criteria: efficiency, effectiveness, and safety.

Purpose

The purposes of this laboratory session are:

1. To provide an opportunity to practice pushing, pulling, lifting, carrying, and to learn the principles of stability.
2. To provide an opportunity to experiment with a number of methods in order to evaluate the effects.
3. To provide an opportunity for experimenting with a number of objects varying in weight, size, shape, and friction in order to determine the effect of these factors on body mechanics.

Procedures

1. Choose a partner of similar size. Stand facing, palms of hands together, legs in a front-stride position, knees bent in a half-crouch.
    a. Try to push your partner backward; keep the back straight, use the leg muscles, and lean forward. Try it with arms straight and then with arms bent. Your partner should attempt to remain stable and resist being moved.
    b. Same as above except try to pull partner forward as you move backward.
    c. Same as above, except try pushing and pulling while facing sideward; push while facing backward; pull while facing forward.
2. Using a blanket, beach towel, mat, or gym scooter, pull partner across the floor while he or she sits on the "chariot."
    a. Using good body mechanics, face partner and walk backwards.
    b. Face away from the partner and walk forward.

    c.   Face sideward and walk sideward.

    d.   Grasp the blanket (rope or handle) close to the partner, making a short handle, while pulling.

    e.   Lengthen the handle and note the difference in pulling.

3.   Practice lifting, carrying, and lowering a variety of objects that the instructor has placed around the room.

Results

Which seems best?

1. Pushing ☐   Pulling ☐
2. Bent-arm pushing ☐   Straight-arm pushing ☐
3. Backward ☐   Forward ☐   Sideward ☐

Which way seemed best for pulling the "chariot"?

1. Forward ☐   Backward ☐   Sideward ☐
2. Long handle ☐   Short handle ☐

Which factors were important in pushing and pulling?

	Most important	Next in importance	Least important
Size	☐	☐	☐
Shape	☐	☐	☐
Weight	☐	☐	☐
Location in space	☐	☐	☐

Conclusions and Implications

Explain the implications of the above questions to a daily life activity or to a sport. Examples: blocking in football, pushing a stalled car, or carrying a forty-pound suitcase in an airport.

Body Mechanics in Sports

Name _____ Section _____ Date _____

In sports, as in daily life, there are certain principles of movement that, when applied, make you more efficient. These are known as the principles of body mechanics.

Purpose

The purposes of this laboratory session are:

1. To show that sports performance can be improved by following certain principles of body mechanics.
2. To demonstrate with one sports skill (jumping) how proper body mechanics can improve performance.
3. To identify some of the principles of body mechanics in actual sports situations.

Procedures

With a partner, practice jumping five different ways as described below. Use the best of three tries as your score for each different way of jumping. Record your scores for each jump in the results section.

Perform the five jumps (standing long jump) as follows:

1. With both feet behind a starting line, jump forward with both feet as far as possible.
   a. *Jump 1*—Do the jump with the arms held crossed against the chest.
   b. *Jump 2*—Do the jump with the arms held tightly against your sides.
   c. *Jump 3*—Throw the arms vigorously forward and up as you jump.
   d. *Jump 4*—Take one short hop from behind the line before jumping; swing the arms forward and up.
   e. *Jump 5*—Take one short hop before jumping but keep the arms at your sides.
2. Measure the jump distance to the point where the body touched nearest the take-off line.

Expected Results

Before you do the five jumps, read how each is to be performed.
On which jump do you expect to perform best?
1 ☐ 2 ☐ 3 ☐ 4 ☐ 5 ☐
On which jump do you expect to perform worst?
1 ☐ 2 ☐ 3 ☐ 4 ☐ 5 ☐

Results

What was your best score on each of the five jumps?

Jump 1 _____ inches

Jump 2 _____ inches

Jump 3 _____ inches

Jump 4 _____ inches

Jump 5 _____ inches

Conclusions and Implications

Did you perform best on the jump expected? Yes ☐ No ☐
Were you able to jump equally far on all five jumps? Yes ☐ No ☐
If not, why not?

Explain the reasons why you did better or poorer on different jumps and tell what mechanical principles were involved.

Did you find a difference on the first, second, and third trial of each type of jump? If so, how do you explain these differences?

Posture

<u>Name</u>   <u>Section</u>   <u>Date</u>

Purposes

The purposes of this laboratory session are as follows:

1. To learn to recognize postural deviations and thus become more posture conscious.
2. To determine one's own faults in order that a preventive and corrective program might be instituted.

Procedures

1. Wear as little clothing as possible (bathing suits are recommended) and remove shoes and socks.
2. Work in groups of two or three, with one person acting as the "subject" while partners serve as "examiners"; alternate roles.
3. Use the posture evaluation in Chart 21.1 to determine your posture score.
4. Rate your posture score using Chart 21.2.

Expected Results

What do you expect your posture rating to be?

Excellent ☐   Poor   ☐
Very good ☐   Very poor ☐
Marginal   ☐

Results

Record your posture score. _____

Record your posture rating. _____

Conclusions

Were you aware of the deviations that were found? Yes ☐ No ☐
List the deviations that were moderate or severe.

Implications

What will you do about your postural faults? List specific exercises (or habits)
you need to practice to correct each deviation listed in the conclusions. If you
were checked as having some of the symptoms of scoliosis, see your instructor
for a more thorough examination and possible referral to a physician.

Evaluating Posture

There is probably no one best posture for all individuals, but there are some
basic and common posture problems that can be relatively easy to identify.

Procedures

1. Stand by a vertically hung plumb line.
2. Using Chart 21.1, check the deviations found by indicating their severity
   as follows: 0—none; 1—slight; 2—moderate; 3—severe.
3. Total the score and determine your posture rating from Chart 21.2.

Chart 21.1　Posture Evaluation

Side View	Points	Back View	Points
Head forward	_____	Tilted head	_____
Sunken chest	_____	Protruding scapulae	_____
Round shoulders	_____	Symptoms of scoliosis:	
		Shoulders uneven	_____
Kyphosis	_____	Hips uneven	_____
Lordosis	_____	Lateral curvature of spine (Adams position)	_____
Abdominal ptosis	_____	One side of back high (Adams position)	_____
Hyperextended knees	_____		
Body lean	_____		
		Total score _____	

Chart 21.2　Posture Rating Scale

Classification	Total Score
Excellent	0–2
Very good	3–4
Marginal	5–7
Poor	8–11
Very poor	12 or more

Care of the Back

Name _____ Section _____ Date _____

Purpose

The purpose of this laboratory session is to determine if you have some muscle imbalance and to learn exercises suitable for preventing backaches and correcting lordosis.

Procedures

1. Secure a partner and administer the muscle tests to each other. (Details appear on pp. 227, 228.) Record results of tests in the results section of this laboratory.
2. Under the direction and supervision of the instructor, perform the exercises described in Appendix A. Two or three repetitions of each exercise will be adequate for the purposes of this laboratory.

Expected Results

Do you have any back problems? Yes ☐ No ☐
Do you expect to have any difficulty with the tests of muscle imbalance?
Yes ☐ No ☐

Results and Conclusions

1. On test number 1, was there evidence that you have shortened lumbar and/or hip flexor muscles? Yes ☐ No ☐
2. a. On test number 2, was there evidence that you have short hamstrings?
        Yes ☐ No ☐   Right ☐ Left ☐
    b. Was there evidence of short lumbar and/or hip flexor muscles?
        Yes ☐ No ☐
3. On test number 3, was there evidence that you have short hip flexors?
        Yes ☐ No ☐   Right ☐ Left ☐

4. Did you have difficulty performing any of the exercises? Yes ☐ No ☐
If so, which ones?

How do you account for this difficulty?

Implications

If your answers to the questions are positive, what does this suggest to you in terms of your susceptibility to backache?
What specific exercises might help correct your muscle imbalance?

Testing for Back Weakness and Muscular Imbalance

Test 1—Back-Wall Test

Stand with the back against a wall, with head, heels, shoulders, and calves of legs touching the wall as shown in the diagram. Try to flatten the neck and hollow of your back by pressing your buttocks down against the wall. Your partner should just be able to place a hand in the space between the wall and the small of your back. If this space is greater than the thickness of his hand, you probably have lordosis with shortened lumbar and hip flexor muscles.

Test 2—Supine Leg Lift

Lie on your back with hands behind your neck. The partner on your right should stabilize your right leg by placing his/her left hand on the knee. With the right hand, your partner should grasp the left ankle and raise the left leg as near to a right angle as possible. In this position (as shown in the diagram), the lower back should be in contact with the floor. The right leg should remain straight and on the floor throughout the test. If the left leg bends at the knee, short hamstring muscles are indicated. If the back arches and/or the right leg does not remain flat on the floor, short lumbar muscles or hip flexor muscles (or both) are indicated. Repeat the test on the opposite side.

Test 3—Knee to Chest

Lie on your back on a table or bench with the left leg extended beyond the edge of the table (approximately one-third of the thigh off the table). Bring right knee to chest and pull it down tightly with hands. The lower back should remain flat against the table as shown in the diagram. The left thigh should remain on table. If the left thigh lifts off the table while the right knee is hugged to chest, a tight hip flexor (iliopsoas) on that side is indicated. Repeat on opposite side.

Stress

Name _____ Section _____ Date _____

The purpose of this laboratory session is to determine the amount of stress resulting from the application of various physical and emotional stressors.

One method of measuring stress is heart rate. Although increase in heart rate can represent the desirable effects of physical overload on the heart, it can also reflect wear and tear on the heart as a result of constant demands that are not part of a plan of progressive overload. These constant demands produce stress that prevents desirable and necessary heart rest. Stress is also reflected in the rate of wear and tear on other body systems.

Purposes

The purposes of this laboratory session are as follows:

1. To identify the relative stress caused by different physical and emotional stressors.
2. To determine the amount of time required to recover from the various stressors.

Procedures

Determine your resting heart rate. Next you will be exposed to five different stressors. After each stressor is applied, count your heart rate for thirty seconds. Allow three minutes after each stressor to lower the heart rate. Record your heart rate for each stressor in the results section. Exchange data with another student so that records can be compared.

Expected Results*

Which do you think will cause the greatest increase in heart rate?
Emotional stressors ☐   Physical stressors ☐
Who do you think will have the biggest heart rate change under stress?
You ☐   Your partner ☐

___

*Typically, women will have slightly higher resting heart rates than men.

Results

Record stressors and thirty second heart rates on the chart that follows.

Stressor	Heart Rate	
	Self	**Partner**
1.		
2.		
3.		
4.		
5.		

Darken the bar for each of the five stressors to indicate heart rate after each of the stressors are applied.

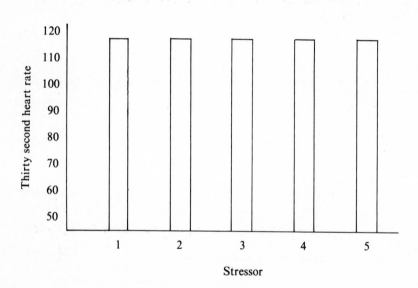

Conclusions and Implications

Did your partner react to the stress in the same way as you did?
Yes ☐ No ☐ Explain.

Does previous experience affect the way you respond to stress?
Yes ☐ No ☐ Explain.

Explain the fact that some people do not experience much stress from physical exercise.

Evaluating Stress Levels

Name _____ Section _____ Date _____

Purpose

The purpose of this laboratory is to help you evaluate your current stress level. Research shows that when people are stressed they are more susceptible to certain diseases. Some stress-related diseases include heart disease, ulcers, allergy, hypertension, and insomnia. People with high stress levels need to recognize the causes and effects of stress and need to consider ways of avoiding, coping with, or reducing stress. Exercise and relaxation are important therapeutic techniques.

Procedures

1. Look at the list of stressful life events given in Chart 24.1. Circle the score opposite each event that seems to be true for you.
2. Add up all of the circled numbers. Record your score.
3. Look up your rating on Chart 24.2.
4. Interpret your score by answering the questions below.

Expected Results

Do you think you will have a high score on the stress test? Yes ☐ No ☐

Results

Record your score on the test _____

What is your rating? _____

Conclusions and Implications

What does your stress score suggest in terms of possible future illnesses?

Do you feel that you need to do anything to reduce your stress level?

Chart 24.1 Stressful Life Events

Event	Score
Death of spouse	100
Divorce	73
Marital separation	65
Jail term	63
Death of close family member	63
Personal injury/illness	53
Marriage	50
Fired from work	47
Marital reconciliation	45
Retirement	45
Change in family member's health	44
Pregnancy	40
Sex difficulties	39
Addition to family	39
Business readjustment	39
Change in financial status	38
Death of close friend	37
Change in number of marital arguments	35
Mortgage/loan over $10,000	31
Foreclosure of mortgage/loan	30
Change in work responsibilities	29
Son/daughter leaves home	29
Trouble with in-laws	29
Outstanding achievement	28
Spouse begins work	26
Start or finish school	26
Change in living conditions	25
Revision of personal habits	24
Trouble with boss	23
Change in work hours, conditions	20
Change in residence	20
Change in schools	20
Change in recreational habits	19
Change in church activities	19
Change in social activities	18
Mortgage/loan under $10,000	18
Change in sleeping habits	16

Chart 24.1—*Continued*

Event	Score
Change in number of family gatherings	15
Change in eating habits	15
Vacation	13
Christmas season	12
Minor violation of law	11

This test is adapted from the Social Readjustment Scale devised by Thomas Holmes and Richard Rahe. Used by permission.

Chart 24.2 Rating Scale for Stressful Life Events

Rating	Score	Implication for Illness
Low stress	150 or less	This indicates that a person has a 35% chance of getting a stress-related disease in the next two years.
Moderate stress	151–300	51% chance of getting a stress illness in the next two years.
High stress	301 or higher	80% chance of getting a stress illness in the next two years.

Tension, Relaxation, and Tension Relieving Exercises

Name   Section   Date

Purpose

The purpose of this laboratory session is to learn to recognize signs of excess tension in oneself and in others by observation of symptomatic mannerisms and by manually testing ability to relax. If time permits, perform the relaxation exercises in Appendix B before executing the lab.

Procedures

1. Choose a partner; designate one partner as the subject and the other as the tester. Alternate roles.
2. The subject should lie supine in a comfortable position and try to consciously relax as described in Concept 15. An individual may do this alone, or the instructor may wish to direct the entire group in this procedure.
3. The tester should kneel beside the subject's right hand and remain very still and quiet while the subject is concentrating.
4. After five minutes have elapsed, the tester should observe the subject for signs of tension according to the procedures outlined on the next page.
5. Record your relaxation rating in the results section of this report. (Use Chart 25.1 to determine your rating.)

Expected Results

Are you a tense person? Yes ☐ No ☐
What will your tension-relaxation rating be?

Relaxed   ☐   Moderately tense   ☐
Mildly tense   ☐   Markedly tense   ☐

Results

What is your tension score? _____

What is your relaxation rating? _____

Conclusions and Implications

Were you aware of your own tensions? Yes □ No □
Was it more difficult to relax than you expected? Yes □ No □
Did your awareness of your partner make it more difficult to concentrate?
Yes □ No □
Can you concentrate on your breathing without altering its rhythm?
Yes □ No □
Could you learn to consciously release muscular tension with additional prac-
tice? Yes □ No □
Could you learn to release tension while sitting or standing with your eyes
open? Yes □ No □
Do you think your score today is typical of your normal tension level?
Yes □ No □
What implications does this concept have for you in terms of your daily life
(e.g., sleeping, studying, taking exams, performing on stage, etc.).

Evaluating Muscular Tension

A trained person can diagnose neuromuscular hypertension by observation
and by manual testing. While there is insufficient time in this course to master
either the technique of relaxing or the techniques of evaluation, it is possible
to learn the procedures for both.

Procedures

1. Following the procedures outlined on the previous page, look for visual
   signs of tension outlined in section A of Chart 25.1. Place a check mark
   in the appropriate column.
2. Quietly and gently, the tester should grasp the subject's right wrist with
   his fingers, and slowly raise it about three inches from the floor, letting
   it hinge at the elbow; then let the hand drop. Observe the signs of tension
   outlined in section B of Chart 25.1. Record results.
3. After all visual and manual symptoms have been recorded on the chart,
   determine the total number of symptoms checked "yes."
4. Find your total score on Chart 25.2 to determine your rating.

Chart 25.1 Signs of Tension

	No	Yes
Visual Symptoms		
Frowning		
Twitching		
Eyelids fluttering		

Breathing
  shallow
  rapid
  irregular		

Mouth tight		
Swallowing		
Manual Symptoms		
Assistance (subject helps lift arm)		
Resistance (subject resists movement)		
Posturing (subject holds arm in raised position)		
Perseveration (subject continues upward movement)		

Total number of "yes" checks _____

Chart 25.2 Tension-Relaxation Rating Scale

Classification	Total Score
Excellent (relaxed)	0
Very good (mild tension)	1– 3
Marginal (moderate tension)	4– 6
Poor (tense)	7– 9
Very poor (marked tension)	10–12

A Cardiovascular Fitness Program—Aerobics

Some of the cardiovascular health benefits that are purported to result from regular progressive exercise include the development of a stronger heart muscle, healthier arteries, lower resting heart rate, better oxygen supply to working muscles (including the heart) and improved coronary collateral circulation. One program that claims all of these benefits is the Aerobics Program developed by Dr. Kenneth Cooper.

Purpose

The purposes of this laboratory session are:

1. To give you an opportunity to experience a part of an exercise program designed to develop cardiovascular fitness.
2. To familiarize you with an exercise program that can be continued as part of your normal life's pattern.

Procedures

1. Read about the Aerobics Program in Concept 18, page 127.
2. Select one aerobics activity and perform it, earning as many aerobics points as you can during the laboratory period.

Expected Results

Will you be able to earn three to six points without undue fatigue?
Yes ☐ No ☐
Is thirty minutes enough time to spend in earning the desired number of points? Yes ☐ No ☐

Results

What activity did you choose to perform? _____

How many points did you earn? _____

How many days a week would you have to do the same exercise to earn thirty

points a week?_____

Conclusions and Implications

Did you do as well as expected?
Yes ☐ No ☐
Was the exercise within your level of capacity? Yes ☐ No ☐ Explain.

Would the Aerobics Program be a good fitness program for you?
Yes ☐ No ☐
Do you think you will continue this type of program? Yes ☐ No ☐ Why?

The Adult Fitness Program

Lab **27**

Name_____ Section_____ Date_____

The President's Council on Physical Fitness and Sports has developed a complete progressive exercise program. A special book titled *Adult Physical Fitness* outlines several exercise programs that range from very simple to quite difficult. The manual suggests that an individual do a self-test and then begin with the program that best meets his or her individual needs.

Purpose

The purposes of this laboratory session are:

1. To give you an opportunity to experience a part of an exercise program designed to develop total physical fitness.
2. To acquaint you with an exercise program that can be continued as part of your normal life's pattern.

Procedures

1. Read about the Adult Physical Fitness Program in Concept 18, page 128.
2. Perform the sample program described in Appendix D.

Results

Did you complete the program of exercises in thirty minutes? Yes ☐ No ☐

If not, how much more time did you need? _____ minutes

Conclusions and Implications

Was the program too easy? Yes ☐ No ☐
Was it too difficult? Yes ☐ No ☐ Explain.

Will the Adult Fitness Program be a good one for you? Yes ☐ No ☐
Do you think *you* would continue this type of program? Yes ☐ No ☐
Why?

The XBX and 5BX
Physical Fitness Programs

Name_____ Section_____ Date_____

The Royal Canadian Air Force developed the XBX plan of exercise for women and the 5BX for men to help air force personnel become and stay physically fit. Since the time of the program's development, many lay people have selected the XBX and 5BX programs as their regular exercise program.

Purpose

The purposes of this laboratory session are:

1. To give you an opportunity to experience a part of an exercise program designed to develop total physical fitness.
2. To familiarize you with an exercise program that can be continued as part of your normal life's pattern.

Procedures

1. Read about the XBX and 5BX programs in Concept 18, page 128.
2. Perform the sample program described in Appendix E.

Results

How long did it take you to complete the program of exercises? _____ minutes

Was the program too easy? Yes ☐ No ☐
Too difficult? Yes ☐ No ☐ Explain.

Conclusions and Implications

Will the Royal Canadian Air Force XBX or 5BX be a good program for you?
Yes ☐ No ☐
Would you like to continue this type of program? Yes ☐ No ☐ Why or why
not?

A Continuous Rhythmical Endurance Exercise Program

Name   Section   Date

When an individual attempts to find a personal exercise program that best meets his or her own fitness needs, the individual should consider the following criteria: (1) will the program help improve or maintain *all* of the health-related aspects of fitness, and (2) is the program interesting enough to stimulate continued participation. One program that meets the above criteria is a progressive rhythmical endurance circle exercise program. The following program has been used quite successfully with adult groups. In fact, research shows that people participating in these exercises for six to ten weeks show significant improvements in *all* aspects of health-related fitness. Those who have used these circle exercises acknowledged that people who begin this type of program are likely to continue, especially if several people organize to perform the exercises as a group.

Purpose

The purposes of this laboratory session are:

1. To give you an opportunity to experience an exercise program designed to develop the health-related aspects of physical fitness with emphasis on cardiovascular fitness.
2. To acquaint you with an exercise program that can be continued as part of your normal life's pattern.

Procedures

1. Read about the program in Concept 18, page 129.
2. Perform the program as outlined in Appendix F. You may choose to exercise ten, fifteen, or twenty minutes depending on your level of fitness.

Results

Were you able to complete the entire exercise program? Yes ☐ No ☐

Conclusions and Implications

Did you exercise as long as you expected? Yes ☐ No ☐
What is your feeling concerning the advantages and disadvantages of this type of an exercise program?

Do you think circle exercises would be a good fitness program for you? Yes ☐ No ☐ Why or why not?

Do you think you will continue this type program later in life? Yes ☐ No ☐ Why or why not?

Speed Play or Fartlek

Name _____ Section _____ Date _____

This type of program, originally developed in Sweden, is a combination of fast running, slow running, walking, and a limited number of fast calisthenics. Though designed originally as a training technique for athletes it has been adapted as a program for people just interested in improving their fitness.

Purpose

The purposes of this laboratory session are:

1. To give you an opportunity to experience an exercise program designed to develop cardiovascular fitness and, to a lesser extent, other aspects of health-related physical fitness.
2. To acquaint you with an exercise program that can be continued as part of your normal life's pattern.

Procedures

1. Read about the Speed Play program in Concept 18, p. 129.
2. Perform the program described in Appendix G. You may choose to walk or jog instead of performing all of the exercises if the program is too vigorous for your current level of fitness.

Results

Were you able to complete the entire Speed Play program? Yes ☐ No ☐
Do you think you would continue this type of program? Yes ☐ No ☐
Why?

What type of an interval training program would be best for you? Describe.

Interval Training

Name _____ Section _____ Date _____

Interval training is the name used to describe a method of anaerobic or intermittent exercise training. Originally developed as a method of conditioning for athletes, it is now used by many individuals as part of their regular program for physical fitness development. Interval training involves running relatively short distances at a relatively high intensity, followed by low intensity running, or resting. Swimming and other forms of exercise can also be used for interval training.

Purpose

The purposes of this laboratory session are:

1. To give you an opportunity to experience interval training or an anaerobic exercise program for developing cardiovascular fitness.
2. To familiarize you with an interval training program that can be continued for a lifetime.

Procedures

1. Read about interval training in Concept 18, p. 130.
2. Perform the sample interval training program described in Appendix H.

Results

Were you able to complete the entire interval training program?
Yes ☐ No ☐

If not, how long were you able to continue? _____

Conclusions and Implications

Was the interval training program a good one for you? Yes ☐ No ☐
If not, do you prefer aerobics? Yes ☐ No ☐

Do you think you would continue this type of program?
Yes ☐ No ☐　　　Why?

What type of an interval training program would be best for you? Describe.

Jogging

Lab **32**

Name _____ Section _____ Date _____

Jogging is a form of aerobic exercise that has become extremely popular as a method of developing cardiovascular fitness. It has a major advantage in that it does not require a great deal of skill, and for this reason almost any individual can enjoy the benefits of this form of exercise.

Purpose

The purposes of this laboratory session are:

1. To give you an opportunity to experience one type of jogging program that can be used to develop and maintain cardiovascular fitness.
2. To acquaint you with the basic techniques of jogging.

Procedures

1. Work with a partner and rate each other on jogging techniques. Make a note on Chart 32.1 if you have any problems in your technique.
2. Using proper jogging technique, jog for fifteen minutes at your own individual cardiovascular threshold of training. (Determine your threshold of training from Chart 4.1, p. 139.

Results

What is your cardiovascular threshold of training? _____ bpm

What was your heart rate after your fifteen minute jog? _____ bpm
During your fifteen minute jog, did you reach your threshold of training?
Yes ☐ No ☐
With the help of a partner, note any problems in technique on Chart 32.1. (Read the jogging information in Appendix I before rating your partner's jogging technique.

Chart 32.1   Jogging Technique

Source of Problem	Severity of Problem	
	None	Needs Work
Foot placement		
Length of stride		
Arm movement		
Body position		

Do you feel that you can solve any jogging problems you have?
Yes ☐ No ☐ No problems ☐

Conclusions and Implications

Do you think that jogging is a good type of exercise for you?
Yes ☐ No ☐ Explain.

Do you think that you will include jogging in your exercise program for use in later life? Yes ☐ No ☐ Explain.

Weight Training
or Isotonic Exercise

Lab **33**

Name   Section   Date

Weight training is a type of isotonic exercise that requires you to lift a weighted bar or dumbbell in order to overload specific muscles. Recent evidence indicates weight training is appropriate for both men and women.

Purpose

The purposes of this laboratory session are:

1. To give you an opportunity to experience a sample weight training program.
2. To acquaint you with a strength program that can be continued throughout your life.

Procedures

1. Read about weight training in Concept 18, p. 131.
2. Perform the weight training exercises using the weights and repetitions listed in Chart 33.1. (This is a sample program that would have to be modified to meet your individual needs as described in Appendix J. The *sample program* is *not* intended as a program for regular use.

Chart 33.1 Sample Program—Weight Training

Exercise	Sets	Repetitions	Beginning Weight Men	Beginning Weight Women
Shoulder shrug	3	6	60 pounds	40 pounds
Military press	3	6	50 pounds	40 pounds
Half knee squats	3	6	60 pounds	40 pounds
Curls	3	6	40 pounds	30 pounds
Forearm extension behind neck	3	6	25 pounds	15 pounds
Toe raises	3	6	60 pounds	40 pounds
Pull to chin	3	6	30 pounds	20 pounds

For exercise details see pages 297–301.

Results

How long did it take you to complete the program? _____ minutes
Was the program too long? Yes ☐ No ☐
Too easy? Yes ☐ No ☐
Too difficult? Yes ☐ No ☐ Explain.

Conclusions and Implications

Will weight training be a good program for you? Yes ☐ No ☐
Would you like to continue this type of program? Yes ☐ No ☐ Why or why not?

Isometric Exercise

Name_____Section_____Date_____

Isometric exercises were first popularized by German scientists and later used extensively by coaches for preparation in football. This type of exercise has since been adapted for use in regular exercise programs. Isometrics involves static contractions of the muscles with no movement of the body parts.

Purpose

The purposes of this laboratory session are:

1. To give you an opportunity to experience a sample isometric exercise program.
2. To acquaint you with strength exercises that you may wish to include as a part of your exercise program for a lifetime.

Procedures

1. Read about isometric exercises in Chapter 7, pages 112–48.
2. Perform the isometric exercises, repetitions, and durations suggested below. (This is a sample program that needs to be modified to meet your individual needs as described in Appendix K, page 301. The sample program is *not* intended as a program for regular use.)

Chart 34.1 Sample Program—Isometric Exercises

Exercise	Repetitions	Duration
Shoulder pull	3	8 seconds
Chest push	3	8 seconds
Curl	3	8 seconds
Wall seat	3	8 seconds
Leg extension	3	8 seconds

For exercise details see pages 301–306.

Results

Was the program too hard? Yes ☐ No ☐
Too easy? Yes ☐ No ☐ Explain.

Conclusions and Implications

Will isometrics be a good exercise program for you? Yes ☐ No ☐
Explain.

Isotonic Exercises for Endurance and Mild Strengthening

Name   Section Date

In addition to weight training, there are other types of isotonic exercises that use gravity as the resistance. These can be modified to be suitable for those who are not able to lift heavy weights. These exercises can develop limited strength, but are primarily good for muscular endurance. They are frequently used for "figure development" by women, but are appropriate for anyone needing muscular endurance and limited strengthening, such as in postural correction.

Purpose

The purposes of this laboratory session are:

1. To give you an opportunity to experience gravity resisted exercises.
2. To familiarize you with exercises you may wish to include in your lifetime exercise program for muscular endurance, figure/physique control, and posture correction.

Procedures

1. Read about the exercises in Appendix L.
2. Perform the exercises as described. Do ten repetitions of each exercise or as many as you can do in the time allotted by your instructor.

Results

Do you think you need to use any of these exercises? Yes ☐ No ☐ If so, which ones?

Conclusions and Implications

How would you use these exercises in your regular exercise program?

Name an advantage of this type of program that is not listed among the advantages in Appendix 13.

Were any of the exercises too easy for you? If so, list them here.

Were any of the exercises too difficult for you? If so, list them here.

Tell how to modify each of the exercises you listed above to make it better fit your ability.

Flexibility Exercises

Flexibility is not an aspect of health-related fitness that is built without effort. To attain flexibility it is necessary to stretch muscles regularly.

Purpose

The purposes of this laboratory session are:

1. To give you an opportunity to experience different flexibility exercises.
2. To acquaint you with a flexibility program that can be continued throughout your life.

Procedures

1. Read about the flexibility exercises in Appendix M.
2. Perform each of the exercises three times as described in Appendix M.

Results

Were you able to do all of the exercises? Yes ☐ No ☐
Were the exercises difficult? Yes ☐ No ☐
Could you tell which of your muscles were inflexible by performing the exercises? Yes ☐ No ☐ Which ones?

Conclusions and Implications

Will you choose any of these flexibility exercises for your lifetime program of exercise? Yes ☐ No ☐
If yes, which ones?

If no, why will you not use these exercises?

Sports for Physical Fitness

Name   Section   Date

Sports should be considered with the other types of exercise amd physical activity programs as a means for achieving health-related physical fitness. As noted in Concept 12, sports have various advantages and disadvantages as fitness programs. However, because there are so many different kinds of sports, it is really necessary to consider each sport individually when planning your exercise program. You should consider participation in the sport that is most likely to meet your own personal needs and interests.

Purpose

The purpose of this experiment is to explore the use of different sports as a part of your personal physical fitness program.

Procedures

1. On Chart 37.1 check any of the ten most popular sports in America in which you especially like to participate.
2. Also on Chart 37.1, check the sports that you feel skilled in (ones in which you have enough skill to enjoy playing a game without more lessons).
3. Perform, in or out of class, two or three different sports, each for thirty to sixty minutes.
4. On Chart 37.2 list the sports you played in the results section.
5. Check the parts of fitness in which you think you improved by playing that sport. Refer to Table 12.1, page 81.

Results

Chart 37.1 Sports Interests and Proficiencies

Sports	Check If Interested	Check If Proficient
Bowling	☐	☐
Tennis	☐	☐
Basketball	☐	☐
Softball	☐	☐
Baseball	☐	☐
Golf	☐	☐
Volleyball	☐	☐
Football	☐	☐
Frisbee	☐	☐
Table Tennis	☐	☐
Others (write in)		
_____	☐	☐
_____	☐	☐

Chart 37.2 Fitness Benefits

Benefit	Sport _____	Sport _____	Sport _____
Cardiovascular fitness	☐	☐	☐
Flexibility	☐	☐	☐
Body leanness	☐	☐	☐
Strength	☐	☐	☐
Muscular endurance	☐	☐	☐

Conclusions and Implications

Which sports do you feel you might actually include in your exercise program for a lifetime? Discuss.

Planning Your Personal Exercise Program

Name   Section   Date

It is hoped that every person will desire to develop and maintain physical fitness through exercise and activity. A physically *fit* person may be described as one who possesses the ability to work at peak efficiency in daily life and in any emergency situation that might arise. A fit person possesses buoyant health and performs well in the health-related aspects of physical fitness, including cardiovascular fitness, muscular endurance, strength, and flexibility. A fit person also possesses a relatively lean body.

The physically educated person possesses efficient movement skills and is reasonably proficient in a variety of sports and other physical activities. He or she also has a knowledge of and a desirable attitude toward exercise, sports, dance, good body mechanics, relaxation, and proper health habits.

It is one of the purposes of this book to present information that might contribute to the physical education of the reader. The measure of its success will be your decision to engage in adequate physical activity in the future.

Purpose

The purposes of this laboratory session are:

1. To plot a personal profile to be used in making decisions about your future patterns of activity and exercise.
2. To develop your own personalized exercise program, which can be continued for a lifetime.
3. To try out your personal exercise program.
4. To evaluate your personal exercise program to see if it meets the purposes for which it was intended.

Procedures

1. Plot your personal physical activity evaluation profile on Chart 38.1 (men) or Chart 38.2 (women). Circle the score you achieved on each of the tests taken during Labs 5 to 22.
2. Check your ratings on the various physical aspects in the appropriate boxes presented in the "results" section.

3. Using the information from items 1 and 2 above, plan a weekly program and record it on Chart 38.3. Include all of the exercises you feel you should do (including sports and games) on a regular basis to meet your physical activity needs. (Review Concept 19 "Planning Your Exercise Program."

4. Perform *one day's* activities from your exercise plan during class time. Ask your instructor for help if you have questions about your exercise plan.

Results

1. Circle your scores on Chart 38.1 (men) or Chart 38.2 (women).
2. Check the boxes that best reflect your performance.

	Attitude about exercise	Strength and muscular endurance	Flexibility	Cardiovascular fitness	Body fatness	Posture, feet, and back	Skill-related fitness
Excellent	☐	☐	☐	☐	☐	☐	☐
Adequate for my needs	☐	☐	☐	☐	☐	☐	☐
Need work	☐	☐	☐	☐	☐	☐	☐
Very poor	☐	☐	☐	☐	☐	☐	☐

3. Write in your exercise program on Chart 38.3.

Chart 38.1 Personal Evaluation Profile for Men

Very Poor	Poor	Marginal	Very Good	Excellent	Classification	
0–5	6–7	8–14	15–17	18	H F Scale	
0–5	6–7	8–14	15–17	18	Social	**Attitude**
0–5	6–7	8–14	15–17	18	Recreational Relaxational	**Scale,**
0–5	6–7	8–14	15–17	18	General	**First**
0–20	21–31	32–56	57–68	69–72	Total	**Test**
0–5	6–7	8–14	15–17	18	H F Scale	
0–5	6–7	8–14	15–17	18	Social	**Attitude**
0–5	6–7	8–14	15–17	18	Recreational Relaxational	**Scale,**
0–5	6–7	8–14	15–17	18	General	**Second**
0–21	21–31	32–56	57–68	69–72	Total	**Test**
1.48−	1.50	1.60	1.80			
1.5	1.59	1.79	1.89	1.90	12-Minute Run	**Cardio-**
≥ 125	124–115	114–95	94–85	< 84	Step Test	**vascular**
33	34–36	37–45	46–53	≥ 54	Bicycle Test	**Fitness**
85	86–94	95–110	111–130	> 131	Left Grip	
90	91–104	105–125	126–140	> 141	Right Grip	
200	201–276	277–389	390–459	> 460	Back Strength	
300	301–351	352–420	421–475	≥ 476	Leg Strength	**Strength**
675	676–825	826–1045	1046–1250	> 1251	Total Strength	**Tests**
4.80	4.81–5.20	5.21–6.95	6.96–7.25	≥ 7.26	Strength Per/Lb/Wt	
0–6	7–11	12–24	25–34	≥ 35	Sitting Tuck	**Muscular Endurance**
0–3	4–6	7–10	11–14	≥ 15	Chins	
3	4–6	7–10	11–13	≥ 14	Test I	**Flexibility**
0	1–3	4–5	6	> 7	Right Up	
− 3	− 2–1	0–2	3–6	> 7	Left Up Test II	
≥ 20	18–19	15–17	11–14	10	% Fat	
≥ 12	8–11	5–7	3–4	0–2	Posture	
10–12	7–9	4–6	1–3	0	Tension-Relaxation	
0–29	30–59	60–79	80–89	90–100	Balance	**Motor**
≥ 18.9	18.7–18.8	16.8–18.6	15.9–16.7	15.8	Agility	**Fitness**
5′9″	5′10″–6′3″	6′4″–7′8″	7′9″–8′5″	≥ 8′6″	Power Jump	**Tests**
0–2	3–4	5–10	11–13	14–15	Coordination	

Conclusions and Implications

Do you think you will perform your personal program regularly for the next year? Yes ☐ No ☐ Discuss.

Chart 38.2 Personal Evaluation Profile for Women

Very Poor	Poor	Marginal	Very Good	Excellent	Classification	
0–5	6–7	8–14	15–17	18	H F Scale	
0–5	6–7	8–14	15–17	18	Social	**Attitude**
0–5	6–7	8–14	15–17	18	Recreational Relaxational	**Scale,**
0–5	6–7	8–14	15–17	18	General	**First**
0–20	21–31	32–56	57–68	69–72	Total	**Test**
0–5	6–7	8–14	15–17	18	H F Scale	
0–5	6–7	8–14	15–17	18	Social	**Attitude**
0–5	6–7	8–14	15–17	18	Recreational Relaxational	**Scale,**
0–5	6–7	8–14	15–17	18	General	**Second**
0–20	21–31	32–56	57–68	69–72	Total	**Test**
below .90	.90–1.09	1.10–1.30	1.40–1.49	1.5	12 Minute Run	**Cardio-**
$\geq$ 125	124–115	114–95	94–85	< 84	Step Test	**vascular**
29	30–35	36–41	42–46	$\geq$ 47	Bicycle Test	**Fitness**
39	40–47	48–70	71–76	$\geq$ 77	Left Grip	
48	49–55	56–75	76–85	$\geq$ 86	Right Grip	
94	95–124	125–214	215–240	$\geq$ 241	Back Strength	
104	105–144	145–225	226–260	$\geq$ 261	Leg Strength	**Strength**
279	280–369	370–587	588–664	$\geq$ 665	Total Strength	**Tests**
2.19	2.20–2.89	2.90–4.59	4.60–5.29	$\geq$ 5.30	Strength Per/Lb/Wt	
0–4	5–7	8–15	16–21	$\geq$ 22	Sitting Tuck	**Muscular**
0			1	2	Chins	**Endurance**
0–3	4–6	7–11	12–14	$\geq$ 15	Test I	
0	1–4	5–6	7	> 8	Right Up	**Flexibility**
− 3	−2–1	0–5	6–7	> 8	Left Up Test II	
$\geq$ 28	23–27	18–22	16–17	15	% Fat	
$\geq$ 12	8–11	5–7	3–4	0–2	Posture	
10–12	8–11	4–6	1–3	0	Tension-Relaxation	
0–29	30–59	60–79	80–89	90–100	Balance	
$\geq$ 23.5	22.4–23.4	18.7–22.3	17.5–18.6	17.4	Agility	**Motor**
4'1"	4'2"–4'7"	4'8"–5'9"	5'10"–6'7"	$\geq$ 6'8"	Power Jump	**Fitness**
0–1	2–3	4–9	10–12	13–15	Coordination	**Tests**

Chart 38.3   Personal Exercise Program (Regular Weekly Schedule)

Directions:
1. List the activities you would do for each day of the week.
2. Indicate what part or parts of fitness will be developed by each activity.
3. If you do not plan to exercise on a given day, leave it blank.
4. Prepare your activities for Monday through Wednesday on this sheet and for Thursday through Sunday on the backside of this sheet.

	Describe Activity	**Reason for Activity**
Monday		
Tuesday		
Wednesday		

Describe Activity	Reason for Activity

Thursday

Friday

Saturday

Sunday

Physical Activity for a Lifetime   Lab 39

Name _____ Section _____ Date _____

As the typical American grows older, his or her physical fitness tends to decline. At least one study indicates that health-related physical fitness begins to decline in the average American woman in her early teens and in the average American man in his late teens. This decline occurs in spite of the fact that our greatest potential for fitness is between ages twenty-five and thirty.

Much of the decrease in physical and mental function that accompanies aging is a result of disuse rather than age. We are all capable of considerably more physical fitness later in life than is characterized by the typical American.

Purpose

The purposes of this laboratory session are:

1. To estimate your fitness needs at age forty.
2. To plan a program for yourself at age forty.
3. To determine the difference in exertion for your current program and your program for later life.

Procedures

1. Assume that your age is forty (or the age of a parent or relative near that age). Look up your cardiovascular threshold of training for that specific age. Guess your resting heart rate (it tends to go up as you get older and less fit). Record it in the results section.
2. Estimate what exercise would make you reach the cardiovascular threshold of training for a person near forty. (Make this determination on the basis of how fit you expect to be at forty or how fit the person is whose age you are assuming.) Write this exercise down in the results section and note the rate (e.g., one mile in seven minutes).
3. List three flexibility exercises and three strength or muscular endurance exercises that you think you should be performing (list only those you really think you could do at that age). Record in the results section.
4. Perform the cardiovascular exercise for fifteen minutes and do the flexibility and strength-muscular endurance exercises.

Results

What will your cardiovascular target zone be at age forty?

_____bpm

What exercise(s) would you do to get your heart rate above the level noted for age forty? _____   _____

List three flexibility exercises you would do at age forty.

Exercise	**Repetitions**
1. _____	_____
2. _____	_____
3. _____	_____

List three strength or muscular endurance exercises you would do at age forty.

Exercise	**Repetitions**
1. _____	_____
2. _____	_____
3. _____	_____

How much easier for you were these exercises than the exercises in your own program?

Do you really think you will be fit enough to do the above listed exercises at age forty?

Could your parent of the same sex or a relative of about forty do the exercises you have selected? Yes ☐ No ☐ Why or why not?

At age forty do you expect to be more or less fit than the typical person at that age? More Fit ☐ Average ☐ Less Fit ☐ Explain.

Could you help a person forty or over plan an exercise program?
Yes ☐ No ☐ Explain.

Reassessing the Values of Physical Activity

Name _____ Section _____ Date _____

In Lab 1, an assessment was made of your personal feelings about physical activity. Before making a decision concerning future exercise and physical activity habits, a reassessment might be helpful.

Purpose

The purpose of this laboratory session is to help you to detect any change in attitude that may have occurred during the course of this class.

Procedures

Read each of the sixteen items in Chart 40.1 and answer them either as "strongly agree," "agree," "undecided," "disagree," or "strongly disagree." Give the answer that best indicates the way *you* feel. Try not to use the response "undecided" unless absolutely necessary. Do not look at your first test. Score the sixteen items usng the scoring method on page 278.

Expected Results

Do you think your attitude test scores will be different from your scores the first time you took the test? Yes ☐ No ☐
Check the changes that you think have occurred.

	Same	Higher	Lower
Health and fitness	☐	☐	☐
Social scale	☐	☐	☐
Relaxation	☐	☐	☐
General	☐	☐	☐
Total test	☐	☐	☐

Results

After scoring your test, write your rating on each scale of the attitude test below and note whether your score increased or decreased.

	Rating Test 1	Rating Test 2	+	same	−
Health and Physical Fitness Scale					
Social Scale					
Recreation-Relaxation Release Scale					
General Attitude Scale					
Test Total					

Conclusions and Implications

Do you think the sixteen-item test could accurately detect changes in your attitude? Yes ☐ No ☐ Explain.

What is your attitude about physical activity at this time?

Chart 40.1 Attitude Test

Attitude Scale First Test	Strongly Agree	Agree	Un-decided	Disagree	Strongly Disagree	SCORE
1. Physical education is all right for those who like sports but is not for me.	☐	☐	☐	☐	☐	_____
2. Physical exercise and activity are as dangerous to health as they are valuable.	☐	☐	☐	☐	☐	_____
3. I enjoy taking part in a sport just to get away from it all.	☐	☐	☐	☐	☐	_____
4. I like to participate best in those games that involve working as a team.	☐	☐	☐	☐	☐	_____
5. Physical activity is one way to rid yourself of the worries and tensions of everyday life.	☐	☐	☐	☐	☐	_____
6. Probably one of the main values of sports is to fill leisure time in our automated society.	☐	☐	☐	☐	☐	_____
7. I would only enroll in physical education if it were a graduation requirement.	☐	☐	☐	☐	☐	_____
8. The time some people spend exercising could probably be better spent in other ways.	☐	☐	☐	☐	☐	_____
9. Sports and games build social confidence.	☐	☐	☐	☐	☐	_____
10. Industry might be wise to substitute exercise breaks for coffee breaks.	☐	☐	☐	☐	☐	_____
11. Competition in sports is often a way to destroy good friendships.	☐	☐	☐	☐	☐	_____
12. Most jobs provide all the exercise and activity a person needs.	☐	☐	☐	☐	☐	_____
13. Everyone should have skill in several sports that can be used later in life.	☐	☐	☐	☐	☐	_____
14. Social dancing and other similar forms of activity are a waste of time.	☐	☐	☐	☐	☐	_____
15. Health and physical fitness are basic to all of life's activities.	☐	☐	☐	☐	☐	_____
16. I would recommend that everyone take physical education because of the important nature of the subject.	☐	☐	☐	☐	☐	_____

Score the attitude test as follows:

1. For items 1, 2, 7, 8, 11, 12, and 14 give one point for *strongly agree,* two for *agree,* three for *undecided,* four for *disagree,* and five for *strongly disagree.* Put the correct number on the blank to the right of these statements.

2. For items 3, 4, 5, 6, 9, 10, 13, 15, and 16 give five points for *strongly agree,* four for *agree,* three for *undecided,* two for *disagree,* and one for *strongly disagree.* Put the correct number on the blank to the right of these statements.

3. Add the scores for items 2, 8, 12, and 15. This total represents your health and fitness attitude score.

4. Add the scores for items 4, 9, 11, and 14. This total represents your social attitude score.

5. Add the scores for items 3, 5, 6, and 13. This total represents your recreation-relaxation attitude score.

6. Add the scores for items 1, 7, 10, and 16. This total represents your general attitude score.

7. Circle your scores on Chart 40.2 and record them in the results section.

Chart 40.2 Attitude Rating Scale

	Attitude Scale First Test					Attitude Scale Second Test				
	HF Scale	Social	Recreation-Relaxation	General	Total	HF Scale	Social	Recreation-Relaxation	General	Total
Excellent (Ex)	18	18	18	18	69–72	18	18	18	18	69–72
Good	15–17	15–17	15–17	15–17	57–68	15–17	15–17	15–17	15–17	57–68
Marginal (M)	8–14	8–14	8–14	8–14	32–56	8–14	8–14	8–14	8–14	32–56
Poor	6–7	6–7	6–7	6–7	21–31	6–7	6–7	6–7	6–7	21–31
Very Poor (VP)	0–5	0–5	0–5	0–5	0–20	0–5	0–5	0–5	0–5	0–20

Exercises for the Care of the Back

The treatment for painful spines ranges from surgical fusion to more conservative measures such as procain injections, muscle relaxant pills, ethyl chloride spray, traction, bed rest, heat, massage, and therapeutic exercise. Exercise is not a cure-all and should not be used indiscriminately for backaches. If a doctor recommends exercise for the back, or if an individual is susceptible to back strain and/or simply wishes to prevent its occurrence, then be assured, proper exercise will be invaluable.

The exercises presented here are preventive and remedial exercises for the back. Some are designed primarily to strengthen the abdominals and to stretch the lumbar muscles; others are designed to strengthen back muscles. Omitted from this series of exercises are those that stretch shortened hip flexors. If it is determined that you need to stretch the iliopsoas muscles, consult your instructor. If you have had surgery or an injury, you should wait until your physician advises you to start exercising. If you have been inactive for a period of time, it would be wise to perform these exercises for several days before tackling a job that might strain your back. Start slowly and gradually increase the number of repetitions; perform the exercises three times daily for maximum benefits. If soreness occurs the next day, reduce the frequency until strength is increased and soreness ceases to occur.

1. Deep Breathing. In the hook-lying position, with arms at sides, take a deep breath, expanding the chest as much as possible; exhale slowly, allowing the chest to return to its normal position. Keep the back and neck flat. Repeat very slowly five or six times. (mild back stretcher)

2. Alternate Knee-to-Chest. In the hook-lying position, draw one knee up to the chest and pull it down tightly with the hands, then slowly return to the original position. Repeat with the other knee. Repeat with each leg ten to twenty times. (stretches lumbar muscles)

3. Trunk Curl. Lie on the back with the knees bent. Roll the head and neck forward, then the shoulders. Roll as far forward as possible without lifting the lower back off the floor. Hold. Return to start and repeat. (strengthens abdominals)

4. Bent Knee Sit-up. Lie on the back with knees bent. Roll the head, neck, and shoulders forward in sequence. Lift the back off the floor. Return to starting position and repeat. Arms may be placed at the sides, across the chest or behind the head. (strengthens abdominals)

5. Double Knee-to-Chest. In the hook-lying position, draw both knees to the chest and pull them down tight against the chest with the arms. Hold this position for twenty-five seconds. Return to starting position and repeat five or six times. Before raising the knees, tighten the abdominal muscles and hold the back flat. (stretches lumbar muscles)

6. Alternate Leg Extension. In the hook-lying position, draw one knee to the chest, then extend the knee and point the foot toward the ceiling. Return to the starting position by drawing the knee back to the chest before sliding the foot to the floor. Repeat with other leg. Repeat cycle four or five times. (stretches lumbar muscles)

7. Double Leg Extension. In the hook-lying position, draw both knees to the chest, then extend both legs toward the ceiling, keeping the lower back flat. Return to the starting position by drawing the knees to the chest before placing the feet on the floor. Repeat three or four times. (stretches lumbar muscles) (*Note:* This is a more strenuous exercise and the weak person should not attempt it until the other exercises have been performed three or four weeks.)

8. Hip Abduction. In the hook-lying position, let the knees fall apart alternately, right and left as far as they will go, thirty or forty times. (stretches hip flexors and adductors)

9. Isometric Contractions. In the hook-lying position, tighten the abdominal muscles and try to flatten the lower back against the floor. At the same time, tighten the hip and thigh muscles. Hold the contractions for six seconds, then relax. Repeat five or six times. Breathe normally during the contraction—do not hold the breath. (strengthens abdominals)

10. Cat Backs. Kneel on all fours. Contract the abdominals strongly, tilting the pelvis backward and making the back hump upward while dropping the head. Hold the rounded back position for six seconds and then relax, letting the back sway and abdomen sag as the head is lifted. Repeat five or six times. (strengthens abdominals)

11. Knee-to-Nose Touch. Kneel on all fours. Drop the head and try to touch the nose with one knee. Then extend that leg backward parallel with the floor (avoid arching the back). Return to the starting position. Alternate legs ten to twenty times. (stretches lumbar muscles and strengthens gluteals)

The following exercises are designed to strengthen the back muscles:

1. For those who do *not* have weak abdominals and/or lordosis:

Prone Arm and Leg Lift. Lie prone with the arms extended in front of the head. Raise: (a) the right arm toward the ceiling and return; (b) the left arm and return; (c) both arms and return; (d) repeat with legs—right, left and both; (e) try right arm and right leg; (f) left arm and left leg; (g) right arm and left leg; (h) left arm and right leg; and (i) both arms and both legs. (strengthens upper and lower back and hip extensors)

2. For those *with* weak abdominals and/or lordosis:

2. Upper Trunk Lift. Lie on table or bench with upper half of body hanging over the edge. Have a partner stabilize the feet while the trunk is raised parallel to the floor. Start with the hands under the thighs; as strength develops, place hands behind neck. Do not raise past the horizontal, or arch the back. (strengthens upper back)

Tension Relieving Exercises

1. Head Circle. Roll the head slowly in a large circle, first clockwise and then counterclockwise. Close your eyes and let your mouth fall open during the exercise. Repeat several times.

2. Shoulder Lift. Hunch the shoulders as high as possible and then let them drop. Repeat several times. Inhale on the lift; exhale on the drop.

3. Trunk Stretch and Drop. Stand and reach as high as possible; tiptoe and stretch every muscle, then collapse completely, letting knees flex and trunk, head, and arms dangle (see Trunk Swing Illustration). Repeat two or three times.

4. Trunk Swings. Following the trunk drop (described above), bounce gently with a minimum of muscular effort. Set the trunk swinging from side to side by shifting the weight from one foot to the other, letting the heels come off the floor alternately. Then with a slight springing movement of the lower back, gently bob up and down, keeping the entire body (especially the neck) limp.

5. Tension Contrast. With arms extended overhead, lie on your side; tense the body as "stiff as a board," then "let go," and relax letting the body fall either forward or backward in whatever direction it loses balance. Continue "letting go" for a few seconds after falling and allow yourself to feel like you are still "sinking." Repeat on the other side.

The Aerobics Program

To achieve the benefits of the Aerobics Program, an individual should exercise a minimum of three times a week and earn at least thirty points a week from the chart below. At first you may wish to begin by earning ten to fifteen points a week and then work up to thirty.

Aerobics Point Chart

Points	Walking-Running (Time for 1 Mile)	Cycling (Speed for 2 Miles)	Swimming (300 yds.)	Hand-ball, Basket-ball	Stationary Running for 5 Min.	Stationary Running for 10 Min.	Points
0	Over 20 min.	Less than 10 mph	Over 10 min.	Less than 10 min.	Less than 60 steps/min.	Less than 50 steps/min.	0
1	20:00–14:30 min.	10–15 mph	8:00–10:00 min.	10 min.	60–70 steps/min.	50–65 steps/min.	1
2	14:29–12:00 min	15–20 mph	7:30–8:00 min.	20 min.	80–90 steps/min.	65–70 steps/min.	2
3	11:59–10:00 min.	Over 20 mph	6:00–7:30 min.	30 min.		70–80 steps/min.	3
4	9:59–8:00 min.			40 min.		80–90 steps/min.	4
5	7:59–6:30 min.			50 min.			5
6	Less than 6:30 min.			60 min.			6

Used by permission of K. Cooper, *The New Aerobics* (New York: M. Evans and Co., 1970.)

If you plan to use the Aerobics Program as part of your regular exercise plan you should read: *The New Aerobics* by K. H. Cooper and *Aerobics for Women* by K. H. Cooper and M. Cooper.

Aerobic Dance is a modification of Aerobics that has gained much popularity recently. It combines aerobic exercise with dance to provide many exercise benefits. The interested person is referred to Concept 18.

Advantages and Disadvantages of the Aerobics Program

Advantages

1. Develops cardiovascular fitness.
2. Provides a program with a variety of activities.
3. Provides a method of evaluating progress (12-minute run).

Disadvantages

1. Is principally a cardiovascular fitness program, which would have to be supplemented with exercises for other aspects of health-related fitness.
2. Because of individual differences points may vary for activities from individual to individual.

Appendix
D

The Adult Fitness Program of Exercise

The adult physical fitness program as developed by the President's Council on Sports and Physical Fitness is designed as a total program of exercise. A manual is available that includes exercises graduated in intensity from easy to very difficult depending on the needs of the person. As you perform one set of exercises for a period of time and they become easy, you then progress to the next set of exercises. The following is a *sample* program that is presented to give you an idea of the nature of the Adult Fitness Program. If you choose to perform these activities, you should read the *Adult Fitness Manual* (For reference, see Concept 18 reference list, page 132).

Advantages and Disadvantages of the Adult Fitness Program

Advantages

1. Graduated in intensity to meet the needs of a wide variety of people.

2. Develops most all aspects of health-related fitness though it is doubtful that the program would build cardiovascular fitness for all people.

Disadvantages

1. Because it is basically a calisthenics program, it may be difficult to sustain interest in the program over a long period of time.

2. For many, it would need to be supplemented with cardiovascular fitness exercises.

Adult Physical Fitness Exercises

1. Bend and Stretch. Starting position, Stand erect, feet shoulder-width apart.
Action: Count 1. Bend trunk forward and down, flexing knees. Stretch gently in an attempt to touch fingers to toes or floor. Count 2. Return to starting position.
Note: Do slowly, stretch and relax at intervals rather than in rhythm.

2. Knee Lift. Starting position: Stand erect, feet together, arms at sides.
Action: Count 1. Raise left knee as high as possible, grasping leg with hands and pulling knee against body while keeping back straight. Count 2. Lower to starting position. Counts 3 and 4. Repeat with right knee.

Sample Program

Conditioning Exercises	Goal (in Repetitions)
1. Bend and stretch	10
2. Knee lift	10 left, 10 right
3. Wing stretcher	20
4. Half knee bend	10
5. Arm circles	15 each way
6. Body bender	10 left, 10 right
7. Prone arch	10
8. Knee push-up	6
9. Head and shoulder curl	5
10. Ankle stretch	15

Circulatory Activity (Choose One Each Workout)

Walking	½ mile
Rope (skip 15 sec.; rest 60 sec.)	3 series

Note: Exercises 1 and 7 are not recommended for those experiencing low back difficulties.

Used by permission President's Council on Physical Fitness and Sports. *Adult Physical Fitness.* Washington, D.C.

3. Wing Stretcher. Starting position: Stand erect, elbows at shoulder height, fists clenched in front of chest.
Action: Count 1. Thrust elbows backward vigorously without arching back. Keep head erect, elbows at shoulder height. Count 2. Return to starting position.

5. Arm Circles. Starting position: Stand erect, arms extended sideward at shoulder height, palms up.
Action: Describe small circles backward with hands. Keep head erect. Do 15 backward circles. Reverse, turn palms down and do 15 small circles forward.

4. Half Knee Bend. Starting position: Stand erect, hands on hips.
Action: Count 1. Bend knees halfway while extending arms forward, palms down. Count 2. Return to starting position.

6. Body Bender. Starting position: Stand, feet shoulder-width apart, hands behind neck, fingers interlaced.
Action: Count 1. Bend trunk sideward to left as far as possible, keeping hands behind neck. Count 2. Return to starting position. Counts 3 and 4. Repeat to the right.

Appendixes

7. Prone Arch. Starting position: Lie face down, hands tucked under thighs. Action: Count 1. Raise head, shoulders, and legs from floor. Count 2. Return to starting position.

9. Head and Shoulder Curl. Starting position: Lie on back, hands tucked under small of back, palms down.
Action: Count 1. Tighten abdominal muscles, lift head, and pull shoulders and elbows off floor. Hold for four seconds. Count 2. Return to starting position.

8. Knee Push-up. Starting position: Lie on floor, face down, legs together, knees bent with feet raised off floor, hands on floor under shoulders, palms down.
Action: Count 1. Push upper body off floor until arms are fully extended and body is in straight line from head to knees. Count 2. Return to starting position.

10. Ankle Stretch. Starting position: Stand on a stair step, large book, or block of wood, with weight on balls of feet and heels raised.
Action: Count 1. Lower heels. Count 2. Raise heels.

Circulatory Activities

Walking. Step at a lively pace, swing arms, and breathe deeply.

Rope. Any form of skipping or jumping is acceptable. Gradually increase the tempo as your skill and condition improve.

The Canadian XBX and 5BX Programs

The Canadian Air Force Program consists of two separate parts: 5BX for men and XBX for women. These graduated programs are arranged so that a specific number of exercises and repetitions are performed, depending upon your initial fitness. The more fit people select exercises from a chart listing more difficult exercises, while the less fit people select exercises from a chart illustrating less difficult exercises.

The XBX plan contains four charts of ten exercises, with each chart more difficult than the preceding one. Each chart is divided into twelve fitness levels. The 5BX includes six charts of five exercises each with each chart divided into twelve fitness "levels." Intensity of exercise increases progressively as one moves from level to level and from chart to chart. Persons planning to use the program should obtain a copy of the book. A sample program of moderate intensity is presented on the following pages.* The program is selected from the XBX plan for women, but is very similar to the plan for men.

Sample Program	Number of Repetitions
Exercise 1	10
Exercise 2	16
Exercise 3	12
Exercise 4	24
Exercise 5**	26
Exercise 6	28
Exercise 7	28
Exercise 8	22
Exercise 9	8
Exercise 10	140

*Used by permission Royal Canadian Air Force, *Exercise Plans for Physical Fitness.* Queen's Printer, Ottawa, Canada: Revised U.S. Edition, 1962. By special arrangement with *This Week Magazine.*

**Exercises with double asterisks have been modified to avoid possible back problems for those with weak back muscles.

Advantages and Disadvantages of the XBX and 5BX Programs

Advantages

1. Develops most all aspects of health-related fitness though it is doubtful that the program would build cardiovascular fitness in many people.
2. Graduated in intensity to meet the needs of a wide variety of people.

Disadvantages

1. Would need to be supplemented with cardiovascular fitness exercise for many.
2. Because it is basically a calisthenics program, it may be difficult to sustain interest in the program over a long period of time.

XBX and 5BX Exercises

1. Toe Touching. Start. Stand erect, feet about sixteen inches apart, arms overhead. Bend down to touch floor outside left foot. Bob up and down to touch floor between feet. Bob again and bend to touch floor outside right foot. Return to starting position.

Count. Each return to the starting position counts as one repetition.

2. Knee Raising. Start. Stand erect, feet together, arms at sides. Raise left knee as high as possible, grasping knee and shin with hands. Pull leg against body. Keep straight throughout. Lower foot to floor.

Repeat with right leg. Continue by alternating legs.

Count. Left knee raise plus right knee raise counts as one repetition.

3. Lateral Bending. Start. Stand erect, feet twelve inches apart, right arm extended over head, bent at elbow. Bend sidewards from waist to left. Slide left hand down leg as far as possible, and at the same time press to left with right arm. Return to starting position and change arm positions. Repeat to right. Continue by alternating to left, then right.

Count. Bend to left plus bend to right counts as one repetition.

4. Arm Circling. Start. Stand erect, feet twelve inches apart, arms at sides. Make large circles with arms in a windmill action—one arm following other and both moving at same time. Do half the number of repetitions making backward circles and half making forward circles.

Count. Each full circle by both arms counts as one repetition.

5. Sit-ups.** Start. Lie on back, knees bent and together, arms across chest. Roll shoulders and trunk forward to a sitting position. Return to starting position.
Count. Each return to the starting position counts as one repetition.

6. Chest and Leg Raising. Start. Lie face down, legs straight and together, arms stretched sidewards at shoulder level. Raise entire upper body and both legs from floor as high as possible. Keep legs straight. Return to starting position.
Count. Each return to the starting position counts as one repetition.

7. Side Leg Raising. Start. Lie on side with the legs straight along floor, top arm used for balance. Raise upper leg until it is perpendicular to floor. Lower to starting position.
Count. Each leg raise counts as one. Do half the number of repetitions raising the left leg. Roll to other side and do half with the right leg.

8. Modified Push-up. Start. Lie face down, hands directly under shoulders, knees on the floor. Raise body from floor by straightening it from head to knees. In the "up" position, the body should be in a straight line with palms of hands and knees in contact with floor. Lower to starting position. Keep head up throughout.
Count. Each return to the starting position counts as one repetition.

9. Leg-overs—Tuck. Start. Lie on back, legs straight and together, arms stretched sidewards at shoulder level, palms down. Raise both legs from floor, bending at hips and knees until in a tuck position. Lower legs to left, keeping knees together and both shoulders on floor. Twist hips and lower legs to floor on right side. Twist hips to tuck position and return to starting position. Keep knees close to abdomen throughout.
Count. Each return to the starting position counts as one repetition.

10. Run and Half Knee Bends. Start. Stand erect, feet together, arms at sides. Starting with left leg, run in place raising feet at least six inches from floor.
Each time the left foot touches the floor counts as one repetition. After each fifty counts do ten half knee bends.
Half Knee Bends. Start with hands on hips, feet together, body erect. Bend at knees and hips, lowering body until thigh and calf form an angle of about 90 degrees. Do not bend knees past a right angle. Keep back straight. Return to starting position.

The Progressive Rhythmical Endurance Program

Appendix

F

1. Depending upon your physical fitness test scores, you should participate for five, ten, or fifteen minutes. As you become more fit, you should progress to the point where you can exercise continuously for at least fifteen minutes. All persons should begin with the stretching exercises listed in the sample program.
2. Exercise should be done continuously. As you finish a specific exercise, get up and jog in place or in a circle.
3. After progressing to the point where you can exercise for the full fifteen minutes, you should begin jogging after completing all of the exercises. Some participants progress to the point where they perform the fifteen minutes of exercise and jog for an additional five to twenty minutes.

Advantages and Disadvantages of Progessive Rhythmical Endurance Exercises

Advantages

1. Develops all health-related aspects of fitness.
2. Can be kept interesting by changing the different exercises periodically.

Disadvantages

1. Is best when done with a group. Interest may lag if you must exercise by yourself.

A Sample Program* (see exercise illustrations below)

Stretching	5-Minute Circle Exercises	10-Minute Circle Exercises	15-Minute Circle Exercises
All stretching is passive and each exercise is held 5 to 6 seconds 3 standing hamstring stretches 3 lateral trunk stretches 3 sitting trunk stretches 3 back hperextensions	Jog in a circle 1 minute 7 bent knee sit-ups Lateral shuffle in circle 10 side leg-lifts (each leg) 25 side hop-kicks 7 push-ups Jog in a circle	15 jumping jacks 7 knee dips 15 jumping jacks Jog in a circle 5 bent-knee sit-ups Jog backward in a circle 10 back leg-lifts (one leg at a time) 5 long stride steps with each leg Jog in a circle	Jog in a circle 10 knee dips with each leg Jog in a circle 5 bent knee sit-ups 5 side leg-lifts (each leg) 5 interval sprints (first run a lap, walk a lap)

*Adapted from an article by C. B. Corbin, "An Exercise Program for Large Groups," *The Physical Educator* 30:46–47, March 1973. Used by permission.

Some general suggestions for using this exercise program are:

1. Stretch first to establish a pattern of regular stretching and to help eliminate possible soreness associated with the regular exercise program.
2. Start "too easy" rather than "too hard." You can always increase intensity after you determine your reaction to the exercise. You may wish to start out exercising for five or ten minutes and gradually progress to fifteen minutes.
3. If you exercise in a group, you may want to select a daily leader to choose the exercises. This can help motivate group members.
4. Vary the exercises daily but make sure all body parts are exercised.
5. Walk outside the circle if you find you need a slower pace. If the exercises are too difficult, start with what you can handle, but try to exercise continuously even if it is just walking at first.
6. Use whatever exercises are appropriate for your individual needs. The ones listed are merely suggestions.

Appendix
G

"Speed Play" or Fartlek Exercise

"Speed Play" (originally called Fartlek, the Swedish word for speed play) features varied speed running, walking, and some calisthenics. The program is designed to be psychologically stimulating by introducing a change in scenery and changing the pace of running. Those who prefer this type of running feel that it offers more diversity than jogging. Ideally, speed play is done over a course that provides a variety of terrain as opposed to being performed on a track. It can, however, be done on a track.

Advantages and Disadvantages of Speed Play or Fartlek Exercise

Advantages

1. A good means of achieving cardiovascular fitness and, to a lesser extent, other health-related fitness aspects.
2. Psychologically stimulating because of the break in monotony from changing speeds and scenery.

Disadvantages

1. The fast "anaerobic" sprints may be inappropriate for beginners and some older runners.
2. Primarily a cardiovascular program.
3. You must have more than a little information to plan a good speed play program of the appropriate intensity.

You can plan your own speed play program using your own course, which may include up and downhill running (common in the foothills of Sweden where it was developed) and other variations. The following is a sample program of moderate intensity.

A Sample Program*

1. Jog easily for three minutes.
2. Perform brisk calisthenics—no rest between exercises.
   a. Trunk stretch—With the feet spread, reach through the legs as far as possible. Hold for eight seconds. Repeat three times. (See page 292.)
   b. Do five to ten bent-knee sit-ups. (See page 280.)
   c. Run in place for fifty steps.
   d. Do five to ten push-ups or modified push-ups. (See page 289.)
   e. Do ten side leg raises with each leg. (See page 290.)
3. Run 200 yards at ¾ speed. Run on grassy area if possible.
4. Walk 200 yards.
5. Repeat 3 and 4.
6. Jog for two minutes.
7. Run 100 yards at ¾ speed.
8. Walk 100 yards.
9. Repeat 7 and 8.
10. Jog for two minutes.

*If this *sample* program is too vigorous for your current level of fitness, walk instead of performing the exercise as outlined.

Interval Training

Interval training is a type of anaerobic exercise that involves alternate running and resting. Interval training is considered to be intermittent exercise and to be effective, one should use the threshold of training and fitness target zone guidelines discussed in the section on cardiovascular fitness on page 27.

Advantages and Disadvantages of Interval Training

Advantages

1. Anaerobic or interval exercise is a good method for building cardiovascular fitness.
2. Proponents argue that alternate running and walking is more interesting than the more regular nature of jogging.
3. If planned properly, you can do more work for improving fitness in a shorter period of time.

Disadvantages

1. Interval sprints may be inappropriate for beginners and some older people.
2. Interval training is designed primarily as a cardiovascular fitness program.

For longer distances (more than 100 yards), running should be estimated at approximately eighty percent of your maximum running speed. Rest periods for these longer runs should be of the same length as the running and should not be complete rests but should consist of walking or slow jogging. Shorter runs may be done above 80 percent of maximum speed. Rests should end when the heart rate returns to 120.

A Sample Program

1. Jog for three minutes to warm up.
2. Run for 440 yards around a track or elsewhere at 80 percent of maximum speed.
3. Walk 220 yards.
4. Repeat 2 and 3.
5. Run 100 yards at 80 percent effort or faster. Immediately after exercise, count your ten-second heart rate. Continue to count the heart rate for ten-second intervals until the heart rate for one ten-second period times 6 equals 120. Then repeat the 100-yard run.
6. Do five 100-yard runs with alternate rests. Walk or slowly jog during rests. (If no watch or clock is available, walk for about 100 years or jog about 150 yards between runs.) If you plan to use interval running regularly, you should get a watch and determine accurately the length of your rest period.
7. Repeat steps 2 and 3.

Jogging is a type of slow running that can be used to improve your level of cardiovascular fitness. To be effective, you should jog fast enough to elevate your heart rate to the threshold of training and in the fitness target zone. Refer to Table 5.1 for some general guidelines and Chart 4.1 for information about the target heart rate for improving your cardiovascular fitness.

There are some techniques that every jogger should be familiar with before starting a jogging program.

1. *Foot Placement*—The heel of the foot hits the ground first in jogging. Your heel should strike before the rest of the foot (but not vigorously) and then you should rock forward and push off with the ball of your foot. Contrary to some opinion, you should *not* jog on your toes. (A flat foot landing can be all right as long as you push off with the ball of the foot.) The toes should point straight ahead. The feet should stay under the knees and should *not* swing out to the sides as you jog.
2. *Length of Stride*—For efficiency, you should have a relatively long stride. Your stride should be at least several inches longer than your walking stride. If necessary, you may have to "reach" to lengthen your stride. Most older people find it more efficient to run with a shorter stride.
3. *Arm Movement*—While you jog you should work with the arms as well as the legs. The arms should be bent at about 90 degrees and should swing freely and alternately from front to back. The arms should swing in the direction you are moving and not from side to side. Keep the arms and hands relaxed.
4. *Body Position*—While jogging the upper body should be nearly erect. The head and chest should be held up and there should not be a conscious effort to lean forward as is the case in sprinting or fast running.
5. Refer to page 124 for a discussion of some of the common problems experienced by joggers.

Weight Training

Weight training is perhaps the most effective type of training to improve muscular strength. There are as many different weight-training exercises as there are different muscles in the body. However, there are a few exercises that require overload of the major muscle groups. These exercises are presented on the following pages within this appendix.

Before beginning a weight training program you should review the guidelines for strength development on Table 7.1 and the Principles of Isotonic Strength on Table 7.2.

Also, prior to beginning a regular weight-training program it is important to test yourself to determine the optimal weights to be lifted for each exercise. This is done by trial and error. Begin lifting *too little* weight at first. Determine the maximum amount you can lift for four repetitions of each exercise. Do one set of four repetitions at ½ maximum, the next set at ¾ maximum, and the final set at maximum weight. As you improve, increase the repetitions until you can do eight in each set. Then increase the weight and resume four repetitions.

Advantages and Disadvantages of Weight Training

Advantages

1. Weight training is probably the best method available for developing strength and, to a lesser extent, muscular endurance.
2. Weight training can result in significant changes in appearance that are favorable to both men and women.

Disadvantages

1. Weight training does little to improve the health-related aspects of physical fitness other than strength and muscular endurance.

Sample Weight Training Exercises

Shoulder Shrug

Purpose

Strengthen the muscles of the shoulders and arms.

Position

1. Palms toward body.
2. Bar touching thighs.
3. Legs straight.
4. Feet together.

Movement

1. Lift shoulders (try to touch ears).
2. Roll shoulders smoothly backward.
3. Roll shoulders down and forward.
4. Repeat maximum number of times.

Military Press

Purpose

Strengthen the muscles of the shoulders and arms.

Position

1. Palms forward (chest position, front grip).
2. Hands spread (slightly more than shoulder width).
3. Bar touching chest.
4. Feet spread (comfortable distance).
5. Feet flat, legs straight.

Movement

1. Move bar to overhead position (arms straight).
2. Lower to chest position.
3. Repeat.

Appendixes

Half Squats

Purpose

Strengthen the muscles of the thighs and hips.

Position

1. Begin in standing position.
2. Rest bar behind neck on shoulders.
3. Spread hands (comfortable position).
4. Feet at 45° angle.

Movement

1. Squat slowly.
2. Back straight, eyes ahead.
3. Bend knees to 90°, keep knees over feet.
4. Pause, then stand.
5. Repeat.

Curls

Purpose

Strengthen the muscles of the upper front part of the arms.

Position

1. Palms away from body (reverse grip).
2. Arms spread in order not to touch body.
3. Bar touching thighs.
4. Spread feet (comfortable position).

Movement

1. Move bar to chin.
2. Keep body straight.
3. Keep elbows forward of center line of body.
4. Don't allow elbows to touch body.
5. Lower to original position.
6. Repeat.

Elbow Extension Behind Neck

Purpose

Strengthen the muscles of the back part of the upper arms (triceps).

Position

1. Front grip.
2. Hands together at center of bar.
3. Feet spread, body straight.
4. Rest bar behind neck on shoulders.
5. Point elbows upward.

Movement

1. Hold upper arms stationary.
2. Raise weight overhead.
3. Return bar to original position.
4. Repeat.

Toe Raises

Purpose

Strengthen muscles of the lower back part of the legs (calf).

Position

1. Front grip.
2. Hands wider than shoulder width apart.
3. Bar resting behind neck on shoulders.
4. Legs straight.
5. Balls of feet resting on 2-inch block with heels on floor.
6. *Variations*:
    (a) Toes together, heels apart.
    (b) Feet apart, toes straight ahead.

Movement

1. Rise on toes quickly.
2. Hold for one second.
3. Lower heels to floor.
4. Repeat.

Pull to Chin

Purpose

Strengthen muscles of the shoulders and arms.

Position

1. Front grip (loose).
2. Hands together at center of bar.
3. Bar touching thighs.
4. Feet spread, body straight.
5. Head erect, eyes straight ahead.

Movement

1. Pull bar to chin.
2. Keep elbows close to body.
3. Keep elbows well above bar.
4. Lower to extended position.
5. Repeat.

Isometric Exercise

Isometric exercises are intended primarily to develop muscular strength and endurance. Sixteen different exercises for different body parts are presented here. You should select exercises for your program (if you choose isometric exercise) that meet your own personal needs.

Before performing isometric exercises as part of your exercise program, you should review the guidelines for strength development in Table 7.1 and the Principles of Isometric Exercise in Table 7.2.

Advantages and Disadvantages of Isometric Exercise

Advantages

1. Isometrics are good for developing strength and muscular endurance.
2. Isometrics require little equipment and little space.

Disadvantages

1. Isometric exercises do nothing to promote flexibility and cardiovascular fitness. Isometrics should be avoided by those with high blood pressure or heart disease.
2. It may be hard to motivate yourself for maximal contractions.

Sample Isometric Exercises

All of the following exercises should be held for five to eight seconds and should be repeated several times a day.

3. Forearms parallel to floor.
4. Attempt to pull hands apart with maximum force.

Chest Push

Purpose

Develop muscles of the chest and upper arms.

1. Place left fist in palm of right hand.
2. Keep hands close to chest.
3. Forearms parallel to floor.
4. Push hands together with maximum strength.

Fist Squeeze

Purpose

Develop muscles of the lower arm.

1. Arms extended at side.
2. Clench fists as hard as possible.
3. Repeat.

Shoulder Pull

Purpose

Develop muscles of the upper back and arms.

1. Cup hands and interlock fingers.
2. Keep hands close to chest.

Neck Pull

Purpose

Develop muscles of the neck, upper back, and arms.

1. Interlock fingers behind head.
2. Elbows pointing forward.
3. Force head backward.
4. Pull hands forward with maximum strength.

Strengthen Back

Purpose

Develop muscles of arms, legs, and hips.

1. Loop rope under feet.
2. Stand on rope, feet spread shoulder width.
3. Keep back straight.
4. Bend knees, grasp both ends of rope.
5. Back erect and arms straight, buttocks low.
6. Lift upward with maximum strength.

Overhead Pull

Purpose

Develop muscles of the arms and shoulders.

1. Fold rope in a double loop.
2. Grasp rope overhead, palms outward.
3. Extend arms.
4. Push outward at maximum force.
5. Repeat with palms in.

Curls

Purpose

Develop muscles of the upper arms.

1. Place rope loop behind thighs while standing in a half squat position.
2. Grasp loop, palms up, shoulder width.
3. Lift upward with maximum strength.
4. For reverse curls, repeat gripping with palms down.

Foot lift

Purpose

Develop muscles of legs.

1. Stand on loop with left foot.
2. Place loop around right ankle.
3. Flex knee until taut.
4. Apply maximum strength upward.
5. Repeat forward, to side, with both feet.

Military Press in Doorway

Purpose

Develop muscles of the arms and shoulders.

1. Stand in doorway.
2. Face straight ahead.
3. Hands shoulder width apart, elbows bent.
4. Tighten leg, hip, and back muscles.
5. Push upward as hard as possible.

Arm Press in Doorway

Purpose

Develop muscles of the arms.

1. Stand in doorway.
2. Back flat on one side of doorway, hands placed on other side.
3. Push with maximum strength.

Leg Press in Doorway

Purpose

Develop muscles of the legs.

1. Sit in doorway facing side of door frame.
2. Grasp molding behind head.
3. Keep back flat on side of doorway, feet against other side.
4. Push legs with maximum strength.

Wall Seat

Purpose

Develop muscles of the leg and hips.

1. Assume half-sit position.
2. Back flat against wall.
3. Knees bent to 90°.
4. Push back against wall with maximum strength.

Appendixes

Triceps Extension

Purpose

Develop muscles of upper arm.

1. Grasp towel at both ends.
2. Hold left hand at small of back.
3. Right hand over shoulder.
4. Pull towel with maximum force.
5. Repeat exercise by changing position of hands.

Leg Extension

Purpose

Develop muscles of thigh.

1. Place towel around right ankle.
2. Knee bent at 90° angle.
3. Grasp towel with both hands behind back.
4. Extend leg downward with maximum force.
5. Repeat exercise by changing legs.

Waist Pull

Purpose

Develop muscles of the abdomen and arms.

1. Grasp ends of towel, palms in.
2. Towel around back of waist.
3. Elbows flexed to right angle.
4. Pull forward on towel with maximum strength while contracting abdomen and flattening back.

Bow Exercise

Purpose

Develop muscles of arms, shoulders and upper back.

1. Take archer's position with bow (towel) drawn.
2. Left elbow partially extended.
3. Right hand at chin, right arm parallel to floor.
4. Grasp towel and pull arms away from each other.
5. Exchange positions of hands and repeat.

Gluteal Pinch

Purpose

Develop muscles of the buttocks.

1. Lie prone, heels apart and big toes touching.
2. Pinch the buttocks together; hold several seconds.
3. Slowly relax.
4. Repeat several times.

Pelvic Tilt

Purpose

Develop muscles of the abdomen and buttocks.

1. Assume a supine position with the knees bent and slightly apart.
2. Press the spine down on the floor and hold for five seconds.
3. Keep abdominals and gluteals tightened.

Appendix L

Isotonic Exercises for Muscular Endurance and Mild Strengthening

The exercises suggested here should be performed as described until the person is able to increase the repetitions to approximately twenty-five or more for some exercises; then additional weight should be added.

Advantages and Disadvantages of Isotonic Exercises for People with Limited Strength

Advantages

1. Suitable for persons with a wide range of strength levels.
2. Suitable for figure or physique control and postural correction.
3. Designed for muscular endurance and mild strengthening.

Disadvantages

1. These exercises will not increase cardiovascular fitness and have only limited ability to increase strength.

Sample Isotonic Exercises

Bent Knee Let-downs

For those who cannot do bent-knee push-ups.

Purpose

Develop muscles of the arms, shoulders, and chest.

Let-downs

Assume a bent-knee push-up position and slowly lower the body to the floor, keeping the body line straight; return to the starting position in any manner.

Full-length Push-ups

Purpose

Develop muscles of arms and chest.

Full-length Push-ups

Take front-leaning rest position, arms straight. Lower chest to floor. Press to beginning position in same manner. Repeat exercise as many times as possible up to thirty-five.

Bent Knee Push-ups

For those who cannot do full-length push-ups.

Purpose

Develop muscles of the arms, shoulders, and chest.

Push-ups

Assume the push-up position. Lower the body until the chest touches the floor; return to the starting position keeping the body straight.

Modified Pull-ups

Purpose

Develop muscles of the arms, shoulders, and chest.

Pull-ups

Hang (palms forward and shoulder width apart) from a low bar (may be placed across two chairs), heels on floor, with the body straight from feet to head; pull up, keeping the body straight, and touch the chest to the bar, then lower to the starting position. (Stronger persons may hang from a bar vertically and pull up.)

Pull-ups (Chinning)

Purpose

Develop muscles of arms and shoulders.

Pull-ups (Chinning)

Hang from bar, palms forward, body and arms straight. Pull up until chin is over bar. Repeat as many times as possible up to thirty-five.

Reverse Sit-ups

Purpose

Develop the lower abdominal muscles and correct abdominal ptosis.

Reverse Sit-ups

Lie on the floor, bend the knees, place the feet flat on the floor, and place arms at sides; life the knees to the chest raising the hips off the floor; return to the starting position.

Bent-knee Sit-ups

Purpose

Develop the upper abdominal muscles and correct ptosis.

Sit-ups

Assume a hook-lying position with arms crossed and hands on shoulders; roll up, making elbows touch knees, then roll down to the starting position.

Leg Extension Exercise

Purpose

Develop muscles of the hips.

Leg Extension

Assume a knee-chest position, hands on floor with arms extended as far as possible; extend right leg upward in line with trunk; then lower. Continue repetitions, repeat with other leg.

Prone Back Lift

Purpose

Develop muscles of the upper back. Correct kyphosis and round shoulders.

Prone Back Lift

Lie prone (face down) with hands clasped behind the neck. Pull the shoulder blades together, raising the elbows off the floor; slowly raise the head and chest off the floor by arching the upper back; return to the starting position; repeat. Caution: Do not arch the lower back; lift only until the sternum (breast bone) clears the floor.

Side Leg Raises

Purpose

Develop muscles on outside of thighs.

Side Leg Raise

Lie on the side and raise the top leg toward the ceiling, then return. Do the same number of repetitions with each leg.

Lower Leg Lift

Purpose

Develop muscles on the inside of thighs.

Lower Leg Lift

Lie on the side with the upper leg (foot) supported on a bench; raise the lower leg toward the ceiling; repeat on opposite side.

Forward Lunge

Purpose

Develop muscles of the legs and hips.

Forward Lunge

Stand tall, feet together. Take a long step forward with the left foot touching the right knee to the floor. Return to the starting position and step out with the other foot. Repeat, alternating left and right.

Sitting Tucks or "V Sit"

Purpose

Develop muscles of abdomen and legs.

Sitting Tucks or "V Sit"

Sit on the floor so that the back and feet are off the floor. Interlock fingers behind the head. Alternately draw the legs into the chest and extend the feet away from the body. Keep feet and back off the floor. Repeat as many times as possible up to thirty-five.

Stationary Leg Change

Purpose

Develop muscles of the legs and hips.

Stationary Leg Change

Crouch on the floor with weight on hands, left leg bent under the chest, right leg extended behind. Alternate legs; bring right leg up while left leg goes back. Repeat as many times as possible up to fifty.

Appendix
M

Flexibility Exercises

Before you use flexibility exercises in your regular program of exercise, you should review the guidelines for flexibility development on page 55 (Table 8.3) and the table comparing the advantages of passive and active flexibility exercises on page 54 (Table 8.2).

Specific instructions for performing each exercise are provided opposite each exercise illustration.

Advantages and Disadvantages of a Flexibility Exercise Program

Advantages

1. Flexibility exercises can serve as "limbering up" exercises in addition to developing flexibility.
2. Flexibility exercises can complement strength and muscular endurance exercises and keep muscles from becoming too short or "muscle-bound."

Disadvantages

1. Flexibility exercises do not promote all health-related fitness aspects.

Sample Flexibility Exercises

3. To. Stretch Muscles on Inside of Thighs. Sit with the knees apart and the legs crossed at the ankles. Place the hands on the inside of the knees and push toward the floor. Hold for several seconds and repeat. Useful for pregnant women or anyone whose thighs tend to rotate inward causing knock-knees and foot pronation.

1. To Stretch the Calf Muscles and Achilles Tendons. Stand with the toes on a thick book or lower rung of a stall bar; hold on to a support with hands; lower heels toward floor as far as possible; hold several seconds. Repeat several times. If an active stretch is desired, bounce gently.

4. To Stretch the Lower Back. Lie supine, arms at sides, draw bent knees to chest, then straighten legs so they are over the head and trunk, parallel to floor (do not allow buttocks to go beyond head); hold several seconds; return to starting position by bringing bent knees back to chest. Repeat several times. Avoid getting the weight over the neck and avoid straight-leg lowering. Useful for backache and lordosis.

2. To Stretch Lower Back and Hamstring Muscles. Stand with one foot on a bench; keeping both legs straight, bend the trunk forward, trying to touch the head to the knee; hold for a few seconds; return to starting position and repeat with opposite leg. As flexibility improves, the arms can be used to pull the chest toward the legs. Useful in relief of backache and correction of lordosis. If an active stretch is desired, bounce gently.

5. Pectoral Stretch. Stand erect in doorway with arms raised shoulder height, elbows bent and hands grasping doorjambs; step forward with either foot, forcing chest forward; repeat several times. Useful for round shoulders, kyphosis, and sunken chest.

7. Flexibility Stunt. (A) Grasp a broomstick, or wand, with palms down about shoulder's width apart; (B) Reach the end of broomstick and the left hand between the legs; (C) Step with left leg around the outside of the arm and between the stick and the body; (D) Slide the stick over the left knee, left hip, and back; and (E) Step the right foot over the stick and stand holding the stick in front of body, palms up.

6. Lateral Trunk Flexibility. Stand with feet shoulder width apart, hands on hips. Stretch left arm over head to right. Bend to right at waist reaching as far to right as possible with left arm. Repeat to left side with right arm reaching over head to left. Repeat several times.

8. Mosher Exercise—For Relief of Dysmenorrhea. In a supine position with the knees bent and feet on the floor, suck in the abdomen and tip the pelvis backward. Try to press the low back flat against the floor. Hold for six seconds, then try to "blow up" abdomen (balloon), pushing it out until it stretches. Relax and repeat.

Some suggest that this exercise can be of benefit if performed after exercise as well as during the warm-up; also good conditioning for snow skiing.

Face the wall with feet together three to four feet from the wall. Keeping the body straight lean forward and support the upper body on the wall. Keep the heels on the floor. Hold for six to twelve seconds, stretching the calf muscles and Achilles tendon.

11. Exercises for Leg Soreness (Shin Splints). "Shin splints" are a common source of muscle pain that results from exercise, particularly exercise that involves bouncing on the legs, such as in basketball or even jogging on a hard surface. Regular passive stretching can help reduce "shin splint" soreness. This exercise may be performed before your regular exercise program as a warm-up. Some suggest that it may be done after exercise as a prevention against future soreness. NOTE: If pain persists, is severe, or other evidence of muscle injury exists, discontinue this exercise until you get a medical diagnosis of the exact nature of your problem.

Kneel with the front of the lower leg in contact with the floor. The toes should be pointed backward with the top of the foot in contact with the floor. Gently lean the upper body back thus stretching the "shin" muscles (also good to increase strength of abdominals and hip flexors on the return movement).

9. Billig's Exercise—For Dysmenorrhea (painful menstruation). Menstrual cramps are a problem experienced by many women. This exercise, if done regularly, can help relieve menstrual pain. This exercise can be done before exercise or it can be done as a part of your regular exercise program. The exercise is for women, but men may choose to learn the exercise so that they may pass it on to women who may benefit from it.

Stand with side to a wall and place the elbow and forearm against the wall at shoulder height. *Tilt the pelvis backward tightening the gluteal and abdominal muscles.* Place opposite hand on hip and push the hips toward the wall. Push forward and sideward (45°) with the hips. *Do not twist the hips.* A stretch should be felt in the abdominal region. Hold this position for several seconds. Keep knees straight and the chest high. Repeat several times as necessary.

10. Sore calf muscles are another problem common to people who participate in regular exercise. Passive stretching of the calf muscles during a warm-up can help relieve the soreness of these muscles.

References

"All the News That's Fit." *Fitness for Living,* vol. 15, July–August, 1971, p. 150.

Almekinder, E., and LaPoint, J. S. "Current Development in Exercise Structure." *Scholastic Coach* 46 (November 1976):54.

American Alliance for Health, Physical Education and Recreation. *Nutrition for Athletes.* Washington, D.C., 1971.

American College of Sports Medicine. "Position Statement on the Use and Abuse of Anabolic—Androgenic Steroids in Sports." *Medicine and Science in Sports* 9 (1977):xi.

———. "Position Statement on the Recommended Quantity and Quality of Exercise for Developing and Maintaining Fitness in Healthy Adults." *Medicine and Science in Sports* 10 (Fall 1978):vii.

———. "Weight Loss in Wrestlers: Position Stand of American College of Sports Medicine." Madison, Wisconsin, in Alsen, P.E. editor, *Conditioning and Physical Fitness*, Dubuque, Ia.: Wm. C. Brown Company Publishers, 1978.

American Physical Therapy Association. "Take Three Steps, Stoop Down, Pick up a Pencil." 1980, p. 2–3.

Armstrong, R. B., et al. "Structure and Function of Skeletal Muscle." *Physician and Sports Medicine* 5 (May 1977):34.

Astrand, P. O., and Rodahl, K. *Textbook of Work Physiology.* 2d ed. New York: McGraw-Hill Book Company, 1977.

Bailey, Covert. *Fit or Fat.* Boston: Houghton Mifflin Co., 1978.

Barber, T. S., et al., eds. *Biofeedback and Self-Control.* Chicago: Aldine-Atherton, 1971.

Barnard, R. J. "The Heart Needs a Warm-up Time." *The Physician and Sports Medicine* 4 (1976):40.

Benson, H. *The Relaxation Response.* New York: William Morrow and Co., Inc., 1975.

Bishop, R. D., and Hay, J. G. "Basketball: The Mechanics of Hanging in the Air." *Medicine and Science In Sports* 11, no. 3 (1979):274–277.

Bogert, L. J., Briggs, G. M., and Calloway, D. H. *Nutrition and Physical Fitness.* 9th ed. Philadelphia: W. B. Saunders Co., 1973.

Boyer, J. L. "Effects of Chronic Exercise on Cardiovascular Function." *Physical Fitness Research Digest* 2 (July 1972):1.

———. "Mechanisms by Which Physical Activity May Reduce the Occurrence or Severity of Coronary Heart Disease." *Physical Fitness Research Digest* 2 (October 1972):1.

———. "Mechanisms by Which Physical Activity May Reduce the Occurrence or Severity of Coronary Heart Disease." *Physical Fitness Research Digest* 2 (October 1972):1.

Broer, M. *Efficiency of Human Movement.* 3d ed. Philadelphia: W. B. Saunders Co., 1973.

Brown, L. H., and Wilmore, J. H. "The Effects of Maximal Resistance Training on the Strength and Body Composition of Women Athletes." *Medicine and Science in Sports* 6 (1974):174.

Brown, R. S. "The Prescription of Exercise for Depression." *The Physician and Sports Medicine* 6 (December 1978):34.

Brunner, B. C. "How Will Today's Physical Education Classes be Remembered in 1989?" *Journal of Health, Physical Education and Recreation* 40 (February 1969):42.

Bunn, W. *Scientific Principles of Coaching.* Englewood Cliffs, N.J.: Prentice-Hall, Inc. 1972.

Bunnell, R. H., DeRitter, E., and Rubin, S. H. "Effect of Feeding Polyunsaturated Fatty Acids with a Low Vitamin E Diet on Blood Levels of Tocopheral in Men Performing Hard Physical Labor." *American Journal of Clinical Nutrition* 28 (July 1975):706.

Burt, J. J., Blyth, C. S.; and Rierson, H. A. "Effects of Exercise on the Coagulation—Fibrinolysis Equilibrium." *Journal of Sports Medicine and Physical Fitness* 4 (1964):213.

Butler, R. N. "Psychological Importance of Physical Fitness." *Testimony on Physical Fitness for Older Persons.* Washington, D.C.: National Association for Human Development, 1975.

Campbell, C. J., et al. "Muscle Fiber Composition and Performance Capabilities of Women." *Medicine and Science in Sports* 11 (1979):260.

Cantwell, J. D.; Watt, E. W.; and Piper, J. H. "Fitness, Aerobic Points, and Coronary Risk." *The Physician and Sports Medicine* 7 (August 1979):79.

Carmack, M. A., and Martens, R. "Measuring Commitment to Running: A Survey of Runners Attitudes and Mental States." *Journal of Sport Psychology* 1(1979):25.

Carr, R. *The Yoga Way to Release Tension.* New York: Coward, McCann & Geoghegan, Inc., 1974.

Carroll, C., and Miller, D. *Health: The Science of Human Adaptation.* Dubuque, Ia: Wm. C. Brown Company Publishers, 1979.

Castelli, W. P., et al. "HDL, Cholesterol, and Other Lipids in Coronary Heart Disease." *Circulation* 55 (May 1977):767.

Clarke, D. H. "Adaptations in Strength and Muscular Endurance Resulting from Exercise." In *Exercise and Sport Sciences Reviews,* Edited by Jack H. Wilmore. New York: Academic Press, 1973. pp. 74–102.

Clarke, D. H., and Henry, F. M. "Neuromuscular Specificity and Increased Speed from Strength Development." *Research Quarterly* 32 (1961):315.

Clarke, H. H., ed. "Toward a Better Understanding of Muscular Strength." *Physical Fitness Research Digest* 3 (January 1973):1.

————, ed. "Circulatory-Respiratory Endurance." *Physical Fitness Research Digest* 4 (July 1973):1.

————, ed. "Development of Muscular Strength and Endurance." *Physical Fitness Research Digest* 4 (January 1974):1.

————, ed. "National Adult Physical Fitness Survey." *Physical Fitness Research Digest* 4 (April 1974):1.

————, ed. "Strength Development and Motor Sports Improvement." *Physical Fitness Research Digest* 4 (October 1974):1.

————, ed. "Exercise and Fat Reduction." *Physical Fitness Research Digest* 5 (April 1975):1.

————, ed. "Joint and Body Range of Movement." *Physical Fitness Research Digest* 5 (October 1975):1.

————, ed. "Exercise and Fat Reduction." *Physical Fitness Research Digest* 5 (1975):1.

————, ed. "Diet and Exercise in Relation to Peripheral Vascular Disease." *Physical Fitness Research Digest* 6 (1976):11.

————, ed. "Update: Exercise and Some Coronary Risk Factors." *Physical Fitness Research Digest* 9 (July 1979):1.

Compton, D., et al. "Weight Lifter's Blackout." *Lancet*, December 1973.

Conner, J. F. et al. "Effects of Exercise on Coronary Collateralization: Angiographic Analysis of Six Patients in a Supervised Exercise Program." *Medicine and Science in Sports* 8 (Fall 1976):145.

Conrad, C. C. "Physical Fitness for the Elderly." *Testimony on Physical Fitness for Older Persons*. Washington, D.C.: National Association for Human Development, 1975.

Consolazio, C. F., Johnson, H. L., and Nelson, R. A. "Protein Metabolism During Intensive Physical Training in the Young Adult." *American Journal of Clinical Nutrition* 28 (January 1975):29.

Cooper, D. L. "Drugs and the Athlete." *Journal of the American Medical Association* 221 (August 28, 1972):1107.

Cooper, D. L., and Fair, J. "Stretching Exercises for Flexibility." *The Physician and Sports Medicine* 5 (1977):114.

Cooper, K. H. *The Aerobics Way*. New York: M. Evans and Co., 1977.

Corbin, C. B. "A Study of Spectator Attitudes About Sportsmanship." *Texas Association of Health, Physical Education and Recreation Journal* 40 (1971):6.

————, "Overload." *Encyclopedia of Sport Sciences and Medicine*. New York: The Macmillan Company, 1971.

————, "Mental Practice." In *Ergogenic Aids and Muscular Performance*. Edited by W. P. Morgan. New York: Academic Press, 1972.

————, "Attitudes Toward Physical Activity of Champion Woman Basketball Players." *International Journal of Sport Psychology* 7 (1976):14.

————. *Becoming Physically Educated in the Elementary School*, 2d ed. Philadelphia: Lea and Febiger, 1976.

Corbin, C. B., ed. *A Textbook of Motor Development*. 2d ed. Dubuque, Ia.: Wm. C. Brown Company Publishers, 1980.

Corbin, C. B., and Laurie, D. R. "Exercise for a Lifetime: An Educational Effort." *The Physician and Sports Medicine* 6 (January 1978):50.

Corbin, C. B., and Lindsey, R. *Fitness for Life*. Glenview, Ill.: Scott, Foresman and Co. 1979.

Corbin, C. B., and Noble, L. "Flexibility." *Journal of Physical Education and Recreation*, June 1980.

Costill, D. L.; Cole, R.; Miller, E.; Miller, T., and Wynder, S. "Water and Electrolyte Replacement During Repeated Days of Work in the Heat." *Aviation Space Environmental Medicine* 46 (June 1975):795.

Costill, D. L., et al. "Skeletal Muscle Enzymes and Fiber Composition in Male and Female Track Athletes." *Journal of Applied Physiology* 40 (1976):149.

Costill, D. L., et al. "Lipid Metabolism in Skeletal Muscle of Endurance Trained Males and Females." *Journal of Applied Physiology* 47 (1979):787.

Cratty, B. J. *Social Dimensions of Physical Activity*. Englewood Cliffs, N.J.: Prentice-Hall, Inc., 1967.

Csikszentmihalyi, M. *Beyond Boredom and Anxiety*. San Francisco: Jossey-Bass, 1977.

Cunningham, D. A., et al. "The Effects of Training: Physiological Responses." *Medicine and Science in Sports* 11 (1979):379.

Daniels, L., and Worthingham, C. *Therapeutic Exercise.* 2d ed. Philadelphia: W. B. Saunders Co. 1977.

Dawber, T. R. "Risk Factors in Young Adults: The Lessons from Epidemiologic Studies of Cardiovascular Disease—Framingham, Tecumseh, and Evans County." *Journal of the American College Health Association* 22 (1973):84.

Dedmon, R. E. "An Industry Health Management Program." *The Physician and Sports Medicine* 7 (November 1979):56.

deVries, H. A. *Physiology of Exercise.* 3d ed. Dubuque, Ia: Wm. C. Brown Company Publishers, 1980.

————. "What Research Tells Us Regarding the Contribution of Exercise to the Health of Older People." *Testimony on the Physical Fitness of Older People.* Washington, D.C.: National Association for Human Development, 1975, pp. 3–7.

Dodge, D. L., and Martin, W. T. *Social Stress and Chronic Illness.* Notre Dame, Indiana: University of Notre Dame Press, 1970.

Dressendorfer, R. H. "Serum Lipid Levels in Male Runners." *The Physician and Sports Medicine* 7 (January 1979):119.

Ecker, T. "Angle of Release in Shot Putting." *Athletic Journal* 50 (February 1970):52.

Eckstein, R. "Effect of Exercise and Coronary Artery Narrowing on Coronary Collateral Circulation." *Circulation Research* 5 (1957):230.

Eitzen, D. S., and Sage, G. H. *Sociology of American Sport.* Dubuque, Ia.: Wm. C. Brown Company Publishers, 1978.

Ellis, M. J. *Why People Play.* Englewood Cliffs, N.J.: Prentice-Hall, Inc. 1973.

Elrich, H. "Exercise and the Aging Process." *Testimony on Physical Fitness for Older Persons.* Washington, D.C.: National Association for Human Development, 1975.

Fait, H. F. *Special Physical Education: Adapted, Corrective, Developmental.* 4th ed. Philadelphia: W. B. Saunders Co., 1978.

Fardy, P. S. "Cardiovascular Function of Former Athletes." *The Physician and Sports Medicine* 6 (August 1978):34.

Farfan, H. F. *Mechanical Disorders of the Low Back.* Philadelphia: Lea and Febiger, 1973.

Fast, J. *Body Language.* New York: Pocket Books, 1971.

Federal Trade Commission News, Washington, D.C., 23 July 1970.

Feffer, H. L. "All About Backaches—Latest Advice from a Specialist." *U.S. News and World Report* 71 (September 20, 1971):74.

Finneson, B. E. *Low Back Pain.* Philadelphia: J. B. Lippincott Co., 1973.

Fisher, A. C. *Psychology of Sport.* Palo Alto, Calif.: Mayfield, 1976.

Fisher, D. D. *I Know You Hurt But There's Nothing to Bandage.* Beaverton, Oregon: Touchstone Press, 1978.

Fox, S. M.; Naughton, J. P.; and Skinner, J. S. "Physical Activity in Prevention of Coronary Heart Disease." *Annals of Clinical Research* 3 (1971):404.

Frederick, C. J. "Suicide in the United States." *Health Education* 8 (November-December 1977):17.

Freed, D. L. J.; Banks, A. J.; Longson, D.; and Burley, D. M. "Anabolic Steroids in Athletics: Crossover Double-blind Trial on Weightlifters." *British Medical Journal* 2 (May 1975):471.

Fried, J. J. "Biofeedback: Teaching Your Body to Heal Itself." *Family Health*, February, 1974; and *Readers Digest*, May, 1974, p. 110.

Friedman, L. W., and Galton, L. *Freedom from Backaches.* New York: Simon & Schuster, 1973.

Friedman, M., and Rosenman, R. H. *Type A Behavior and Your Heart.* New York: A. A. Knopf, 1974.

Gench, B. E. "Cardiovascular Adaptations for College Women to Training at Pre-determined Individualized Heart Rate Levels for Varied Durations." *The Foil,* p. 56, 1975.

Gettman, L. R., et al. "The Effect of Circuit Weight Training on Strength, Cardio-vascular Function, and Body Composition of Adult Males." *Medicine and Science in Sports* 10 (1978):171.

Glass, D. C., and Singer, J. E. *Urban Stress: Experiments on Noise and Social Stressors.* New York: Academic Press, 1972.

Glasser, W. *Positive Addiction.* New York: Harper & Row, 1976.

Goldberg, A. L., et al. "Mechanism of Work-Induced Hypertrophy of Skeletal Muscle." *Medicine and Science in Sports* 7 (1975):248.

Gollnick, P. D. "The Muscle Biopsy: Still a Research Tool." *The Physician and Sports Medicine* 8 (January 1980):50.

Grandjean, E. *Fitting the Task to the Man.* London: Taylor and Francis, Ltd., 1969.
———. *Ergonomics of the Home.* New York: Halsted Press, 1974.

Greene, E., and Bilger, A., ed. *Winter's Protective Body Mechanics.* Ref. ed. New York: Springer Publishing Co. 1973.

Greist J. H. "Running Out of Depression." *The Physician and Sports Medicine* 6 (December 1978):49.

Gunderson, E. K. E., and Rahe, R. H., eds. *Life Stress and Illness.* Springfield, Ill.: Charles C Thomas, Publisher, 1974.

Hammond, J. *Understanding Human Engineering.* Vancouver, B. C.: David & Charles, 1978.

Harris, L. and associates. *The Perrier Study: Fitness in America.* New York: Great Waters of France, 1979.

Hartung, G. H., and Squires, W. G. "Exercise and HDL Cholesterol in Middle Aged Men." *The Physician and Sports Medicine* 8 (January 1980):74.

Hartung, G. H. et al. "Relation of Diet to High Density—Lipoprotein Cholesterol in Middle-Aged Marathon Runners, Joggers, and Inactive Men." *New England Journal of Medicine* 302 (1980):357.

Hay, J. *Biomechanics of Sports Techniques,* 2d ed. Englewood Cliffs, N.J.: Prentice-Hall, Inc. 1978.

Herkowitz, J. "Social Psychological Correlates to Motor Development." *A Textbook of Motor Development.* 2d ed. Edited by C. B. Corbin. Dubuque, Ia.: Wm. C. Brown Company Publishers, 1980.

Hernlund, V., and Steinhaus, A. H. "Do Mechanical Vibrators Take Off or Redistribute Fat?" *Journal of the Association of Physical and Mental Rehabilitation* 11:3 (1957):96.

Hinson, M. L., and Rosenswieg, J. "Comparing the Three Best Ways of Developing Strength." *Scholastic Coach* 41 (1972):34.

Hinson, M. L., et al. "Isokinetics: A Clarification." *Research Quarterly* 50 (1979):30.

Hirsch, J., and Knittle, J. L. "Cellularity of Obese and Nonobese Adipose Tissue." *Federation Proceedings* 29(1970):1518.

Hodgson, J. D. "Leisure and the American Worker." *Journal of Health, Physical Education and Recreation* 43 (1972):38.

Holland, G. J. "The Physiology of Flexibility: A Review of the Literature." *Kinesiology Review,* p. 49, 1968.

Holt, L. E. "Comparative Study of the Three Stretching Techniques." *Perceptual and Motor Skills* 31 (1970):611.

Hupperich, F. L., and Segerseth, P. O. "The Specificity of Flexibility in Girls." *Research Quarterly* 21 (1970):25.

"Ideas on Bedding and Backaches." *Forecast for Home Economics* 19 (May 1917):44.

Jackson, A. S., and Frankiewicz, R. J. "Factorial Expressions of Muscular Strength." *Research Quarterly* 46 (May 1975):206.

Jacobson, E. *Anxiety and Tension Control.* Philadelphia: J. B. Lippincott Co., 1964.

Jesse, J. P. "Misuses of Strength Development Programs in Athletic Training." *The Physician and Sports Medicine* 7 (October, 1976):46.

Jette, M., et al. "A Simple Field Procedure for Estimating Ideal Body Weight in Male." *Research Quarterly* 50 (1979):396.

Kannel, W. B., et al. "The Framingham Study." *American Journal of Internal Medicine* 74 (1971):1.

Kasch, F. W. "The Effects of Exercise on the Aging Process." *The Physician and Sports Medicine* 4 (1976):65.

Katch, F. I., and McArdle, W. D. *Nutrition, Weight Control, and Exercise.* Boston: Houghton Mifflin Co., 1977.

Kavanaugh, T. "Postcoronary Joggers Need Precise Guidelines." *The Physician and Sports Medicine* 4 (1976):63.

Kennedy, J. F. "The Soft American." *Sports Illustrated* 13 (December 1960):15.

Kenyon, G. S. "Six Scales for Assessing Attitudes Toward Physical Activity." *Research Quarterly* 39 (1968):566.

Klein, K. K., and Allman, F. L. *The Knee in Sports.* Austin, Texas: Jenkins, (n.d.)

Klump, F. "Overcoming Overprotection of the Elderly." *The Physician and Sports Medicine* 4 (1976):107.

Klumpp, T. G. "Physical Activities and Older Americans." *Testimony on Physical Fitness for Older Persons.* Washington, D.C.: National Association for Human Development, 1975.

Kostrubala, T. *The Joy of Running.* New York: Simon & Schuster, 1977.

Kournakis, P. Pharmocological Conditioning for Sporting Events." *American Journal of Pharmacy* 144 (September-October 1972):151.

Kraus, H. *Backache, Stress, and Tension.* New York: Simon & Schuster, 1965.

Kraus, H. "Ecology and Backache." *Journal of Physical Education* 69 (March 1972):111.

Kraus, H., and Raab, W. *Hypokinetic Disease.* Springfield, Ill.: Charles C Thomas, Publisher, 1961.

Kugelmass, J. A. "How to Keep From Getting Tired." *Capper's Farmer*, May, 1959.

Kulund, D. N. "Long-Term Effects of Playing Tennis." *The Physician and Sports Medicine* 7 (April 1979):87.

Kuntzleman, C. "Dangerous Exercise: Which, When, Why." *Fitness for Living*, January-February, 1971.

Lamb, L. E. "Staying Youthful and Fit." *Testimony on Physical Fitness for Older Persons.* Washington, D.C.: National Association for Human Development, 1975.

———, "Androgens and Exercise." *Medicine and Science in Sports* 7, no. 1 (1975):1.

———. "Anabolic Steroids and Strength and Power-Related Athletic Events." *JOPER* 51 (February 1980):59.

Lawrence, J. D., et al. "Effects of Alpha-tocopherol Acetate on the Swimming Endurance of Trained Swimmers." *American Journal of Clinical Nutrition* 28 (March 1975):205.

Lawther, J. D. *The Learning and Performance of Physical Skills.* (2d ed. Englewood Cliffs, N.J.: Prentice-Hall, Inc., 1977.

Ledaux-Personnet, M. "Nutrition and the Athlete." *CAHPER Journal*, March-April, 1979, pp. 30–36.

Lehtonen, A., et al. "The Effects of Exercise on High Density (HDL) Lipoprotein Apoproteins." *Acta Physiologica Scandinavica.* 106 (1979):487.

Lewis, S., and Gutin, B. "Nutrition and Endurance." *American Journal of Clinical Nutrition* 26 (September 1973):1011.

Lindsey, R. "Figure Wrapping: Can You Believe It?" *Fitness for Living*, March-April 1972, p. 54.

Lindsey, R.; Jones, B.; and Whitley, A. *Body Mechanics.* 4th ed. Dubuque, Ia.: Wm. C. Brown Company Publishers, 1979.

Little, C. "The Athlete's Neurosis—A Deprivation Crisis." *Acta Psychiatrica Scandinavica* 45 (1969):187.

Mamaliga, E. *Body Development Through Weight Training.* Minneapolis: Burgess, 1976.

Martens, R. *Social Psychology and Physical Activity.* New York: Harper & Row, 1975.

Mayer, J. *A Diet For Living.* New York: David McKay Company, Inc., 1975. Consumers Union edition, 1976.

Mayhew, J. J., and Gross, P. M. "Body Composition Changes in Young Women with High Resistance Weight Training." *Research Quarterly* 45 (1974):433.

Michele, A. A. *Orthotherapy.* New York: M. Evans and Co., 1971.

Miller, D. J. and Nelson, R. C. *Biomechanics of Sports.* Philadelphia: Lea and Febiger, 1973.

Mirken, G. "Carbohydrate Loading: A Dangerous Practice." *Journal of the American Medical Association* 233 (March 26, 1973):1151.

Morehouse, L. E. and Gross, L. *Total Fitness in 30 Minutes a Week.* New York: Simon & Schuster, 1975.

Morris, J. N., et al. "Vigorous Exercise in Leisure Time and Incidence of Coronary Heart Disease." *Lancet* 1 (1973):323.

Murray, R. O., and Duncan, C. "Athletic Activity in Adolescence as an Etiological Factor in Degenerative Hip Disease." *Journal of Bone and Joint Surgery* (British) 53 (August 1971):406.

Nash, J. B. *Philosophy of Recreation and Leisure.* Dubuque, Ia.: Wm. C. Brown Company Publishers, 1960.

Noland, M., and Kearney, J. T. "Anthropometric and Densiometric Responses of Women to Specific and General Exercise." *Research Quarterly* 49 (1978):322.

Northrip, J. W., et al. *Biomechanics Analysis of Sport.* 2d ed. Dubuque, Ia.: Wm. C. Brown Company Publishers, 1979.

Ogilvie, B., and Tutko, T. "Sport: If You Want to Build Character, Try Something Else." *Psychology Today* 5 (1971):60.

———. "A Survey and Critical Analysis of Practices Found in Selected Commercial Reducing Salons." Unpublished paper, Oklahoma State University Library, Stillwater, Oklahoma, 1971.

Oscai, L. B. "The Role of Exercise in Weight Control." In *Exercise and Sports Science Reviews.* Edited by J. H. Wilmore. New York: Academic Press, 1973.

———. "Exercise or Food Restriction: Effect of Adipose Cellularity," *American Journal of Physiology* 27 (1974):902.

Paffenbarger, R. S., et al. "Current Exercise and Heart Attack Risk." *Cardiac Rehabilitation* 10 (1979):1.

Parizkova, J. and Rogozkin, V., ed. *Nutrition, Physical Fitness and Health.* Baltimore: University Park Press, 1978.

Pipes, T. V., and Wilmore, J. H. "Isokinetic vs. Isotonic Strength Training in Adult Men." *Medicine and Science in Sports* 7 (1975):262.

Plowman, S. A., and Falls, H. B. "Youth Fitness Test Revision." *JOPER* 49 (1978):22.

————. "Fitness Testing in the Schools: Revision of the AAHPER Fitness Test." *Implementation of Aerobics Programs*. Washington: AAHPERD, 1979.

Pollock, M. B.; Purdy, C. O.; and Carroll, C. R. *Health: A Way of Life*. Glenview, Ill.: Scott, Foresman and Co., 1979.

Pollock, M. L. "How Much Exercise Is Enough?" *The Physician and Sports Medicine*. 6 (June 1978):50.

Pollock, M. L. "Effects of Fitness of Aging." *The Physician and Sports Medicine* 6 (August 1978):45.

Pollock, M. L.; Gettman, L. R.; Milesis, C. A.; Bah, M. D.; Divistine, L.; and Johnson, R. B. "Effects of Frequency and Duration of Training on Attrition and Incidence of Injury." *Medicine and Science in Sports*. 9 (1977):31.

Pollock, M. L., and Jackson, A. J. "Body Composition: Measurement and Changes Resulting From Physical Training." *Proceedings of the NCPEAM* 77 (1977):125.

Pollock, M. L.; Wilmore, J. H.; and Fox, S. M. *Health and Fitness Through Physical Activity*. New York: John Wiley and Sons, 1978.

Presidents Council on Physical Fitness and Sports. *PCPFS Newsletter*. Special Edition, May 1973, pp. 1–27.

Puranen, J. "The Medial Tibial Syndrome." *Journal of Bone and Joint Surgery* (British) 56, no 13. (November 1974):712.

Raab, W. "Loafer's Heart." *Archives of Internal Medicine* 101(1958):194.

Radd, A. "Statement on Physical Fitness and the Elderly." *Testimony on Physical Fitness for Older Persons*. Washington, D.C.: National Association for Human Development, 1975.

Rasch, P. J. "The Present Status of Negative (Eccentric) Exercise: A Review." *American Corrective Therapy Journal* 28 (1974):77.

Rasch, P., and Burke, R. *Kinesiology and Applied Anatomy*. 6th ed. Philadelphia: Lea and Febiger, 1978.

Rechnitzer, P. A. et al. "A Controlled Prospective Study of the Effects of Endurance Training on the Recurrence Rate of Myocardial Infarction." *American Journal of Epidemiology* 102 (1975):358.

Ribisl, P. "When Wrestlers Shed Pounds Quickly." *The Physician and Sports Medicine* 2 (1974):30.

Riss, J. F. "Health Control Through Bio-feedback." *Modern Maturity*, January, 1973, p. 67.

Rivera, M. L. "Effects of Static, Ballistic, and Modified Proprioceptive Neuromuscular Stretching Exercises on the Flexibility and Retention of Flexibility in Selected Joints." Unpublished masters thesis, University of Kansas, Lawrence, Kansas, 1979.

Robb, M. D. *The Dynamics of Motor Skill Acquisition*. Englewood Cliffs, N.J.: Prentice-Hall, Inc., 1972.

Rochmis, P., and Blackburn, H. "Exercise Tests: A Survey of Procedures, Safety, and Litigation." *Journal of the American Medical Association* 217 (August 23, 1971):1066.

Rogers, J. L. "PNF: A New Way to Improve Flexibility," *Track Technique* 12 (Winter 1978):2345.

Rosentswieg, J. "Motor Development in Adolescence and Adulthood." In *A Textbook of Motor Development*, 2d ed. Edited, by C. B. Corbin, Dubuque, Ia.: Wm. C. Brown Company, Publishers, 1980.

Ryan, A. J. "Backache and What To Do About It." *Fitness for Living*, May-June, 1970, p. 78.

————. "Hazardous Exercises." *Fitness For Living*, September-October, 1970, p. 4.

————. "Are You Hamstrung?" *Fitness for Living,* March-April 1971, p. 59.

————. "What Causes Low Back Pain?" *The Physician and Sports Medicine* 2 (1974):36.

Sargent, J. D.; Green, E. D.; and Walters, E. D. "The Use of Autogenic Feedback Training in a Pilot Study of Migraine and Tension Headaches." A speech delivered to the American Association for the Study of Headaches, July 17, 1972, San Francisco, Calif.

Sarno, J. E. *Therapeutic Exercise for Back Pain.* In Therapeutic Exercise, 3d ed., Chap. 9. Edited by J. V. Basmajian, Baltimore: Williams and Wilkins, 1978.

Schlesinger, Z. "Life Threatening Vagal Reaction to Physical Fitness Test." *Journal of the American Medical Association* 226 (November 26, 1973):1119.

Schmidt, R. A. *Motor Skills.* New York: Harper & Row, 1975.

Schontz, F. C. *The Psychological Aspects of Physical Illness and Disability.* New York: The MacMillan Company, 1975.

Schultz, P. "Flexibility: Day of the Static Stretch." *The Physician and Sports Medicine* 7 (November 1979):109.

Selye, H. *Stress Without Distress.* Philadelphia: J. B. Lippincott Co. 1974.

Sheehan, G. "Case Against Loading." *Runners World.* 11:46, August, 1976.

Shepard, R. J. *Men at Work.* Springfield, Ill.: Charles C Thomas, Publisher, 1974.

Shepard, R. J. *Endurance Fitness.* 2d ed. Toronto: University of Toronto Press, 1977.

Shepard, R. J., and Kavanagh, T. "What Exercise to Prescribe for the Post-MI Patient." *The Physician and Sports Medicine* 3 (1975):57.

Sherrill, C. *Adapted Physical Education and Recreation.* Dubuque, Ia.: Wm. C. Brown Company Publishers, 1976.

Sherrill, R. "Before You Believe Those Exercise and Diet Ads." *Todays Health* 49 (August, 1971):34.

Simonelli, C., and Eaton, R. P. "Reduced Triglyceride Solution: A Metabolic Consequence of Chronic Exercise." *American Journal of Physiology* 243 (March 1978):221.

Sinning, W. E. "Use and Misuse of Anthropometric Estimates of Body Composition." *JOPER* 51 (February 1980):43.

Smith, Matthew. "What Arnold Schwarzenegger Hath Wrought." *Los Angeles* magazine, January 1980, p. 162.

Smith, N. J. "Gaining and Losing Weight in Athletics." *Journal of the American Medical Association,* 236 (July 1976):149.

Stanton, G. A. Diet and Exercise in Coronary Heart Disease." *Lancet* 2 (August 10, 1974):351.

Steinhaus, A. *Toward an Understanding of Health and Physical Education.* Dubuque, Ia.: Wm. C. Brown Company Publishers, 1963.

Svoboda, M. "Addressing Weight Management in Physical Education." *JOPER* 51 (February 1980):49.

Swartz, F. C. "Statement on Physical Fitness and the Elderly." *Testimony on Physical Fitness for Older Persons.* Washington, D.C.: National Association for Human Development, 1975.

Terauds, J. "Optimal Angle of Release for the Competition Javelin as Determined by Its Aerodynamic and Ballistic Characteristics." *Biomechanics IV.* Edited by R. C. Nelson and C. A. Morehouse. Baltimore: University Park Press, 1974.

————. *Modern Treatment of Tense Patients.* Springfield, Ill.: Charles C Thomas, Publishers, 1970.

Tichauer, E. R. *Biomechanical Basis of Ergonomics*. New York: John Wiley and Sons, 1978.

Turner, R., and Ball, K. "The Cardiologist's Responsibility for Preventing Coronary Heart Disease." *American Heart Journal* 91 (February 1976):139.

Van Oteghen, S. L. "Two Speeds of Isokinetic Exercise as Related to the Vertical Jump Performance of Women." *Research Quarterly* 46 (March 1975):78.

―――. "Isokinetic Conditioning for Women." *Scholastic Coach* 44 (1974):87.

Wells, K., and Lutgens, K. *Kinesiology*. 6th ed. Philadelphia: W. B. Saunders Co. 1976.

Whiting, H.T.A. *Acquiring Ball Skills*. Philadelphia: Lea and Febiger, 1971.

Williams, R. S., et al. "Physical Conditioning Augments the Fibrinolytic Response to Venous Occlusion in Healthy Adults." *New England Journal of Medicine* 302 (1980):987.

Woodworth, R. S., and Schlosberg, H. *Experimental Psychology*, 3d ed., London: Methuen, 1972.

Zuti, W. B., and Golding, L. A. "Comparing Diet and Exercise as Weight Reduction Tools." *The Physician and Sports Medicine* 4 (1976):49.

Index

Circulatory
fitness, 23
Circulatory system, 7, 60
Cleaning, floor, 91
Climate, 68
Climbing, 76
Clothing
ill-fitting, 100
See also Garments
Clubs, health, 123
Cocaine, 125
Colitis, 106
Collateral circulation, 31
Colon, irritable, 107
Concentric, 41
contractions, 46, 171
isotonic exercises, 46
Conditioning, cardiovascular, 124
Congenital poor posture, 100
Congestive heart failure, 31, 32
Conscious relaxation, 109
Constipation, 106
Continuous
exercise, 23
fitness program, 26, 28
lift, 89
Rhythmical Exercise, 127, 129
Contortionist, 51
Contractions
concentric, 171
eccentric, 171
Control, fat, 81
Cooper, Kenneth, 161, 241
Coordination, 7, 75, 77, 94
evaluating, lab, 213–16
Coronary Collateral Circulation Theory, 33,
36–37
Coronary heart disease, 4, 17, 31
rehabilitation, 32
risk factors, exercise and, 38
Coronary occlusion, 31, 32
Coronary thrombosis, 31, 34
Counseling, 108
Cramps, 71
Crash diets, 61, 72
Creeping obesity, 64
Cureton, Thomas, 129
Curls, 299, 303

Dancer, 51
Death rate, normal, related to obesity, 60
Deep breathing, 279
Deep knee bends, 122
Defects, foot, 100
Degenerative diseases, 4, 60
Dehydration, 67, 124
Depression, 106

Diabetes, 17
Diarrhea, 67, 106
Diet, 39, 59, 68
crash, 61, 72
fad, 72
high protein, 124
low carbohydrate, 70
Disc
herniated, 97
ruptured, 98
slipped, 102
Disease
conditions and poor posture, 100
degenerative, 4, 60
heart, 106, 233
hypokinetic, 4, 101
infectious, 4
Ischemic heart, 124
Dishwashing, 91
Distance, 94
Ditchdigger, 75
Diuresis, 106
Diver, 57
Diving, 92
Dizziness, 98
Double-jointedness, 51
Double knee-to-chest, 280
Double leg extension, 280
Double leg lifts, 121
Drugs, 108
hazards of, 124
Duke University Center for the Study of
Aging, 145
Duration, 15, 26, 27, 47, 54, 62, 257
Dynamic stretch, 51
Dynamometer, strength, 175
Dysmenorrhea, 51, 56, 312, 313

Eccentric, 41
contractions, 46, 171
Ectomorph (thin), 59
Edema, 106
Effective living, 5
Effectiveness, 87, 97, 217
Efficiency, 87, 97, 217
Efficient movement, 5
Elasticity, 51
Elbow extension behind neck, 300
Electrical stimulation, 102
Electric muscle stimulators, 120
Emotional
fitness, 8
imbalance, 107
problems, 100
state, 68
storm, 31, 37
tensions, 82

Hypertension, 17, 31, 32, 38, 233
    neuromuscular, 105, 107, 108
Hypertonus, 107
Hyperventilation, 119, 125
Hypokinetic diseases, 4, 17, 18, 19, 20, 31,
    101

Illinois Agility Run Test, lab, 207–9
Illnesses
    emotionally-related, 9
    psychosomatic, 9
Imagery, 109
Imbalance, emotional, 107
Inactivity, 38, 100, 101
Indigestible fiber (bulk) in foods, 67
Indigestion, 106
Infection
    bacterial, 21
    viral, 21
Infectious diseases, 4
Inflammation, 55
Inflated, constricting or nonporous garments,
    121
Informal exercise program, 127
Injury, knee, 99
Insomnia, 106, 107, 233
Intensity, 15, 26, 27, 47, 54, 62
Interactions, social, 82
Intermittent
    exchange, 23
    exercise, 27
    exercise training, 251
    fitness program, 28
Interval Training, 127, 130, 295
    lab, 251–52
Intima, 25
Intrauterine device, 119
Ironing, 91
Ischemic heart disease, 124
Isokinetic, 41
    exercise, 44
Isometric
    contractions, 280
    exercise, 43, 45, 46, 122, 301–6
    exercise, lab, 257–58
    strength, evaluating, lab, 175–77
    strength, rating scale, chart, 177
Isotonic exercise, 41, 43, 45, 46
    for endurance and strengthening, lab,
        259–60
    lab, 255–56
    for muscular endurance and mild
        strength, 306–10
    strength, evaluating, lab, 171–74

Jack spring, 153
Jacobson's Progressive Relaxation Method,
    109

Jelly, royal, 71
Jogging, 5, 63, 79, 80, 124, 127, 130, 146,
    296
    lab, 253–54
Jump, long, 92
Jumping, 92, 93, 219

Kasch Three-Minute Step Test, 165
Kidney
    congestion, 71
    system, 60
Kilogram, 67
Kinesiology, 123
Knee
    hyperextended, 97, 99
    injury, 99
    lift, 285
    push-up, 287
    raising, 289
    to chest, 228
    -to-nose touch, 281
Kyphosis, 97, 99

Labor, manual, 75
Labor Department, 4
Lateral bending, 289
Lateral trunk flexibility, 312
LDL, 35
Lecithin, 71
Leg
    extension, 305
    extension exercise, 308
    length, 55
    lift, prone arm and, 281
    lifts, double, 121
    lowering the, 153
    -overs, tuck, 291
    press in doorway, 304
    sit-ups with straight, 121
    soreness, 313
    strength, 175
Letting go, 109
Lifetime
    exercise, 141–46
    physical activities, 79
    physical activity for a, lab, 271–73
Lifetime sports, 5, 79
    guidelines, 82
    learning, 79–84
    and physical activities, learning, 79–84
Lift
    boys, 89
    continuous, 89
    frequent, 89
    girls, 89
    maximum 89

men, 89
    occasional, 89
    women, 89
Lifters, weight-, 125
Lifting, 87, 88, 90, 217
    suggested maximums, table, 89
Lifts, double leg, 121
Ligaments, 52
Linear motion, 87
Lines, postural, 99
Lipid, 31
    Deposit Theory, 33, 34
Lipoproteins, 31, 34
Liter, 23
Living, effective, 5
Loafer's Heart Theory, 33, 37
Lobotomy, frontal, 108
Locomotor movements, 87, 92
Long jump, 92
Lordosis, 99, 100
    lumbar, 97, 98
Low back pain, 4
Low density lipoproteins, 35
Lower back
    flexibility test of, 185
    stretch, 311
Lower leg lift, 309
Lower trunk lift, 174
Lumbar, 119
    lordosis, 97, 98
    muscles, 52
Lungs, 23

Machines
    motor-driven cycles and rowing, 120
    rolling, 120
Maintenance, 63
Making weight, 67
Maneuver, Valsalva, 119, 125
Manual labor, 75
Marathon runs, 70
Mass, 87
Massage, 120
Maximal oxygen uptake, 23, 27, 161
Mechanics, body, 87–94
    for daily living, 88–91
    in sports, 92
Media (muscle), 25
Meditation, Transcendental, 109
Membrane, synnovial, 119
Mental
    activity, reduce, 109
    fitness, 8
    health benefits of activity, table, 10
    practice, 79
Mesomorph (muscular), 59
M.E.T., 59

Military press, 298
    in doorway, 304
Milk, 70
Miller, H.G. "Dad", 144
Minerals, 68
Modified
    pull-ups, 307
    push-up, 290
Mosher exercise, 312
Motion
    linear, 87
    rotary, 87, 90
Motor-driven cycles and rowing machines,
    120
Motor skill aspects, 77
Movement
    arm, 91
    efficient, 5
    locomotor, 87, 92
    meaning of, 113
    personality, 113, 115
Muscle
    -bound, 56
    electric, stimulators, 120
    fiber, 41
    mass, 68
    tests, 225
    tissue, three types, 42
Muscular
    fatigue, 101
    imbalance tests, 227–28
    tension, evaluating, 238–39
Muscular endurance, 7, 8, 17, 19, 41, 81, 82,
    151, 265
    fitness target zone, 47
    general guidelines, 47
    lab, 179–81
    rating scale, chart, 181
    strength and, 41–49
    threshold of training, 47
Myositis, tension, 98, 101, 102

Narcotics, 125
Neck
    pain, 98
    and poor posture, 100
    pull, 302
Nerve, sciatic, 98
Nervousness, 107
Nervous system, autonomic, 105
Neuromuscular hypertension, 105, 107, 108
Nomogram, 167, 169, 190–91
Nutrition, 123
    exercise and, 67–72
    exercise and, lab, 199–201

Obesity, 4, 17, 38, 59, 60, 61, 187
    creeping, 64

Occasional lift, 89
One foot balance, 153
Organic foods, 71
Orthopedic problems, 56
Over-breathing, 119
Overfat, 59, 60
Overhead pull, 303
Overlearning, 79, 83
Overload, 14
    principle, 13, 44
    progressive, 229
Overweight, 59, 60
Oxygen
    -carrying capacity of the blood, 25
    maximal, uptake, 161
    Pump theory, 33

Pain, 101
    in arm, 98
    in neck, 98
    referred, 97, 101
    in shoulder, 98
Painkillers, 108
Painting, 91
Paralysis by analysis, 79
Parasympathetic nervous system, 32
Passive
    exercise, 120
    exercise machines, 61
    stretch (static stretch), 52, 53
    vs. active stretching exercises, 54
Pectoral stretch, 312
Pelvic tilt, 306
Peptic ulcer, 107
Peripheral circulation, 39
Personal exercise program, planning your,
        lab, 265–69
Personality
    movement, 113, 115
    problems, 100
Perspiration, 67
Phospholipids, 34
Physical activities
    choice of, 5
    learning, 79–84
    lifetime sports and, learning, 79–84
Physical activity
    activity rating scale, chart, 150
    for adolescents, 142
    for adults, 143
    for aesthetic experience, 114
    attitude test, chart, 149
    for children, 141
    as games of chance, 114
    guidelines, 82
    for a lifetime, lab, 271–73

as a means of achieving health and
        physical fitness, 114
    for older adults, 143
    reassessing the values, lab, 275–78
    for recreation and relaxation, 114
    seven reasons why, 114
    for social purposes, 114
    for thrills and excitement, 114
    to meet a challenge, 114
    the values of, lab, 147–50
Physical fitness, 7–11
    lab, 151–54
    sports for, lab, 263–64
    stunts, lab, 153–54
Physical health benefits of activity, table, 9
Physical stressors, 106
Physiological fatigue, 105
Physiology, 123
Pillows and tables, vibrating, 120
PNF technique, 55
Poke neck, 97
Position, swan, 122
Positive addiction, 115
Postural
    deviations, correction of, 100
    lines, 99
Posture, 97–103
    evaluation, chart, 223
    lab, 221–23
    poor, 98–103
    poor, congenital, 100
    poor, and disease conditions, 100
    poor, herditary, 100
    rating scale, chart, 223
Potassium, 70
Power, 7, 75, 77, 151
    evaluating explosive, lab, 211–12
President's Council on Physical Fitness and
        Sport, 127, 128, 144, 243, 284–87
Principle, overload, 13
Principle of progression, 44
Principles of stability, 217
Problems
    emotional, 100
    personality, 100
Programs of exercise
    Adult Physical Fitness, 127, 128
    aerobic dance, 127, 130
    aerobics, 127–28
    calisthenics, 127, 131
    circuit training, 127, 129
    Continuous Rhymical Exercise, 127, 129
    interval training, 127, 130
    jogging, 127, 130
    Royal Canadian XBX and 5BX, 127,
        128, 245
    speed play or fartlek, 127, 129–30

sports exercise, 127, 131–32
strengths and weaknesses, 133
weight training, 127, 131
Progressive rhythmical endurance exercise
  program, lab, 247–48, 291–93
Prolapse, 97
Prone
  arch, 287
  arm and leg lift, 281
  back lift, 309
Proprioceptive neuromuscular facilitation
  technique, 55
Protective Protein Theory, 33, 35
Protein, 68, 69
  high, diet, 124
Protruding abdomen, 98
Psychological fatigue, 105
Psychophysical disorders, 107
Psychosocial, 113
  considerations, 113–17
  stressors, 106
Psychosomatic
  illnesses, 9
  stress, 106
Ptosis, abdominal, 99
Pulling, 76, 87, 90, 217
Pull to chin, 301
Pull-ups (chinning), 308
Pulse, carotid, 155
Pushing, 76, 87, 90, 217

Quick energy foods, 70

RDA, 68
Reaction
  alarm, 105
  time, 7, 75, 77
Receiving a blow, 94
Reciprocal Innervation, 52
Recommended daily allowance, 68
Recreational skills, 3
Reducing salons, 123
Reduction
  spot, 61, 120
  weight, 120
Referred pain, 97, 101
Regular exercise, 21
Relaxation, 105–10
  conscious, 109
  lab, 237–39
  tension-, rating scale, chart, 239
Repetitions, 41, 257
Respiration, reduce, 109
Respiratory
  capacity, 98
  infections, 60
  system, 7, 25, 60

Response, fight or flight, 105
Resting heart rate, 156
Reverse sit-ups, 308
Rhythmical endurance exercise program,
  progressive, lab, 247–48, 291–93
Riding, 80
Risk factor, 32
Rolling machines, 120
Rotary motion, 87, 90
Rounded shoulders, 98
Rowing machines, 120
Royal Canadian Air Force XBX and 5BX
  Fitness Programs, 127, 128, 245,
  288–91
Royal jelly, 71
Run, in place, 154
Run and half knee bends, 291
Running, 92, 199, 207, 249, 251
  efficiency, decreased, 71
Runs, marathon, 70
Ruptured disc, 98
Ryan, A.J., 137

Safety, 217
Sauna, 123
Sauna belts, 121
Sawing, 91
Schizophrenia, 106
Sciatica, 98
Sciatic nerve, 98
Scoliosis, 98, 222
Sedentary living, 4
Set, 41
Sex, 56, 68
  and heart disease, 39
Shiatsu, 108
Shin splints, 56, 313
Shorts, 121
Shoulder
  flexibility, 185
  lift, 282
  pain, 98
  pull, 302
  shrug, 298
Shoulders, rounded, 98
Shoveling, 91
Side leg raises, 290, 309
Sit-and-reach exercise, 53
Sitting, 76
Sitting tucks or V sit, 179, 309
Sit-ups, 290
  with straight legs, 121
Skeletal muscle tissue, 42
Skill analysis, 79